NEW EXPANSIVE
POETRY

THEORY • CRITICISM • HISTORY

EDITED BY

R. S. GWYNN

STORY LINE PRESS
1999

©1999 by R. S. Gwynn
First American Printing

Published by Story Line Press, Three Oaks Farm, P.O. Box 1240, Ashland, OR 97520-0055
www.storylinepress.com

This publication was made possible thanks in part to the generous support of the Nicholas Roerich Museum, the Andrew W. Mellon Foundation, the National Endowment for the Arts, and our individual contributors.

The front cover image is a 1934 Coit Tower fresco, "Library," by Bernard B. Zakheim; reprinted by permission of Coit Tower, San Francisco Recreation & Park Department, San Francisco Art Commission; color photograph by Don Beatty.

Front cover design by Paul Moxon
Book design by Lysa McDowell

Library of Congress Cataloging-in-Publication Data

New expansive poetry : theory, criticism, history / edited by R.S. Gwynn. -- [Rev. ed.]
    p.   cm.
    Rev. ed. of: Expansive poetry / edited by Frederick Feirstein. 1989.
    Includes bibliographical references.
    ISBN 1-885266-69-3
    1. American poetry--20th century--History and criticism. 2. Narrative poetry, American--History and criticism. 3. Poetry--History and criticism--Theory, etc. 4. Literary form. I. Gwynn, R. S. II. Expansive poetry
PS325.N48 1999   99-21411
811'.5409--dc21   CIP

CONTENTS

THE NEW NARRATIVE

BIOGRAPHICAL NOTES

An Expansive Moment:
Introduction to the Revised Edition

R. S. Gwynn

A decade has passed since the appearance of Frederick Feirstein's original edition of *Expansive Poetry*, and those years have witnessed the arrival of the poets and poetry it championed at a secure place in the contemporary canon. Still, when *Expansive Poetry* was first published in 1989, the two related movements in contemporary American poetry which occasioned the essays it contained were largely uncharted. The canon of the new narrative could then boast only a handful of successful book-length and shorter narrative poems, and the new formalism lacked any defining anthologies providing a body of poems by which readers could judge its merits. In the ensuing decade both movements have prospered to a degree that has surpassed the expectations of even their most ardent early supporters.

In recent years narrative poems by Robert McDowell, Dana Gioia, Mark Jarman, Sydney Lea, David Mason, Marilyn Nelson, Frederick Pollack and others have found enthusiastic critics and audiences eager to read poetry of a type that has been virtually extinct in the second half of our century. Anthologies such as *A Formal Feeling Comes: Poems in Form by Contemporary Women*, edited by Annie Finch, and *Rebel Angels: 25 Poets of the New Formalism*, edited by Jarman and Mason, have gathered some of the key texts on which the new formalism can either stand or fall. If neither movement has yet marked contemporary American poetry in as raucously public a way as the Beats or the Confessional Poets did forty years ago (and one can hardly imagine its poets actively seeking such notoriety), both new narrative and new formalist poetry continue to attract critical attention to a degree that, on the present scene, is rivaled only by the avant-garde Language poets.

The continued success of expansive poetry can best be measured by the objective benchmarks of contemporary poetry—the aforementioned anthologies and critical articles; the emergence of younger poets doing sustained work in form and narrative; the success of magazines and journals, like *The Formalist, Janus,* and *Sparrow,* devoted to formalist poetry, and the new *Pivot,* devoted to narrative poetry; the New York Barnes and Noble Story Line and Expansive Poetry reading series; the West Chester Poetry Conference focusing on form and narrative; and even the uneasy sanction of the Associated Writing Programs, in the form of a panel on new formalism at its annual convention. If these signs of the times are indicative, it is indeed an expansive moment in American poetry.

The term "expansive poetry" was coined by Wade Newman in an essay, "The Expansive Movement in American Poetry," which appeared in a special issue of *Crosscurrents 8.2 (1989)*, edited by Dick Allen. As Dana Gioia made clear, early, in his essay "Notes on the New Formalism and the Revival of Traditional Forms in Poetry" (*The Hudson Review,* vol. 40, no. 3):

> Like the new tonal composers, the young poets now work-
> ing in form reject the split between their art and its tra-
> ditional audience. They seek to reaffirm poetry's broader
> cultural role and restore its parity with fiction and drama.
> One critic has already linked the revival of form with the
> return to narrative and grouped these new writers as an
> "expansive movement" dedicated to reversing poetry's
> declining importance to the culture. These young poets
> seek to engage their audience not by simplifying their
> work but by making it more relevant and accessible. They
> are also "expansive" in that they had expanded their tech-
> nical and thematic concerns beyond the confines of the
> short, autobiographical free verse lyric which so domi-
> nates contemporary poetry.

But the term "expansive" has been somewhat problematic from the outset; even *Crosscurrents* misprinted the name "Expansionist Poetry" on its cover. While "expansive poetry" has never found much in the way of general favor among even some of its practitioners, it remains, for good or ill, the most commonly used name for the work of poets whose careers have been consistently intertwined. Still, its defining essence remains elusive. In their introduction to the original edition of this book, Feirstein and Frederick Turner offer a cautious program for its application:

> Our intention is to *expand* [my italics] the possibilities of
> form and content in poetry. We don't want our work as a
> movement to be transformed into a new conformism in
> which superficial elements are reduced to a fashion and a

set of formulae to be duly retailed in the creative writing schools. The reason to use narrative and meter and rhyme is not to be fashionable but to open worlds of reality and imagination to the poet which might otherwise be shut off. If ever our work is taken up as dogma, we expect we will remain true to our natures and attack it.

A lively adversarial spirit abides in these words, representing a stance that is echoed in the sentiments of many new formalist and new narrative poets. Most of them came of age in the 1960s, when Beat, Confessional, and Deep Image poetry, in their respective turns, dominated the poetic *table d'hôte*. They watched bemused while their mentors, the poets of their parents' generation, emerged from mid-life with a vengeance, turning away from tradition toward open form and increasingly subjective approaches to autobiographical material. Dissatisfied by the limited possibilities offered by the '60s *Zeitgeist*, these younger poets, unlike many of their contemporaries, turned back to earlier models — Frost, Hardy, Jeffers, Millay — and in some cases attempted to counter Modernism by recovering and reconstituting the forms and genres of earlier literary periods. This strategy could thus be compared to the way in which post-modern architecture successfully imports the flying buttress and arched nave into a world of concrete and steel or how a return to traditional musical forms can rightly be celebrated as "new."

In the curious manner of literary dialectic, this return to tradition can be seen as yet another manifestation of a generation's revolt against the authority of its elders — not this time as wild-eyed revolutionaries urging even further extremes but as counter-insurgents in the Culture Wars — hence Jarman and Mason's designation of them as "rebel angels." One poet associated with new formalism has confessed that he is by nature so "contrarian" that had he been raised in an age of sonnets, he might well have written only free verse. In *The Reaper Essays*, Mark Jarman and Robert McDowell state that their aim in promoting narrative poetry was, in some measure, "adversarial — aimed to explode the complacency of contemporary letters." By the late 1970s, the tribal music of Poetryland — the murky manifestos of Projective Verse and breath-units, the proliferation of cut-rate knock-offs of "Howl" and "Daddy," the shamanism of the deep image and the multiform brain — had begun to resemble ritualized incantations, mumbled by the multitudes but comprehended by few, and a sense emerged that certain types of poetry had overstayed their welcome.

That said, what directions remained for younger poets who were not content to remain part of the status quo? Alternatives to the aesthetic impasse were found in two very different ways: the Language poets attempted to go further into disorder and subjectivity, dispensing with an audience entirely; the new formalist and new narrative poets, returning to a more accessible vision, have claimed that an audience is entirely indispensable. Perhaps this desire to embrace a larger readership is the essence of what "expansive" connotes; these poets are giving the elusive common reader the missing ingredients that are most often lamented by those who claim to have given up on modern poetry. Indeed, if we are to think of expansive poetry as a truly populist movement (and I, for one, do, in the most honorable senses of the term), then its poets have simply responded to the audience's call (as opposed to arrogantly disregarding it) for formal elements that can be *heard* and narrative qualities that can be *understood*.

In preparing this revised edition of *Expansive Poetry*, I have striven to remain true to Frederick Feirstein's conception, but I have also tried to strengthen some aspects of the original. Several selections which were only tangentially related to the matter at hand have been replaced by more pertinent ones, including important essays on the New Narrative by David Mason and Thomas M. Disch; I have also added Brad Leithauser's "Metrical Illiteracy," an essay which has been much alluded to in discussions of expansive poetry but which has heretofore been hard to find. One criticism of the first edition was that it did not provide any clear historical perspective for expansive poetry; to that end, I have included essays by Meg Schoerke and Keith Maillard which place new formalism in its larger cultural and historical contexts. The latter essay replaces Paul Lake's "Toward a Liberal Poetics" (Lake is represented elsewhere here), offering a comprehensive discussion of the genesis of new formalism and the ensuing controversies that have surrounded it.

Another charge which was leveled against *Expansive Poetry* was that it misrepresented the true state of contemporary American poetry by focusing exclusively on the work of white male poets. As Feirstein has said elsewhere, "I had asked several women to contribute but some were reluctant to do so because they didn't want to be associated with a project advocating form when form was considered patriarchal." It took a few years for this assumption to be successfully challenged by Annie Finch's anthology, *A Formal Feeling Comes*, and then by Jarman and Mason's *Rebel Angels*. To further illustrate the diversity of the movement more accurately, I have added selections by a dozen women poets and critics; many of their comments address the question of how contemporary women poets both subsume and subvert the "patriarchal authority" that some critics have claimed as an inherent component of traditional poetic forms. Also, I have wrestled with the problem of whether or not to retain several selections about which I, both as an editor and also as a critic who has written about expansive poetry, have reservations. I have reprinted one such essay because of its historical importance to the movement, because of its widely admired speculative nature, and because I trust the discerning reader to judge its conclusions fairly for him- or herself.

Finally, I am aware that the reader will encounter many cross-referenced critics, poets, and poems in the essays in *New Expansive Poetry*. For this, I make no apology; as it is in all literary movements, personal friendships and professional alliances play roles equally as important as a shared aesthetic credo, and it is inevitable that many of these poet-critics should discuss the work of those whose work and temperaments they find most sympathetic to their own. It is unavoidable, too, that Story Line Press should figure so prominently in the pages of one of its own books, for Story Line gave some of these poets, editors, and critics shelter when there was none to be had elsewhere. It is only natural for a group of writers who have weathered more than their fair share of benign neglect, facile dismissal, and downright antagonism to draw their poetic wagons in a tight circle, witness the Imagists and the Black Mountain Poets of earlier decades. "Marginalization," a term that is currently fashionable in academic circles, does not apply solely to the more visible segments of the poetic underclass.

In conclusion, I would like to lend my appreciation to several publications and individuals who perhaps deserve more credit than they have received. One is the *Mississippi Review*, which published in 1977 a special issue called *Freedom and Form: American Poets Respond*. I do not believe that this early, perhaps earliest, shot in the "poetry wars" has received prior mention in the history of the expansive movement. Aside from providing the present editor with the first platform from which he was allowed to sound off on the subject, the issue also included comments and poems by a number of poets whose names and voices appear in the pages that follow. A significant figure in the history of expansive poetry is Lewis Turco, whose *The Book of Forms* and subsequent *The New Book of Forms* helped many young poets to sustain their interest in formal possibilities through many a lean year. Indeed, it was Turco who, in his round-up reviews for the *Dictionary of Literary Biography Yearbook*, first began in the early 1980s to chronicle the activities of a movement he called "neo-formalism." A wider readership for expansive poetry could not have come about without the support of editors like X. J. Kennedy (*Counter/Measures*), Frederick Morgan (*Hudson Review*), Donald Stanford (*Southern Review*), Frederick Turner and, later, Marilyn Hacker (*Kenyon Review*) who proved hospitable to their poets. Finally, there remains the steadfastness of older poets who never entirely forsook their first love and who were generous in their support of younger writers who likewise cherished the tradition. With their example in mind, it seems appropriate to conclude with some remarks that Richard Wilbur made in the *Mississippi Review* twenty years ago:

> It will have to be said and proven, once more, that in art there is no joy without difficulty; that to be "natural" in art is not to blurt but to aim for perfection of utterance; that breadth and depth of vocabulary, good grammar and usage, the making of allusions, and the use of formal means are the ways of achieving fullness and precision; that it is impoverishing to be incurious about the art of the past; that artifice is not necessarily cold; that high art is not necessarily pretentious; that to commit oneself to a form is far more daring than to be "free"; and that Whitman, God love him, is not the only possible touchstone. Once we have come to embrace and apply such notions, it will be clear what force and elegance poetic language should have....

It is a hopeful sign that Wilbur's words, which sounded two decades ago like advice for a prophet who had not yet arrived, are now echoed in the voices of the younger poets and critics who have taken up his challenge as an aesthetic imperative and, perhaps, as a moral one as well.

Notes on the New Formalism

Dana Gioia

1.

Twenty years ago it was a truth universally acknowledged that a young poet in possession of a good ear would want to write free verse. Today one faces more complex and problematic choices. While the overwhelming majority of new poetry published in the U.S. continues to be in "open" forms, for the first time in two generations there is a major revival of formal verse among young poets. The first signs of this revival emerged at the tail end of the 'Seventies, long after the more knowing critics had declared rhyme and meter permanently defunct. First a few good formal books by young poets, like Charles Martin's *Room for Error* (1978) and Timothy Steele's *Uncertainties and Rest* (1979), appeared but went almost completely unreviewed. Then magazines, like *Paris Review* which hadn't published a rhyming poem in anyone's memory, suddenly began featuring sonnets, villanelles, and syllabics. Changes in literary taste make good copy, and the sharper reviewers quickly took note. Soon some of the most lavishly praised debuts, like Brad Leithauser's *Hundreds of Fireflies* (1983) and Vikram Seth's *The Golden Gate* (1986), were by poets working entirely in form.

Literature not only changes; it must change to keep its force and vitality. There will always be groups advocating new types of poetry, some of it genuine, just as there will always be conservative opposing forces trying to maintain the conventional models. The revival of rhyme and meter among some young poets creates an unprecedented situation in American poetry. The new formalists put free verse poets in the ironic and unprepared position of being the *status quo*. Free verse, the creation of an older literary

First published in *The Hudson Review*, Autumn 1987, Copyright © 1987 by The Hudson Review, Inc. Reprinted with permission of the author and publisher.

revolution, is now the long-established, ruling orthodoxy; formal poetry the unexpected challenge.

There is currently a great deal of private controversy about these new formalists, some of which occasionally spills over into print. Significantly, these discussions often contain many odd misconceptions about poetic form, most of them threadbare clichés which somehow still survive from the 'Sixties. Form, we are told authoritatively, is artificial, elitist, retrogressive, right-wing, and (my favorite) un-American. None of these arguments can withstand critical scrutiny, but nevertheless, they continue to be made so regularly that one can only assume they provide some emotional comfort to their advocates. Obviously, for many writers the discussion of formal and free verse has become an encoded political debate.

When the language of poetic criticism has become so distorted, it becomes important to make some fundamental distinctions. Formal verse, like free verse, is neither bad nor good. The terms are strictly descriptive, not evaluative. They define distinct sets of techniques rather than rank the quality or nature of poetic performance. Nor do these techniques automatically carry with them social, political, or even, in most cases, aesthetic values. (It would, for example, be very easy for a poet to do automatic writing in meter. One might even argue that surrealism is best realized in formal verse since the regular rhythms of the words in meter hypnotically release the unconscious.) However obvious these distinctions should be, few poets or critics seem to be making them. Is it any wonder then that so much current writing on poetry is either opaque or irrelevant? What serious discussion can develop when such primary critical definitions fail to be made with accuracy?

2.

Meter is an ancient, indeed primitive, technique that marks the beginning of literature in virtually every culture. It dates back to a time, so different from our specialized modern era, when there was little, if any, distinction between poetry, religion, history, music, and magic. All were performed in a sacred, ritual language separated from everyday speech by its incantatory metrical form. Meter is also essentially a pre-literate technology, a way of making language memorable before the invention of writing.

Trained poet-singers took the events and ideas a culture wanted to preserve—be they tribal histories or magic ceremonies—formulated them in meter, and committed these formulas to memory. Before writing, the poet and the poem were inseparable, and both represented the collective memory of their culture.

Meter is therefore an aural technique. It assumes a speaker and a listener, who for the duration of the poem are intertwined. Even in later literary cultures meter has always insisted on the primacy of the physical sound of language. Unlike prose, which can be read silently with full enjoyment, poetry demands to be recited, heard, even memorized for its true appreciation. Shaping the words in one's mouth is as much a part of the pleasure as hearing the sounds in the air. Until recently education in poetry always emphasized memorization and recitation. This traditional method stressed the immediately communicable and communal pleasures of the art. Certainly a major reason for the decline in poetry's popular audience stems directly from the abandonment of this aural education for the joylessly intellectual approach of critical analysis.

Free verse is a much more modern technique that presupposes the existence of written texts. While it does not abandon the aural imagination—no real poetry can—most free verse plays with the way poetic language is arranged on a page and articulates the visual rhythm of a poem in a way earlier metrical verse rarely bothered to. Even the earliest known free verse, the Hebrew Psalms (which actually inhabit a middle ground between free and formal verse since they follow a principle of syntactic but not metrical symmetry) were created by "the people of the Book" in a culture uniquely concerned with limiting the improvisatory freedom of the bard for the fixed message of the text.

Most often one first notices the visual orientation of free verse in trivial ways (the lack of initial capitals at the beginning of lines, the use of typographical symbols like "&" and "7," the arbitrary use of upper or lower case letters). e. e. cummings spent his life exploiting these tricks, trying to create a visual vocabulary for modern poetry. Eventually, however, one sees how the visual field of the page is essential to the organization of sound in free verse. Printed as run-on lines of prose, a free verse poem reads radically differently from how it does printed as verse (whereas most metrical verse still retains its basic rhythmic design and symmetry). This visual artifice separates free verse from speech. Technological innovation affects art, and it is probably not accidental that the broad scale development of free verse came from the first generation of writers trained from childhood on the shift-key typewriter introduced in 1878. This new device allowed writers to predict accurately for the first time the *look* of their words on the printed page rather than just their sound.

All free verse deals with the fundamental question of how and when to end lines of poetry when there is no regular meter to measure them out. The earliest free-verse matched the line with some syntactic unit of sense (in Hebrew poetry, for instance, the line was most often a double unit of parallel syntactic sense):

> Except the Lord build the house, they labor in
>   vain that build it:
> Except the Lord keep the city, the watchman
>   waketh but in vain.
>
> 2
> It is vain for you to rise up early, to sit up late,
> To eat the bread of sorrows: for so he giveth his
>   beloved sleep.
>
> *(Psalm 127)*

Once free verse leaves the strict symmetry of sacred Hebrew poetry, there is no way for the ear to judge accurately from the sounds alone the metrical structure of a poem (unless the reader exaggerates the line breaks). Sometimes one wonders if even the poet hears the purely aural pattern of his words. Most critics do not. For instance, it has never been noted that the most famous American free verse poem of the twentieth century, William Carlos Williams' "The Red Wheelbarrow," is not only free verse but also two rather undistinguished lines of blank verse:

> so much depends upon a red wheel barrow
> glazed with rain water beside the white chickens.

One reason that these lines have proved so memorable is that they are familiarly metrical—very similar in rhythm to another famous passage of blank verse, even down to the "feminine" endings of the lines:

> To be or not to be, that is the question:
> Whether 'tis nobler in the mind to suffer...

That Williams wrote blank verse while thinking he was pioneering new trails in prosody doesn't necessarily invalidate his theories (though it may lead one to examine them with a certain skepticism). This discrepancy, however, does suggest two points. First, even among its adversaries, metrical language exercises a primitive power, even if it is frequently an unconscious one. Second, the organizing principle of Williams' free verse is visual. What makes "The Red Wheelbarrow" free verse is not the sound alone, which is highly regular, but the visual placement of those sounds on the page.

so much depends
upon

a red wheel
barrow

glazed with rain
water

beside the white
chickens.

Here words achieve a new symmetry, alien to the ear, but no less genuine. The way Williams arranges the poem into brief lines and stanzas slows the language until every word acquires an unusual weight. This deliberate visual placement twists a lackluster blank verse couplet into a provocatively original free verse lyric which challenges the reader's definition of what constitutes a poem. Much of the poem's impact comes from catching the reader off guard and forcing him to reread it in search of what he has missed because nothing of what Williams has said comprises a satisfactory poem in a conventional sense. The element of surprise makes this type of poem a difficult trick to repeat and may explain why so much of the minimalist poetry written in the Williams tradition is so dull. The poetic experience comes in the rereading as the reader consciously revises his own superficial first impression and sees the real importance of Williams' seemingly mundane images. Just as Williams' imagery works by challenging the reader to see the despoiled modern world as charged with a new kind of beauty, so too does his prosody operate by making everyday words acquire a new weight by their unexpectedly bold placement on the page. No aural poem could work in this way.

3.

The current moment is a fortunate one for poets interested in traditional form. Two generations now of younger writers have largely ignored rhyme and meter, and most of the older poets, who worked originally in form (such as Louis Simpson and Adrienne Rich) have abandoned it entirely for more than a quarter of a century. Literary journalism has long declared it defunct, and most current anthologies present no work in traditional forms by Americans written after 1960. The British may have continued using rhyme and meter in their quaint, old-fashioned way and the Irish in their primitive, bardic manner, but for up-to-date Americans it becomes the province of the old, eccentric, and the Anglophilic. It was a style that dared not speak its name, except in light verse. Even the tri-nominate, blue-haired lady laureates now wrote in free verse.* By 1980 there had been such a decisive break with the literary past that in America for the first time in the history of modern English most published young poets could not write with minimal competence in traditional meters (not that this failing bothered anyone). Whether this was an unprecedented cultural catastrophe or a glorious revolution is immaterial to this discussion. What matters is that most of the craft of traditional English versification has been forgotten.

Since 1960 there has also been relatively little formal innovation done by the mainstream either in metrical or free verse. Radical experimentation like concrete poetry or language poetry has been pushed off to the fringes of the literary culture where it either has been ignored by the mainstream or declared irrelevant. At the same time most mainstream poets have done little of the more focused (and less radical) experimentation with meters or verse forms that open up new possibilities for poetic language. Since 1960 the only new verse forms to have entered the mainstream of American poetry have been two miniatures: the double dactyl

---

* The editors of *The Hudson Review* ask, as perhaps they should, if this statement is a sexist stereotype. I offer it rather as investigative journalism based on first-hand knowledge of the work of such contemporary poets as Sudie Stuart Hager, Winifred Hamrick Farrar, Maggie Culver Fry, Helen von Kolnitz Hyer, and the late Peggy Simpson Curry (the official poet laureates of Idaho, Mississippi, Oklahoma, South Carolina, and Wyoming respectively). When such rear-guard, middle-class poets write in free verse, how can that style not be said to belong to the establishment?

and the ghazal, the latter usually in a dilute unrhymed version of the Persian original.

Indeed, the most influential form in American poetry over this quarter-century has been the prose poem, which strictly speaking is not a verse form at all but a stylistic alternative to verse as the medium for poetry. In theory the prose poem is the most protean form of free verse in which all line breaks disappear as a highly-charged lyric poem achieves the ultimate organic form. In recent American practice, however, it has mostly become a kind of absurdist parable having more to do with the prose tradition of Kafka or Borges than the poetic tradition of Baudelaire or Rimbaud. As poetry literally became written in prose, was it any wonder that verse technique suffered?

Likewise, although the past quarter-century has witnessed an explosion of poetic translation, this boom has almost exclusively produced translations of a formally vague and colorless sort. Compared to most earlier translation, these contemporary American versions make no effort whatsoever to reproduce the prosodic features of their originals. One can now read most of Dante or Villon, Rilke or Mandelstam, Lorca or even Petrarch in English without any sense of the poem's original form. Sometimes these versions brilliantly convey the theme or tone of the originals, but more often they sound stylistically impoverished and anonymous. All of the past blurs together into a familiar tune. Unrhymed, unmetered, and unshaped, Petrarch and Rilke sound misleadingly alike.

This method of translating foreign poetry into an already available contemporary style also brings less to the language than the more difficult attempt to recreate a foreign form in English (as Sir Thomas Wyatt did for the Italian sonnet or the anonymous translators of the King James Bible did for the Hebrew Psalms). New verse forms and meters can have a liberating effect on poetry. They allow writers to say things that have never worked in poetry before or else to restate familiar things in original ways. Many of the most important forms in our language were once exotic imports—the sonnet, sestina, ballade, villanelle, triolet, terza rima, pantoum, rubaiyt, haiku, ottava rima, free verse, even the prose poem. Recent translation has done little to expand the formal resources of American poetry. Ironically, it may have done more to deaden the native ear by translating all poetry of all ages into the same homogenous style. Studying great poetry in such neutralized versions, one gets little sense of how the forms adopted or invented by great writers are inseparable from their art. Not only the subtleties are lost but even the general scheme.

This assessment does not maintain that metrical innovation is necessary to write good poetry, that successful poetic translation must always follow the verse forms of the original or that prose is an impossible medium for poetry. It merely examines some current literary trends and speculates on both their origins and consequences. It also suggests that the recent dearth of formal poetry opens interesting possibilities for young poets to match an unexploited contemporary idiom with traditional or experimental forms. Indeed the current movement may even offer poets an opportunity for formal innovation and expansion unprecedented in the language since the end of the eighteenth century, for no age since then has been so metrically narrow or formally orthodox as our own.

4.

For the arts at least there truly is a *Zeitgeist*, especially at moments of decisive change when they move together with amazing synchronization. We are now living at one such moment to which critics have applied the epithet "postmodern," an attractive term the meaning of which no two writers can agree on precisely because it does not yet have one. The dialectic of history is still moving too fast, and events still unforeseen will probably define this moment in ways equally unexpected. One day cultural historians will elucidate the connections between the current revival of formal and narrative poetry with this broader shift of sensibility in the arts. The return to tonality in serious music, to representation in painting, to decorative detail and nonfunctional design in architecture will link with poetry's reaffirmation of song and story as the most pervasive development of the American arts towards the end of this century.

No one today can accurately judge all of the deeper social, economic, and cultural forces driving this revival, but at least one central motivation seems clear. All of these revivals of traditional technique (whether linked or not to traditional aesthetics) both reject the specialization and intellectualization of the arts in the academy over the past forty years and affirm the need for a broader popular audience. The modern movement, which began this century in bohemia, is now ending it in the university, an institution dedicated at least as much to the specialization of knowledge as to its propagation. Ultimately the mission of the university has little to do with the mission of the arts, and this long cohabitation has had an enervating effect on all the arts but especially on poetry and music. With the best of intentions the university has intellectualized the arts to a point where they have been cut off from the vulgar vitality of popular traditions and, as a result, their public has shrunk to groups of academic specialists and a captive audience of students, both of whom refer to everything beyond the university as "the real world." Mainly poets read contemporary poetry, and only professional musicians and composers attend concerts of new music.

Like the new tonal composers, the young poets now working in form reject the split between their art and its traditional audience. They seek to reaffirm poetry's broader cultural role and restore its parity with fiction and drama. The poet Wade Newman has already linked the revival of form with the return to narrative and grouped these new writers as an "expansive movement" dedicated to reversing poetry's declining importance to the culture. These young poets, Newman claims, seek to engage their audience not by simplifying their work but by making it more relevant and accessible. They are also "expansive" in that they have expanded their technical and thematic concerns beyond the confines of the short, autobiographical free verse lyric which so dominates contemporary poetry. Obviously, the return to form and narrative are not the only possible ways of establishing the connection between the poet and the broader public, but it does represent one means of renewal, and if this particular "expansive movement" works, American poetry will end this, its most distinguished century, with more promise to its future than one sees today.

5.

One of the more interesting developments of the last five years has been the emergence of pseudo-formal verse. This sort of writing began appearing broadly a few years ago shortly after critics started advertising the revival of form. Pseudo-formal verse bears the same relationship to formal poetry as the storefronts on a Hollywood backlot do to a real city street. They both look vaguely the same from a distance. In pseudo-formal verse the lines run to more or less the same length on the page. Stanzas are neatly symmetrical. The syllable count is roughly regular line by line, and there may even be a few rhymes thrown in, usually in an irregular pattern.

Trying to open the window on a Hollywood facade, one soon discovers it won't budge. The architectural design has no structural function. Pseudo-formal verse operates on the same principle. It displays no firm concept of how meters operate in English to shape the rhythm of a poem. Though arranged in neat visual patterns, the words jump between incompatible rhythmic systems from line to line. The rhythms lack the spontaneity of free verse without ever achieving the focused energy of formal poetry. They grope towards a regular rhythmic shape but never reach it. Ultimately, there is little, if any, structural connection between the look and the sound of the poem.

There are two kinds of pseudo-formal poems. The first type is more sophisticated. It appears regularly metrical. The first line usually scans according to some common meter, but thereafter problems occur. The poet cannot sustain the pattern of sounds he or she has chosen and soon begins to make substitutions line by line, which may look consistent with the underlying form but actually organize the rhythms in incompatible ways. What results technically is usually neither good free verse nor formal verse. Here, for example, is the opening of a poem by a young writer widely praised as an accomplished formalist. (Most poetry reviewers call any poem which looks vaguely regular "formal.") This passage wants to be blank verse, but despite a few regular lines, it never sustains a consistent rhythm long enough to establish a metrical base:

> From this unpardoned perch, a kitchen table
> In a sunless walk-up in a city
> Of tangled boulevards, he tested
> The old, unwieldy nemesis—namelessness.
> Forgetting (he knew) couldn't be remedied
> But these gestures of identity (he liked to think)
> Rankled the equanimities of time:
> A conceit, of course, but preferable to
> The quarrels of the ego, the canter of
> Description or discoveries of the avant-garde.

At first glance this passage appears to be in blank verse. The poem's first line unfolds as regular iambic pentameter (with a feminine ending). The second line has ten syllables, too, but it scans metrically either as awkward trochees or pure syllabics. A regular iambic rhythm appears again in line three, but now it falls decisively one foot short. Line four begins as

regular blank verse but then abruptly loses its rhythm in word play be-
tween "nemesis" and "namelessness." Line five can only be construed as
free verse. After a vague start line six plays with a regular iambic move-
ment but dissipates itself over thirteen syllables. And so it continues awk-
wardly till the end. Good blank verse can be full of substitutions, but the
variations always play off of a clearly established pattern. They help the
overall meter build a syntactic intensity. Here the poem never establishes a
clear rhythmic direction. The lines never quite become blank verse. They
only allude to it.

The second type of pseudo-formal poem is more common because it is
easier to write. It doesn't even try to make a regular pattern of sound,
however awkwardly. It only wants to look regular. The lines have no audi-
tory integrity, as free or formal verse. Their integrity is merely visual—in a
gross and uninteresting sense. The same issue of *The Agni Review*, which
published the previous example, also contains a poem in quatrains which
has these representative stanzas:

> When at odd moments, business and pleasure
> pale, and I think I'm staring into space,
> I catch myself gazing at a notecard propped
> on my desk, "The Waves at Matsushima."
>
> . . .
>
> and wider than the impossible journey
> from island to island so sheerly
> undercut by waves that no boat could find
> a landing, nor a shipwrecked couple
>
> rest beneath those scrubby pines at the top
> that could be overgrown heads of broccoli,
> even if they could survive the surf, tall
> combers, more like a field plowed by a maniac...

These line lengths seem determined mainly by their typographic width.
Why else does the author break the lines between "pleasure" and "pale" or
"tall" and "combers"? The apparently regular line breaks fall without any
real rhythmic relation either to the meter or the syntax. As Truman Capote
once said, "That's not writing—it's typing." There is no rhythmic integrity,
only incompatible, provisional judgements shifting pointlessly line by line.
The resulting poems remind me of a standard gag in improvisational com-
edy where the performers pretend to speak a foreign language by imitating

its approximate sound. Making noises that resemble Swedish, Russian, Italian or French, they hold impassioned conversations on the stage. What makes it all so funny is that the actors, as everyone in the audience knows, are only mouthing nonsense.

The metrical incompetence of pseudo-formal verse is the most cogent evidence of our literature's break with tradition and the lingering consequences. These poets are not without talent. Aside from its rhythmic ineptitude, their verse often exhibits many of the other qualities that distinguish good poetry. Even their desire to try traditional forms speaks well of their ambition and artistic curiosity. How then do these promising authors, most of whom not only have graduate training in writing or literature but also work as professional teachers of writing, not hear the confusing rhythms of their own verse? How can they believe their expertise in a style whose basic principles they so obviously misunderstand? That these writers by virtue of their training and position represent America's poetic intelligentsia makes their performance deeply unnerving—rather like hearing a conservatory trained pianist rapturously play the notes of a Chopin waltz in 2/4 time.

These young poets have grown up in a literary culture so removed from the predominantly oral traditions of metrical verse that they can no longer hear it accurately. Their training in reading and writing has been overwhelmingly visual not aural, and they have never learned to hear the musical design a poem executes. For them poems exist as words on a page rather than sounds in the mouth and ear. While they have often analyzed poems, they have rarely memorized and recited them. Nor have they studied and learned poems by heart in foreign languages where sound patterns are more obvious to nonnative speakers. Their often extensive critical training in textual analysis never included scansion, and their knowledge of even the fundamentals of prosody is haphazard (though theory is less important than practice in mastering the craft of versification). Consequently, they have neither much practical nor theoretical training in the way sounds are organized in poetry. Ironically this very lack of training makes them deaf to their own ineptitude. Full of confidence, they rely on instincts they have never developed. Magisterially they take liberties with forms whose rudimentary principles they misconstrue. Every poem reveals some basic confusion about its own medium. Some misconceptions ultimately prove profitable for art. Not this one.

6.

In my own poetry I have always worked in both fixed and open forms. Each mode opened up possibilities of style, subject, music, and development the other did not suggest, at least at that moment. Likewise, experience in each mode provided an illuminating perspective on the other. Working in free verse helped keep the language of my formal poems varied and contemporary, just as writing in form helped keep my free verse more focused and precise. I find it puzzling therefore that so many poets see these modes as opposing aesthetics rather than as complementary techniques. Why shouldn't a poet explore the full resources the English language offers?

I suspect that ten years from now the real debate among poets and concerned critics will not be about poetic form in the narrow technical sense of metrical versus non-metrical verse. That is already a tired argument, and only the uninformed or biased can fail to recognize that genuine poetry can be created in both modes. How obvious it should be that no technique precludes poetic achievement just as none automatically assures it (though admittedly some techniques may be more difficult to use at certain moments in history). Soon, I believe, the central debate will focus on form in the wider, more elusive sense of poetic structure. How does a poet best shape words, images, and ideas into meaning? How much compression is needed to transform versified lines — be they metrical or free — into genuine poetry? The important arguments will not be about technique in isolation but about the fundamental aesthetic assumptions of writing and judging poetry.

At that point the real issues presented by recent American poetry will become clearer: the debasement of poetic language; the prolixity of the lyric; the bankruptcy of the confessional mode; the inability to establish a meaningful aesthetic for new poetic narrative; and the denial of musical texture in the contemporary poem. The revival of traditional forms will be seen then as only one response to this troubling situation. There will undoubtedly be others. Only time will prove which responses were the most persuasive.

Tradition and Revolution:
The Modern Movement and Free Verse

Timothy Steele

Free verse is possibly the most significant legacy of the revolution in poetry which occurred in the first quarter of this century. A kind of free verse had existed earlier; in our language, the King James Psalms and the "stave-prose poetry" (to use George Saintsbury's term) of James Macpherson, William Blake, Martin Tupper, and Walt Whitman can be adduced as examples of proto-vers libre. But it was in this century that the theory and practice of Ford Madox Ford, Ezra Pound, T.S. Eliot, and others made free verse a dominant medium for English and American poetry. In an interview in *Antaeus* in 1978, Stanley Kunitz remarks of contemporary poetry: "Non-metrical verse has swept the field, so that there is no longer any real adversary from the metricians." Though Kunitz may be overstating the case, his assessment of prevailing practice is accurate: most verse published today is not in meter. And we have the early modernists, and the success of their revolution, to bless or curse for this situation.

Having now some distance on the revolution, we would do well to examine the ideas with which its leaders explained it and free verse. One of the most crucial of these ideas is that the modern revolution is essentially like earlier revolutions. The modern movement's leaders commonly argue, that is, that theirs is a rebellion against an antiquated idiom and is, as such, precisely the rebellion that "modernists" of all ages have had to undertake to keep poetry vitally engaged with the speech and life of its time. Free verse, according to this argument, does not represent a rejection of traditional poetic discipline, but is rather an innovation of the sort which inevitably accompanies changes in style and taste.

First published in *The Southwest Review*, Summer, 1985, vol. 70, no. 3, Copyright © 1988 by Timothy Steele. Reprinted with permission of the author and publisher.

Author's Note: For this essay, I have used standard editions of the writers discussed, the Loeb Classical Library editions in the case of most of the ancient writers. I have consulted W.B. Stanford's edition of *The Frogs* (London: MacMillan, 1958) and C.O. Brink's edition of the *Ars Poetica* (Cambridge: Cambridge University Press, 1971), and I would like to acknowledge particular debts to both these editors, not only for the careful texts they prepared, but for the lively and illuminating commentaries that accompany the texts.

In one respect, this argument is valid. Poetic conventions evolve, flourish, and eventually turn stale with use. When their art suffers a period of decline, it is only right that poets should try to revive it. This is what good poets have always done; this is what Ford, Pound, Eliot, and their followers were doing when they urged that the styles of Victorian verse had grown creaky and run-down and needed to be replaced by an idiom more genuinely equipped to treat modern life.

In another respect, however, the argument is not so sound. In its advocacy of non-metrical poetry, the modern revolution differed from former revolutions. It differed from that which Euripides led against Aeschylean style and from that which Horace led against the literary excesses of his day; and it differed from — to speak of Eliot's favorite examples — the revolution which Dryden led against Cleveland and the metaphysicals and the revolution which Wordsworth led against the neoclassicists. To be sure, earlier revolutions frequently entailed the elevation of certain verse forms at the expense of once-prominent ones. Wordsworth and the romantics, for instance, cultivated the sonnet, ballad stanzas, and blank verse —forms relatively neglected by the previous age —and generally shunned the balanced couplet, in which so much of the poetry of the previous age had been composed. Yet Wordsworth did not argue, as the modernists of this century did, that non-metrical verse was a suitable means of reforming the faults of predecessors. Indeed, historically considered, non-metrical verse is nothing if not singular, in that, until this century, virtually all Western poetry is informed by the distinction, enunciated as far back as Gorgias (*Helen, 9*) and Aristotle (*Rhetoric, 3.8.1-3*), that prose is organized in the general patterns and periods of rhythm (*rhythmos*) and poetry in the specifically and regularly ordered rhythmical units of meter (*metron*).

The modern movement's leaders seem not to have comprehended or admitted the singularity of non-metrical verse, nor has its singularity been sufficiently appreciated by subsequent poets and critics. Our primary aim in the remarks that follow will be to clarify the nature of the modern movement and free verse and to establish their relationship to previous literary revolutions; and we will do this by examining what Ford, Pound, and Eliot said about the modern movement in general and free verse in particular, and by examining evidence from relevant earlier literary history. Secondarily, we will try to set forth some of the reasons why non-metrical verse became the vehicle by which the modern movement was carried forward, and will sketch, by way of conclusion, some of the implications of the modern movement and free verse for current poetic practice.

* * *

We may begin with Eliot. Though anticipated and influenced in various ways by Ford and Pound, Eliot became the most public and prestigious spokesman for the modern movement, and he consequently received opportunity and encouragement to expound the movement in a more systematic fashion than his co-revolutionaries. Eliot's views of the modern movement and free verse appear most tellingly in two lectures delivered in the forties, "The Music of Poetry" and the second of his Milton papers, to the pertinent passages of which we should now look.

In the Milton lecture, Eliot deals with the modern revolution in general, sounding the theme that it is like the earlier revolutions effected by Dryden and Wordsworth and involves an effort to empty poetry of hot air and to relate poetry meaningfully to contemporary speech:

> I have on several occasions suggested, that the important changes in the idiom of English verse which are represented by the names of Dryden and Wordsworth, may be characterized as successful attempts to escape from a poetic idiom which has ceased to have a relation to contemporary speech. This is the sense of Wordsworth's Prefaces. By the beginning of the present century another revolution in idiom—and such revolutions bring with them an alteration of metric, a new appeal to the ear— was due.

It is important to note here two things. First, Eliot associates "idiom" with "metric." Second, he asserts that, in literary revolutions, an alteration of the former entails an alteration of the latter. Eliot's association of idiom and metric is itself questionable. Though what a poet says is always related to the way in which he says it, idiom and metric are different things. Idiom is immediate and fluid; it changes from generation to generation and can even vary greatly among different groups of contemporaries speaking the same language. Meter, on the other hand, is much less local. It is an abstraction; it comprises a measure or measures by means of which speech can be organized into particular rhythmical patterns. Poets working in entirely different times and idioms can use the same meter; Shakespeare and Wordsworth, though of different eras and outlooks, both employ the iambic pentameter. Indeed, entirely different languages can share the same meters, as, for instance, Greek and Latin share the dactylic hexameter or as Russian and German and English share the iambic tetrameter.

As for Eliot's assertion that alterations of idiom inevitably bring alterations of metric, the assertion is simply not borne out by the testimony of literary history, certainly not by the testimony Eliot himself cites. Wordsworth, throughout the revolution he led, defended the virtues of conventional meter as earnestly as he decried the vices of "poetic diction." Whereas Wordsworth tried to reform poetry by bringing to metrical composition a more vital language than was in fashion at the time, Eliot endeavored to reform poetry, at least in part, by abandoning conventional meter.

To put the matter more comprehensively and to anticipate an issue we will discuss later in greater detail, we may say this of the leaders of the modern literary revolution. With the best of motives and intentions, they objected to the diction and attendant subject matter of Victorian verse. Yet they identified the vague and over-decorative lyricality of Victorian poetry with the metrical system which the Victorians had used but which was not itself Victorian, having been used for centuries by a variety of poets working in a variety of styles. Consequently, the moderns' argument that Victorian diction was outmoded came to include the argument that traditional meter was outmoded. And because the general formal quality of standard meter became identified with the particular stylistic excesses of Victorian verse, an attack on the latter led to an attack on the former. In view of the general soupiness of late Victorian verse, the moderns' conflation of diction and meter is, in one sense at least, perfectly understandable. At the same time, the conflation represents a fundamental confusion and mixing-together of properties that have been, for most of literary history, considered and treated as distinguishable. And unless we understand this point, we will not understand why the modern revolution, which began as a protest against the deficiencies of nineteenth-century verse, developed into a movement directed (in many cases contrary to its own intentions) against traditional poetic technique.

Discussing the objectives he and his early associates entertained, Eliot goes on to say, in his Milton lecture, that they wanted to create a poetry which spoke unaffectedly. They wanted to create poetry, Eliot recalls, which possessed the immediacy of good prose and which took its subjects and vocabulary not from dated canons of taste, but straight from modern life and speech, regardless of their evidently "non-poetic" qualities:

It was one of our tenets that verse should have the virtues of prose, that diction should become assimilated to cultivated contemporary speech, before aspiring to the elevation of poetry. Another tenet was that the subject-matter and the imagery of poetry should be extended to topics and objects related to the life of a modern man or woman; that we were to seek the non-poetic, to seek even material refractory to transmutation into poetry, and words and phrases which had not been used in poetry before.

In "The Music of Poetry," Eliot advances arguments much like those he advances in his Milton paper. Here, too, Eliot characterizes the modern movement as "a period of search for a proper modern colloquial idiom," and contends that the modern revolution is identical to the revolutions led by Dryden and Wordsworth: "Every revolution in poetry is apt to be, and sometimes to announce itself to be a return to common speech. That is the revolution which Wordsworth announced in his prefaces, and he was right: but the same revolution had been carried out a century before by Oldham, Waller, Denham and Dryden; and the same revolution was due again something over a century later."

In addition to speaking of the modern movements in general, Eliot speaks in this essay of free verse in particular, and, with regard to the latter, he makes two points which are of special interest. One point is that the free verse he and his fellow experimentalists wrote was in essence simply a natural expression of a desire for poetic reform. Free verse embodied, Eliot says, not a rejection of poetic discipline, but a dissatisfaction with moribund procedures. "Only a bad poet could welcome free verse as a liberation from form," Eliot affirms. "It was a revolt against dead form, and a preparation for new form or for the renewal of the old."

A second point Eliot urges is that those who question the legitimacy of free verse are misguided. They are misguided, contends Eliot, not only to the extent that they see free verse as an expression of a wish to escape poetic restraint rather than as a revolt against dead form; they are also misguided to the extent that they fail to see that the distinction between metrical and non-metrical verse is basically trivial compared to the more profound distinction between good writing and bad: "As for free verse, I expressed my view twenty-five years ago by saying that no verse is free for the man who wants to do a good job. No one has better cause to know than I, that a great deal of bad prose has been written under the name of free verse; though whether its authors wrote bad prose or bad verse, or bad verse in one style or in another, seems to me a matter of indifference."

In speaking as he does, Eliot embodies attitudes also held by other leaders of the modern movement. These attitudes are especially evident in the literary criticism of Ford Madox Ford, who, though mainly remembered today for his novels, began writing free verse in the nineties and who in the first quarter of this century could rightly claim to be, as he puts it in his *Thus to Revisit*, a volume of reminiscences published in 1921, "the doyen of living writers of *Vers Libre* in English."

Ford's views about the modern movement and free verse appear most clearly in his preface to his *Collected Poems* of 1911, in a long essay entitled "The Battle of the Poets" in *Thus to Revisit*, and in some notes for a lecture on vers libre which he delivered in the twenties in New York City and which Frank MacShane has preserved in his *Critical Writings of Ford Madox Ford*. Ford emphasizes, as Eliot does, that the modern revolution in general was a protest against the outmoded idiom of Victorian verse. In his preface to his *Collected Poems*, Ford discusses the literary revolt which began with his generation and says: "What worried and exasperated us in the poems of the late Lord Tennyson, the late Lewis Morris, the late William Morris, the late—well, whom you like—is not their choice of subject, it is their imitative handling of matter, of words, it is their derivative attitude." Ford develops this theme in *Thus to Revisit*, in which he tells us that, when as a young writer he analyzed the Victorians, he came to the conclusion that their faults in part resulted from lofty attitudinizing and that poetry, if it was to recover from these faults, had to be brought back down to earth and into touch with the solid, workmanlike qualities of good prose. "I had to make for myself the discovery that verse must be at least as well written as prose if it is to be poetry," Ford remarks. "The Victorians killed the verse side of poetry because, intent on the contemplation of their own moral importance, they allowed their sentences to become intolerably long, backboneless, and without construction."

For Ford, as for Eliot, the importance of prose qualities in verse extends to specific issues of diction and subject. Not only must poetry achieve a clarity of meaning and structure comparable to that of prose; poetry must also speak in contemporary terms and address contemporary material, even if such terms and such material are not customarily believed to be "poetic." In *Thus to Revisit*, Ford says that by 1898 he had worked out a "formula" for writing poems, and some of the features of his formula will strike our ears as being very similar to the "tenets" Eliot discusses in his Milton essay. The individual articles of the formula, Ford writes, were

> that a poem must be compounded of observation of the everyday life that surrounded us; that it must be written in exactly the same vocabulary as that which one used for one's prose; that, if it were to be in verse, it must attack some subject that needed a slightly more marmoreal treatment than is expedient for the paragraph of a novel; that, if it were to be rhymed, the rhyme must never lead to the introduction of unnecessary thought; and lastly, that no exigency of meter must interfere with the personal cadence of the writer's mind or the pressure of the recorded emotion.

The faith which Ford attached to these articles is obvious in his preface to his *Collected Poems*, in which he characterizes his verse as having "one unflinching aim—to register my own times in terms of my own time." And Ford significantly relates this "unflinching aim" to earlier poetic revolutions, arguing, no less forcefully than Eliot, that he and poets like him are thus performing a function good poets have always performed, to wit, connecting poetry to the real life of its era: "I would rather read a picture in verse of the emotions and environment of a Goodge Street anarchist than recapture what songs the sirens sang. That after all was what Françoise Villon was doing for the life of his day."

About free verse in particular, Ford makes points much like those Eliot makes about the subject. In *Thus to Revisit*, for instance, Ford speaks of imagism (of which he was one of the eleven charter members represented in Pound's *Des Imagistes* anthology of 1914), and he urges that imagistic vers libre is a rebellion not against poetic rigor, but against the rhetorical vices of the Victorians. "The work is free," Ford says of the imagists' poems, "of the polysyllabic, honey-dripping and derivative adjectives that, distinguishing the works of most of their contemporaries, makes nineteenth-century poetry as a whole seem greasy and 'close,' like the air of a room." Ford also argues, in his lecture on vers libre, that free verse is a natural expression of the desire for (to return to Eliot's phrase) "a proper modern colloquial idiom." Perhaps recalling Wordsworth's definition of a Poet as "a man speaking to men," Ford asserts that "if a man cannot talk like an educated gentleman about things that matter in direct and simple English let him hold his tongue." Ford then cites Wordsworth's pentameter, "Shine,

Poet! in thy place, and be content," and comments: "That is really what vers libre is. It is an attempt to let personalities express themselves more genuinely than they have lately done."

Many of the ideas we find in Eliot and Ford are to be found as well in Pound. For Pound, too, the modern revolution represents an overthrowing of lax style, and shows, in this regard, a healthy resemblance to earlier revolutions. In his "A Retrospect" essay, published in *Pavannes and Divisions* in 1918 but incorporating some materials which had appeared earlier in periodicals, Pound looks back on the beginnings of imagism and free verse, and suggests that they were a salutary protest against the poetry of the nineteenth century, a period he describes as being "a rather blurry, messy sort of a period, a rather sentimentalistic, mannerish sort of a period." Pound tells us that when he and H.D. and Richard Aldington decided in 1912 to form a group dedicated to revitalizing poetry, they adopted as their first principle, "direct treatment of the 'thing' whether subjective or objective"; and in Pound's mind, this is exactly the principle earlier poets embraced when they forged new styles. "In the art of Daniel and Cavalcanti," Pound says in the same essay, "I have seen that precision which I miss in the Victorians, that explicit rendering, be it of external nature or of emotion. Their testimony is of the eyewitness, their symptoms are first hand." Speaking generally of the modern movement, Pound adds: "As to Twentieth century poetry, and the poetry which I expect to see written during the next decade or so, it will, I think, move against poppy-cock, it will be harder and saner.... At least for myself, I want it so, austere, direct, free from emotional slither."

In his 1913 essay, "The Serious Artist," Pound sounds similar themes. Alluding to Stendhal's remark that prose (specifically, the prose of the serious novelist) "is concerned with giving a clear and precise idea of the movements of the spirit," Pound urges that modern poetry must adopt the same objective. In advocating this "new sort" of poetry, Pound tells us, he is really doing nothing except advocating an "old sort," a poetry with the requisite sharpness and immediacy to engage a worthy audience:

> And if we cannot attain to such a poetry, noi altri poeti, for God's sake let us shut up. Let us 'give up, go down,' etcetera; let us acknowledge that our art, like the art of dancing in armour, is out of date and out of fashion. Or let us go to our ignominious ends knowing that we have strained at the cords, that we have spent our strength in

trying to pave the way for a new sort of poetic art—it is not a new sort but an old sort—but let us know that we have tried to make it more nearly possible for our successors to recapture this art. To write a poetry that can be carried as a communication between intelligent men.

Pound also stresses, with Eliot and Ford, that poetry will not recover from its Victorian maladies unless it secures the virtues of good prose. This emphasis is evident in "The Serious Artist" and in his 1929 "How to Read" essay, in both of which Pound observes that, as he puts it in the latter essay, in the nineteenth century "the serious art of writing 'went over to prose.'" The modern poet must in consequence emulate, Pound urges, the scrupulosity and careful workmanship of the modern novelist if poetry is to recover a central position in imaginative literature. No less emphatic on this subject is Pound's 1914 article for *Poetry* on Ford's verse. Here, Pound praises Ford for trying to bring the language of verse up to date and argues that, if modern poets wish to refresh their art, they would do well to follow Ford's attempt to integrate real speech and real life into poetry. Pound hails Ford's "On Heaven" as the "best poem yet written in 'the twentieth century fashion,'" and concludes his consideration of Ford by saying: "I find him significant and revolutionary because of his insistence upon clarity and precision, upon the prose tradition; in brief, upon efficient writing—even in verse."

With respect to free verse, Pound presents ideas that are similar to those presented by Eliot and Ford. Indeed, the clearest portion of the "Re Vers Libre" section of Pound's "Retrospect" essay is a one-sentence paragraph which runs: "Eliot has said the thing very well when he said, 'No *vers* is *libre* for the man who wants to do a good job.'" Pound also cites Eliot's dictum in his review of *Prufrock and Other Observations* for *Poetry* in 1917, and here Pound suggests, as does Eliot himself, that distinctions between formal and free verse are not especially significant when compared to distinctions between good and bad writing. "Conviction as to the rightness or wrongness of *vers libre*," says Pound at the start of that section of his review specifically devoted to Eliot's versification, "is no guarantee of a poet." This notion in turn appears to underlie the "Credo" section of the "Retrospect" essay, in which Pound affirms, evidently referring to formal and free verse: "I believe in technique as the test of a man's sincerity; in law when it is ascertainable; in the trampling down of every convention that impedes or obscures the determination of the law, or the precise rendering of the impulse."

❄ ❄ ❄

Most literary revolutions are led, as the modern one was, by poets who feel that poetry has grown pompous and must be refashioned so that it can speak directly and truly of life. Yet the suggestion that an abandonment of meter is a suitable means of reforming poetry is a particular feature of the modern literary revolution. To establish these points more securely—to establish both the way the modern revolution resembled earlier revolutions and the way it differed from them in its identification of diction with meter and in its advocacy of a poetry "free" of conventional versification—we should now turn to the two ancient literary innovators mentioned above, Euripides and Horace, and to the two English ones to whom Eliot appeals, Dryden and Wordsworth.

Though Euripides did not formally engage (as far as we know) in literary criticism, the fact that he consciously revolutionized tragedy at the end of the fifth century B.C. is borne out in the testimony of subsequent ancient writers. It is equally apparent that the two traits that most marked his innovations are traits we associate with the modernists of our time. First, Euripides objected to the heroic model of previous tragedy and insisted on presenting his characters and their world in a "realistic" manner, however much such a presentation involved what traditionalists considered to be qualities wholly inappropriate to tragic drama. Second, he rejected the elevated rhetoric that had characterized tragic style since Aeschylus' time and wrote rather in a style incorporating the ordinary speech of his day. The first of these traits is noted by, among others, Dio Chrysostom (*Oration*, 52) and Diogenes Laertius (*Lives*, 4.5.6 [*Crantor*]), and is noted as well by Aristotle (*Poetics*, 1460 b33-34), who records that "Sophocles said that he portrayed people as they ought to be and Euripides portrayed them as they are." The second of these traits, the colloquial novelty of Euripides' diction, receives comment from Quintilian (*Institutiones Oratoriae*, 10.1.68) and Longinus (*On the Sublime*, 40.2), and from Aristotle (*Rhetoric*, 3.2.5) in his discussion of art-which-hides-art: "Art is cleverly concealed when the speaker chooses his words from ordinary language (*eiothyias dialektou*) and puts them together like Euripides, who was the first to show the way."

Even if we lacked the evidence of such commentators, we would still have ample testimony about Euripides' innovations and about the controversy they excited. This additional testimony is supplied by Aristophanes' *The Frogs*, which provides perhaps the earliest extended examination of a literary revolution and several lines of which, interestingly, Ford uses as an epigraph to "The Battle of the Poets" essay in *Thus to Revisit*. It will be recalled that the second half of *The Frogs* consists of a formal debate, with Dionysus serving as judge, between Aeschylus and Euripides—the former cast in the role of the somewhat stodgy defender of older conventions, the latter cast in the role of the wily and newfangled parvenu. The debate takes place at Pluto's palace in Hades, where Aeschylus, who has long occupied the honorary Chair of Tragedy, finds his tenureship challenged by the arrival of the recently deceased Euripides (Aristophanes' play was first staged in 405 B.C., the year after Euripides' death); and the charges which Euripides levels at the older Aeschylus, and the terms with which Euripides justifies his own innovations, strikingly resemble statements made by the modernists of our time.

For example, Euripides criticizes Aeschylus as bombastic (*kompophakelorremona*, "boast-bundle-phrased") (839) and argues that Aeschylus' tragedies are works of an overly poetical impostor (*alazon*) (907ff.). So wildly inflated is Aeschylus' style, Euripides says (926), that it is at times downright unintelligible (*agnota*), and, with a colorful metaphor, he alleges that, under Aeschylus' influence, tragedy itself grew into a state of sickly bloating (*oidousan*), which, however, has since been happily alleviated by strong doses of modernity (939ff.). "When I took over Tragedy from you," Euripides' remarks run in David Barrett's recent translation, "the poor creature was in a dreadful state. Fatty degeneration of the Art. All swollen up with high-falutin' diction. I soon got her weight down, though: put her on a diet of particles, with a little finely chopped logic (taken peripatetically), and special decoction of dialectic, cooked up from books and strained to facilitate digestion."

As for his own "new" style, Euripides boasts that he did not rely on the grandiose and fabulous (959). Instead, "I wrote about familiar things [*oikeia pragmat' eisagon*], things the audience knew about." Nor did he, he adds, bludgeon the audience with big words or befuddle them with resonant obscurities; no, he spoke in "human terms" (*phrazein anthropeios*, "language man to man") (1058). Euripides further argues that he avoided inane ornament or "padding" (*stoiben*) (1178) and that his writing was "clear" and "accurate" (*saphes* and *leptos* being the words used in several places to denote these qualities). And, indeed, when Euripides speaks of the way he "reduced" tragedy (941), the term he employs, *ischnana*, indicates not only "spare," but suggests the *ischnos charakter* of the classical plain style itself, of which Euripides was one of the founders. That Euripides ultimately loses the debate—Dionysus favoring Aeschylus because he is a sounder ethical guide than his more stylistically sophisticated rival—does not concern us here. What is important is simply the similarity between Euripides' ideas and innovations and those of the leaders of the modern movement in our century.

Issues like those raised by Euripides' work appear in Horace's literary epistles. It would be wrong to call Horace a Euripidean figure, for Horace repeatedly urges that poetry should feature both moral concern and technical finesse, and seeks to heal the kinds of breaches between ethics and aesthetics depicted in *The Frogs*. Nevertheless, Horace is staunchly opposed to the literary conservatism of his day, and in his epistle to Augustus, he writes: "I am impatient that any work is censured, not because it is thought to be coarse or inelegant in style, but because it is modern (*nuper*).... If novelty (*novitas*) had been as offensive to the Greeks as it is to us, what in these days would be ancient?" (*Epistles*, 2.1.76-77; 90-91). Horace, moreover, persistently objects to the notion that poetic diction is a static and time-hallowed dialect and persistently urges that the language of verse should be meaningfully related to the speech of real men and women.

In the earliest of his literary epistles, Horace discusses the nature of satire, a genre that, he argues, could be much improved if the deficiencies of its originator, Lucilius, were recognized and corrected. Though Horace respects and praises Lucilius, he also says that Lucilius' writing is often "harsh" (*durus*), "turbid" [*lutulentus*], "verbose" (*garrulus*) and generally "slapdash" or "lazy" (*piger*) (*Satires*, 1.4.8-12). "You need terseness [*brevitate*]," Horace urges, recommending an antidote to Lucilius' shortcomings, "that the thought may run on, and not become entangled in verbiage that weighs upon wearied ears" (*Satires*, 1.10.9-10) and adds that so different in general is the diction of satire from what is commonly considered poetic speech that, were one to deprive satirical verses of their "regular beat and rhythm" (*tempora certa modosque*), they would scarcely retain any poetic features whatever (56 ff.). And Horace in fact goes so far as to say that in writing satire he does not view himself as a poet (38-44) and to raise the question of whether satire itself can be deemed verse, so humble and plain is the speech in which it is written (63-65).

There is, however, patently an element of irony in such self-deprecation, and it is clear that Horace is poking fun at those who require that verse always be pitched in the grand manner. Moreover, the points Horace facetiously offers in his early literary epistles reappear in the more serious setting of his later *Art of Poetry*. Here, Horace argues in several contexts that, if plain diction is adroitly managed, if it is characterized by *iunctura* (a skillful weaving together of words), *calliditas* (an artful dexterity of arrangement), and *urbanitas* (an engaging refinement of manner), it is far preferable to a continually elevated style. Such plain diction, Horace furthermore contends, has the advantage of being able to deal, without exaggeration or affectation, with life as it is really lived. With respect to dramatic writing, Horace advises that the poet who has mastered the tools of his trade should then "look to life and manners for a model, and draw from thence living words [*viva voces*]." Such a poetry may seem "without force and art" (*sine pondere et arte*), but it nevertheless "gives the people more delight and holds them better than verses void of thought, and sonorous trifles [*verses inopes rerum nugaeque canorae*]" (318-323). And discussing, in another passage, the quality of *iunctura*, Horace makes much the same argument in a broader and more personal manner: "My aim shall be poetry," he tells us, "so moulded from the familiar that anybody may hope for the same success, may sweat much and yet toil in vain when attempting the same: such is the power of order and connexion, such the beauty that may crown the commonplace" (240-243).

Horace's insistence that poetry should deal with the commonplace as well as the lofty, and his insistence that the poet should draw his speech and matter directly from life, are related to his belief that the language of verse is not an artificial vocabulary, but is derived from and governed by normal usage. Like the modernists of our time, he objects to the coterie styles of his day and to the tendency of many poets to isolate themselves in a rarefied linguistic autonomy. "All mortal things shall perish," Horace cautions in *The Art of Poetry*, "much less shall the glory and glamour of speech endure and live. Many terms that have fallen out of use shall be born again, and those shall fall that are now in repute, if Usage so will it [*si volet usus*], in whose hands lies the judgment, the right and the rule of speech" (68-72). This argument is in turn related to Horace's contention that, as usage changes, the poet has the right to bring into verse what Eliot refers to, in his Milton essay, as "words and phrases which had not been used in poetry before." As Horace sums up the issue, "If haply one must betoken abstruse things by novel terms, you will have a chance to fashion words never heard of by the kilted Cethegi [ancient Romans], and license will be granted, if used with modesty; while words, though new and of recent make, will win acceptance, if they spring from a Greek fount and are drawn therefrom but sparingly" (48-53). And in the same way that Eliot urges in his early essay on Swinburne that a poet should be free to seek language "to digest and express new objects, new groups of objects, new feelings, new aspects," so Horace urges that a poet always should be allowed to import into his work novel terms to treat novel subjects in contemporary life. "And why should I be grudged the right of adding, if I can," Horace asks, "my little fund, when the tongue of Cato and of Ennius has enriched our mother-speech and brought to light new terms for things? It has ever been, and ever will be, permitted to issue words stamped with the mint-mark of the day" (55-59).

Dryden, too, stresses that verse should be written in an unaffected and contemporary idiom. Indeed, this aspect of Dryden provides the governing theme of the three BBC lectures on Dryden that Eliot delivered in 1931 and in which Eliot observed: "What Dryden did, in fact, was to reform the language, and devise a natural, conversational style of speech in verse in place of an artificial and decadent one.... He restored English verse to the condition of speech." Dryden's emphasis on naturalness is evident in much of his writing, perhaps nowhere more so than in two of his earliest and best-known critical pieces, his 1664 dedication of *The Rival Ladies* to the Earl of Orrery and his *Essay of Dramatic Poesy*, which was composed in 1665/66 and published in 1668.

The dedication to *The Rival Ladies* is of particular importance to our concerns, because Dryden explicitly advocates in his remarks to his patron a poetry which has "the elegance of prose." Dryden is using the term "negligence," we should note, not in the sense of "carelessness," but in the sense in which Cicero uses the word in his definition of the plain style—in the sense of "directly and uncosmetically attractive." "There is such a thing even as a careful negligence [*neglegentia*]," writes Cicero. "Just as some women are said to be handsomer when unadorned—this very lack of ornament becomes them—so this plain style gives pleasure even when unembellished: there is something in both cases which lends greater charm, but without showing itself" (*Orator*, 78). Inasmuch as *The Rival Ladies* is not only in meter, but in rhyme, and inasmuch as some critics of Dryden's day were arguing that rhyme in dramatic verse produced an inevitably stilted quality, Dryden is particularly interested in making the point that rhyme can be harmonized with, as he puts it, "ordinary speaking." Infelicities may occur, Dryden concedes, when a poet uses rhyme ineptly; by the same token, however, when rhyme is expertly employed, "the first word in the verse seems to beget the second, and that the next, till that becomes the last word in the line which, in the negligence of prose, would be so." And when used in this happy manner, Dryden continues, "rhyme has all the advantages of prose besides its own."

The virtues of natural style are discussed at greater length in the *Essay of Dramatic Poesy*. Among the many topics the four disputants in the dialogue examine are the condition of English verse in the immediately preceding age and the direction in which contemporary verse might profitably move. And Eugenius, one of the two characters who voice Dryden's own views, makes a number of statements resembling those made by Eliot, Ford, and Pound. For one thing, Eugenius argues that the metaphysical poetry so popular with the previous generation is hopelessly stiff and false. Speaking of John Cleveland's work in particular, Eugenius suggests that using words in an odd or distorted manner may be permissible on occasion, but "to do this always, and never be able to write a line without it, though it may be admired by some few pedants, will not pass" with discriminating readers. Eugenius then contrasts truly fine writing, which speaks "easily" (without peculiarity or strain) to a wide audience, with the type of poetry represented by Cleveland: "Wit is best conveyed to us in the most easy language; and is most to be admired when a great thought comes dressed in words so commonly received that it is understood by the meanest apprehensions, as the best meat is the most easily digested; but we cannot read a verse of Cleveland's without making a face at it, as if every word were a pill to swallow; he gives us many times a hard nut to break our teeth, without a kernel for our pains."

In another section of the dialogue, Eugenius takes a position which is not unlike that which Pound takes in his "Retrospect" essay and which involves the argument that the innovations of newer writers like Waller and Denham are in no way seditious assaults on the art of poetry, but are instead a healthy reaction against the vices of a worn-out mode; and it is noteworthy that at this juncture no one else in the dialogue, not even the hidebound and cantankerous Crites, opposes Eugenius. On the contrary, Dryden reports, "Every one was willing to acknowledge how much our poesy is improved by the happiness of some writers yet living, who first taught us to mould our thoughts into easy and significant words, to retrench the superfluities of expression, and to make our rhyme so properly a part of the verse that it should never mislead the sense, but itself be led and governed by it."

We should observe that, as well as recommending naturalness of style and (to use Pound's phrase) "efficient writing" in verse, Dryden is in general a champion of the literature of his nation and his time. Much of the *Essay of Dramatic Poesy* concerns the Quarrel of the Ancients and the Moderns, which had begun in Italy in the fifteenth century and which continued in England and France down into the eighteenth, and Dryden, though respectful of the achievements of the Greeks and Romans, stoutly defends the claims of the moderns. Modern English dramatists especially, Dryden feels, deserve credit for the originality of their plots and the "just and lively image of human nature" they present. Eugenius and his ally (for the most part) Neander make the points that the ancients tended to recycle the same stories again and again in their plays, and did not present the entertaining and realistic varieties of mood found in many modern dramas. And if it would be an exaggeration to portray Dryden's views in terms of the Poundian programme of "Make It New," it is nevertheless the case that he is interested in, and values, the contemporary in many of the same ways that Pound and Eliot and Ford do.

Before moving to the final section of our essay, we may briefly consider Wordsworth, in whom we find many of the ideas we discovered in the other poets we have examined. In the preface to the second edition of *Lyrical Ballads*, Wordsworth announces that his work is a reaction against "the gaudiness and inane phraseology of many modern writers" and against "POETIC DICTION," which he characterizes as "arbitrary and capricious habits of expression." Such habits, he suggests, are connected with another literary vice, this being the turning aside from real experience in order "to trick out or to elevate nature." Of his own poetry, Wordsworth avows that his object in writing it was "to choose incidents and situations from common life, and to relate or describe them, throughout, as far as was possible in a selection of language really used by men." Wordsworth also informs us that his verse involves a belief that "ordinary things should be presented to the mind," and the poet should not dwell, Wordsworth adds, in a private lexicon and among a circumscribed set of "poetical" subjects; rather, the poet's work should partake of a "general sympathy," and the poet must remember that "Poets do not write for Poets alone, but for men."

Like earlier and later poetic innovators, Wordsworth also contends that the language of poetry should be vitally related to the language of fine prose. For instance, in his preface, he asserts of verse that "the language, though naturally arranged, and according to the strict laws of metre, does not differ from that of prose." He furthermore argues "that not only the language of a large portion of every good poem, even of the most elevated character, must necessarily, except with reference to the metre, in no re-spect differ from that of good prose, but likewise that some of the most interesting parts of the best poems will be found to be strictly the language of prose when prose is well written." And toward the end of this part of his preface, he remarks: "We will go further. It may be safely affirmed, that there neither is, nor can be, an *essential* difference between the language of prose and metrical composition."

As is the situation with other innovators at whom we have been look-ing, Wordsworth wants to write directly and freshly, and he says of his verse overall: "I have at all times endeavoured to look steadily at my sub-ject; consequently, there is I hope in these poems little falsehood of de-scription, and my ideas are expressed in language fitted to their respective importance." The aim is true speech, a poetry that communicates itself to its readers with clarity and energy, a style free of mannerism and literary posturing.

❉ ❉ ❉

If a reader of Roman poetry had fallen asleep in 45 B.C. and had awak-ened twenty-five years later to find Horace's *Odes* on his chest, he might well have been astonished on unrolling the scroll. The poet's material and presentation of it, in any event, would have seemed most unusual. Yet the reader, at least the educated one, would have recognized the verse forms, and if he had wished, he could have traced in his mind their continuity all the way back to the misty beginnings of Greek lyric. Similarly, if an En-glish reader had fallen asleep in 1775 and had awakened a quarter of a century later to find the *Lyrical Ballads* at his bedside, he might well have been startled by the subject and manner of "Tintern Abbey" or "Her Eyes Are Wild." He would, however, have had no difficulty determining that the first was in conventional blank verse and the second in conventional rhymed iambic tetrameters. If a reader had fallen asleep in 1900 and had awakened in 1925 to find Ford's *To All the Dead*, Eliot's *The Waste Land*, and Pound's *A Draft of XVI Cantos*, it is unlikely he would have had the slightest idea of what to make of the versification of the poems.

This is the singularity of the modern movement. It broke with tradi-tional versification. It did not involve, to recall Eliot's phrase, "an alter-ation of metric"—a change from one clear set of principles to another—but rather an escape from metric. Like earlier revolutionaries, those of this century urged that poetry should embody the virtues of lively colloquial speech and genuine thought and feeling; but earlier revolutionaries did not urge, to cite Ford once more, "that no exigency of meter must interfere with the personal cadence of the writer's mind or the pressure of the recorded emotion." Euripides' metrical virtuosity is legendary; and though his choruses were sometimes accused of licentiousness, this charge appears to have been brought against their dance and musical elements as much as their rhythmical character. Horace, however innovative in his treatment of his subject matter, is a master of conventional craft. "My own delight," he says, "is to shut up words in feet" (*me pedibus delectat claudere verba*) (*Satires*, 2.1.28). To speak a moment of Villon, whom Ford and Pound both refer to as a model, he is shockingly original; yet he writes in metrical forms, *ballades* and *rondeaux*, which are extremely strict and which had been bequeathed to him by earlier poets like Deschamps and Machaut.

The same circumstance applies to Dryden and Wordsworth. Though a defender of modern practices, Dryden throughout his criticism emphasizes the value of metrical composition. In fact, one of the common themes of his essays, dedications, and prefaces is that those who have difficulty writing naturally in verse should blame themselves and not their medium. In his dedication to *The Rival Ladies*, Dryden admits that rhyme can result in awkwardnesses, but adds that it does so only, "when the poet either makes a vicious choice of words, or places them, for rhyme sake, so unnaturally as no man would in ordinary speaking." This argument appears as well in the *Essay of Dramatic Poesy*, in which Neander comments at one point that "the necessity of a rhyme never forces any but bad or lazy writers to say what they would not otherwise." The fact that Dryden himself, later in his career, abandoned the use of rhyme in his dramatic works, is not of consequence in the present context, for he makes much the same arguments about unrhymed metrical composition. For instance, in the section of the *Essay* in which Neander discusses rhyme, he also cites a line of blank verse containing two clumsy inversions, "I heaven invoke, and strong resistance make," and remarks: "You would think me very ridiculous if I should accuse the stubbornness of blank verse for this, and not rather the stiffness of the poet." And generally Dryden's attitude about meter seems summarized in a statement he makes in the last paragraph of a *Defense* which he wrote of his *Essay* in the wake of Robert Howard's attack on it. "I have observed," says Dryden, "that none have been violent against verse, but such only as have not attempted it, or have succeeded ill in their attempt."

Wordsworth, too, is a strong defender of meter, and his preface to *Lyrical Ballads* has an eloquent explanation of its values. Indeed, Wordsworth carefully distinguishes the conventions of meter from the conventions of "POETIC DICTION"—arguing that the latter create a harmful barrier between reader and poet, but that the former establish a healthy and necessary bond between the two.

> The distinction of metre is regular and uniform, and not, like that which is produced by what is usually called POETIC DICTION, arbitrary, and subject to infinite caprices upon which no calculation whatever can be made. In the one case, the Reader is utterly at the mercy of the Poet, respecting what imagery or diction he may choose to connect with the passion; whereas, in the other, the metre obeys certain laws, to which the Poet and Reader both willingly submit because they are certain, and because no interference is made by them with the passion, but such as the concurring testimony of ages has shown to heighten and improve the pleasure which co-exists with it.

Wordsworth continues by exploring the nature of meter itself and "the charm which, by the consent of all nations, is acknowledged to exist in metrical language." He speaks of the happy effect of meter for the reader— of the "small, but continual and regular impulses of pleasureable surprise from the metrical arrangement" and of "the pleasure which the mind derives from the perception of similitude in dissimilitude." And Wordsworth speaks as well of the fundamental and wonderful paradox of successful metrical composition: it is speech which is natural, yet which, at the same time, is ordered within and played off against the norm of a fixed line: "Now the music of harmonious metrical language, the sense of difficulty overcome, and the blind association of pleasure which has been previously received from works of rhyme or metre of the same or similar construction, an indistinct perception perpetually renewed of language closely resembling that of real life, and yet, in the circumstance of metre, differing from it so widely—all these imperceptibly make up a complex feeling of delight."

In view of the statements of Dryden and Wordsworth, we may find it hard to comprehend how Eliot could repeatedly justify vers libre by appealing to their authority. In a broader sense, we may find it difficult to comprehend how the modernists of our time could in general argue so forcefully that their revolution, which developed and expressed itself—practically speaking—through non-metrical poems, was just like earlier literary revolutions. Admittedly, the modernists' enterprise was, at least in its initial stages, polemical: they wanted first and foremost their views heard and their verse published and read. And, like all polemicists, they may have tended to avail themselves of evidence which supported their cause and to have suppressed evidence that did not. Yet this is neither a complete nor a fair explanation of their use of the past and their desire, which was without doubt sincere, to reform poetry. We must therefore surmise that there were factors in the cultural life of their times which did not in earlier periods exist or exert a determining power, but which did exist in the modern period and helped to give rise to the concept of non-metrical verse. Before we conclude, it behooves us to take note of several of these factors and the manner in which they have shaped the poetry of our time.

One important factor is the influence of the modern physical sciences on our culture. Though evident as early as the seventeenth century, the influence does not really become pervasive until the technological triumphs of the nineteenth century. And increasingly in that century, one comes across the idea that art is not making the kinds of advances science is and that art should model its methods on those of science so that it, too, can achieve a kind of demonstrable, quantitative "progress." This idea is in turn productive of the notion that art should be "experimental" and that the artist should aspire to "breakthroughs" and "discoveries." Insofar as many of the advances of the modern physical sciences were results of inventions of or refinements of apparatus, artists of the late nineteenth and early twentieth centuries came to be more and more tempted to seek novelties of technique. Pound in particular reflects the influence of the modern physical sciences, in that his literary criticism is saturated with scientific and pseudo-scientific terminology. "THE IDEOGRAMMIC METHOD OR THE METHOD OF SCIENCE" is, for instance, the rallying cry of his *ABC of Reading*, and he appears to have believed that, in heaping together the miscellaneous materials of his *Cantos*, he was following the procedure of a biologist collecting data. Art, of course, is always and necessarily capable of novelty, but traditionally its novelty has resided in its subject matter—the ever-changing manners and morals of human beings and their societies. Then, too, art has always and necessarily shared certain values—clearsightedness, rigor, honesty—with science. However, the tendency to model art on science and to assert that each generation of artists should do something technically new is a feature distinctly of our time. It is also a feature that would naturally encourage poets to try unprecedented procedures, such as writing verse without meter.

Another factor which helped to shape and give sanction to non-metrical verse is the development of "Aesthetics." We use the term today in discussing issues throughout literary history; we have used the term, in fact, in these remarks in a comparison of Horace and Euripides. But the term, however widely useful in its applications, did not even exist until Baumgarten coined it in 1750. And not until the end of the eighteenth century, when Kant elaborated his system of three Critiques—isolating thereby the Beautiful (Judgment) from the True (Pure Reason) and the Good (Practical Reason)—was there a philosophical scheme within which art could claim independence from reason and ethics, and from, by extension, its own history. One argument Eliot, Ford, and Pound all make about their movement is that it involved, as Eliot says in his music essay, "an insistence upon the inner unity which is unique to every poem, against the outer unity which is typical." If every poem is to be regarded, as Eliot suggests, as an object with a unique inner unity or autonomy, it follows that every poem can have or create, so to speak, its own individual prosody.

Aestheticism also encouraged the development of non-metrical verse in another respect. In elevating music as the "purest" of the arts, writers in the aesthetic tradition helped produce a climate of opinion in which literary and visual artists aspired to musicality. The central idea of Eliot's music essay is that poetry has or can have a musical structure and that such a structure is in some fashion superior to a metrical structure. As for Ford and Pound, they both explain vers libre in terms of music, actually construing the vers libre line with eighth-notes, quarter-notes, and half-notes—Ford doing this in his preface to his *Collected Poems* and Pound in his "Tradition" essay. In this regard, Pound's famous remark that the poet should "compose in the sequence of the musical phrase, not in sequence of a metronome" is doubly significant. First, it indicates the degree to which music has, in Pound's mind anyway, supplanted meter as the measure of verse, and, second, it suggests the degree to which meter (the root word of metronome) has come to be viewed as something monotonous and inferior.

Another factor which contributed to the development of non-metrical verse is the rise and triumph of the modern novel. Though people have always told stories, and though traditions of prose fiction go back at least as far as Aesop, from the time of Homer to the eighteenth century, the fiction of prestige is virtually all metrical. Not until the nineteenth century do we, when thinking of the finest fiction writers of the age, think to a great extent of prose writers. A constant theme of the modern poets of our time is that verse has lost a lot of its material to prose fiction and that if poetry is to recover the material, it must assimilate elements and characteristics of the novel. In this context, Ford and Pound's assertion that verse must be at least as well-written as prose could be readily translated into the notion that verse should be written as the novel is written — without meter.

We should mention as well a point the late J.V. Cunningham raises in an interview in *The Iowa Review*. In one respect, the modernists of our time did not understand traditional meter and confused meter with a convention of reading and scanning that developed in the schools in the nineteenth century. This convention, which is still reflected in some textbooks, involves speaking lines of verse in a heavily artificial and sing-song way to bring out their metrical identity:

Of *man's* first *disobed*ience, *and* the *fruit*

Such reading clarified the metrical norm of the line, but it totally obliterates natural degrees of relative stress within the line. It sounds awful, to boot, and can easily lead, as Cunningham suggests it did lead, to the feeling that meter is something stiff and wooden.

This certainly appears to have happened with Pound. His remarks about the metronome, and his related imperative, "Don't chop your stuff into separate iambs," are salutary in that they remind the poet that it is incumbent on him to give his verse rhythmical life. At the same time, these remarks exhibit a startling ignorance of English metrical practice, as does his characterization, in "Treatise on Metre" in the *ABC of Reading*, of the iambic pentameter as "ti tum ti tum ti tum ti tum ti tum...from which every departure is treated as an exception." Good poets do not compose foot by foot; and, given the fact that any complete articulation in English has one and only one primarily stressed syllable and a number of syllables receiving greater or lesser degrees of secondary stress, it would actually be rather difficult to write a "metronomic" line in English, a line, that is, of light and heavy syllables of perfectly equivalent alternating weight. Pound's ti-tumming accounts for the metrical norm of the pentameter line and for the way a student might scan or read the line to bring out its metrical identity, but the ti-tumming does not account for the infinite varieties of rhythmical contour (and they are not "exceptions") that can be struck across the conventional pentameter. Here, for example, are pentameters from poems of Shakespeare, Dryden, Jane Austen, Robert Frost, and Thom Gunn:

> Prosperity's the very bond of love

> Thou last great prophet of tautology

> The day commemorative of my birth

> Snow falling and night falling fast, oh, fast

> Resisting, by embracing, nothingness

Each of these lines is orthodox, yet each has, within the context of that orthodoxy, a personal rhythm. The method of reading and scanning to which Cunningham refers, however, obscures this quality of English meter, and Cunningham is no doubt correct in observing that the understandable hostility to the method or convention came to be directed at meter itself.

We have come to our conclusion. Whether one feels pro or con about the movement Eliot, Ford, and Pound led, one probably should be, if one cares about poetry as a living art—an art existing not simply in texts and anthologies, but practiced by women and men today—troubled by this aspect of the movement: new forms were, it was hoped, to emerge from the experiments with non-metrical verse, or the old forms were supposed to revive. This has not happened. Rather, in the wake of the triumph of the modern revolution, several generations of poets have merely continued to write non-metrically. It is on this point that we should be most skeptical of Eliot's contention that metrical considerations are negligible when compared with the broader question of good and bad writing. As true as it is that meter alone will never produce a fine poem, even a bad poet who writes in meter keeps alive the traditions of metrical composition. When, however, good and bad poets alike devote themselves to non-metrical verse, it is possible that all sense of meter—and of the memorability and symmetry and surprise it can give listeners and readers—will be lost.

This danger, interestingly enough, was evident to Eliot late in his career. At the end of the Milton essay of 1947, he remarks: "We cannot, in literature, any more than in the rest of life, live in a perpetual state of revolution"; and warning against "a progressive deterioration" in poetry, he asks his audience to reflect that "a monotony of unscannable verse fatigues the attention even more quickly than a monotony of exact feet." Were Eliot alive today, he might well feel the same unease expressed in these comments. He and his co-revolutionaries had a valid quarrel with the nineteenth century and rebelled with specific goals in view. Whatever one thinks of their experiments with non-metrical verse, the experiments at least had a purpose. Now, however, the styles and attitudes of the nineteenth century have long since vanished, and the great majority of contemporary poets seem merely following, by rote and habit, a procedure of writing, and breaking up into lines, predictably mannered prose.

The New Formalism and the Return of Prosody

Keith Maillard

1.

Beginning in the early 1980s,[1] a disparate group of young poets who have been called "new formalists" gradually broke the domination that free verse had exercised over American poetry for twenty years. They employed rhyme and meter and all of the poetic devices that had long been associated with poetry before free verse displaced them; they wrote in every imaginable received form and invented some new ones of their own; they expanded the range of poetry beyond the lyric to include neglected genres such as verse dramas and narratives; they, in short, breathed new life into an entire poetic tradition that, if not entirely extinct, had at least been moribund. It is too soon to assess the full impact these poets have had upon the mainstream, but their work might well signal the most crucial shift in North American poetic sensibility since the 1960s.

At the outset, in order to avoid rapidly becoming tangled in confusion, I must offer a few definitions. "Free verse" is an unfortunate term with a troubled history, but long usage has established it to refer simply to poetry that is not metered, and that is the way I will use it. "Meter" means measure. There are many ways to measure a line of poetry, but the standard measure of English language poetry from Chaucer to the twentieth century has been "accentual-syllabic," and when I say "meter," that is the meter I mean. Finally, we are left with "formalist." In the '70s and early '80s, that term would have been applied to those left-overs from the '50s who were still writing metered verse—like Wilbur, Hecht, or Nemerov. Against the backdrop of free verse, however, almost any tightening of construction was bound to look formal, and so "formalist" was also used in a looser sense to refer to free verse poets who wrote in stanzas or "closed" forms.

This is a revised version of an essay which originally appeared in *The Antigonish Review* (St. Francis Xavier University, Antigonish, Nova Scotia, Canada), Number 100, Winter 1995.

By the mid-'80s, however, "neo-formalist" or "new formalist" or even, with the added weight of capitalization implying a critical category, "New Formalist" were used most often to refer to poets writing in meter.

The lists of new formalists one began to see in articles in the mid-'80s varied remarkably, but a core group—the highly visible and vocal champions of metered verse: Brad Leithauser, Dana Gioia, and Timothy Steele— were almost always included, as were Mary Jo Salter and Gjertrud Schnackenberg. After that, the lists varied depending (I suspect) upon whom a critic might have noticed and found the time to read. Strangely enough, Marilyn Hacker, one of the earliest and most accomplished of the new formal poets, was often overlooked, but usually included in lists of new formalists were poets who wrote exclusively in meter—Vikram Seth, Richard Kenney, Melissa Green—and poets who wrote a significant portion of their work in meter—J. D. McClatchy, Alfred Corn, William Logan. Finally, there was left a problematical category which some critics included and others didn't: poets who wrote formal constructions like sonnets in free verse—Molly Peacock—or wrote what I call (and will define later) "semi-metrical verse"—Henri Cole, Norman Williams.

Now, a little over a decade later, as older poets who had been there all along have been "discovered" and an ever increasing number of younger poets are publishing formal verse, the ranks of new formalists have swelled enormously; here is a listing, by no means exhaustive, of additional poets to whom that term has been, or might conceivably be, applied: Elizabeth Alexander, Julia Alvarez, Robert Barth, Bruce Bawer, Rafael Campo, Timothy Dekin, Tom Disch, Suzanne Doyle, Frederick Feirstein, Annie Finch, John Gery, Emily Grosholz, Rachel Hadas, Andrew Hudgins, Mark Jarman, Paul Lake, Sydney Lea, Phillis Levin, Robert McDowell, Charles Martin, David Mason, Marilyn Nelson, Katha Pollitt, Wyatt Prunty, Alan Shapiro, Robert B. Shaw, Michael Stillman, Frederick Turner, Rachel Wetzsteon, Greg Williamson.

A mistake made by nearly everyone who has written about the new formalists is to claim a common ground for them—a shared aesthetic more significant than an interest in meter and received forms—but it is impossible to find any such shared aesthetic; they are a wonderfully diverse lot, and they have, by now, produced an impressive body of excellent work that, in itself, should be enough to justify the reemergence of formal verse. But the debate they have prompted—and sometimes instigated—has been, and continues to be, surprisingly contentious.

The first shot in what might be called "the form war"—an ongoing debate conducted in the pages of American literary journals—was fired by Brad Leithauser in a highly provocative article, "Metrical Illiteracy," which appeared in *The New Criterion* (January, 1983).

> The exploding population of poets, the dizzying diffusion, the sense of open opportunities—clearly these conditions will little profit us so long as a belief persists that a person who is not a decent prosodist can be a decent poet. Or so long as we fail to recognize that metrical illiteracy is, for the poet, functional illiteracy.[2]

This was a deliberate challenge to the majority—the mainstream poets who had been trained in the free verse workshops of the 70s and regarded metrical verse as something as dead as the hoop skirt, and who—well, at least an uncomfortably large number of them—couldn't tell an amphibrach from an antimacassar.

In the same year, Dana Gioia's "The Dilemma of the Long Poem" was published in *The Kenyon Review*. Gioia, who would later emerge as one of the most visible and vocal of the new formal poets, conjures up "an intelligent eighteenth-century reader" to survey recent poetry:

> Where are the narrative poems, the verse romances, ballads, hymns, verse dramas, didactic tracts, burlesques, satires, the songs actually meant to be sung, and even the pastoral eclogues? Are stories no longer told in poetry? Important ideas no longer discussed at length?

Gioia argues for the expansion of American poetry to include genres in addition to the currently fashionable short lyric or long, book-length "epic."[3]

The influential anthology, *Strong Measures: Contemporary American Poetry in Traditional Forms*, was published in 1986. The editors, Philip Dacey and David Jauss, open their introduction by proclaiming the utter domination of free verse: "The revolution is over. The war has been won. As Stanley Kunitz has said, 'Non-metrical verse has swept the field.'" But they point out that "many poets have continued to write in traditional forms," and, to prove it, the editors have filled up their anthology with fascinating examples. Their introduction is a model of clarity and contains a detailed and useful discussion of prosody; they provide an equally useful selected bibliography and an introduction to meter and scansion. They are not championing formal verse over free. "The strongest poetry can be written," they argue, "when all options, formal and free, are open to the poet."[4] That formulation is so simple, so modest, so downright unassailable that it should have put an end to discord, but, given the combative nature of many American poets, it didn't.

In 1987 Leithauser ("The Confinement of Free Verse" in *The New Criterion*)[5] and Gioia ("Notes on the New Formalism" in *The Hudson Review*)[6] again issued pronouncements. Although the tone taken by these two could not be more dissimilar (Leithauser, the owlishly lofty literary critic, circa 1920; Gioia, the no-nonsense businessman giving us the straight scoop), what they have to say is quite similar. Both judge the contemporary mainstream and find it wanting. Leithauser: "Free verse at the moment shows signs of exhaustion." Gioia: "The new formalists put free verse poets in the ironic and unprepared position of being the status quo. Free verse, the creation of an older literary revolution, is now the long-established, ruling orthodoxy; formal poetry the unexpected challenge." Leithauser suggests that free verse needs "to gather to itself a broader collection of effects, a denser music." Gioia wishes to see an end to the wrangling between the proponents of metrical and free verse. "Soon, I believe, the central debate will focus on form in the wider, more elusive sense of poetic structure."

But the wrangling was not about to end. In 1988 another influential anthology was published: Robert Richman's *The Direction of Poetry: An Anthology of Rhymed and Metered Verse Written in the English Language Since 1975*. As a compiler of formal verse, Richman cannot be faulted; nearly every American poet anyone might wish to label new formalist is included—along with the older poets who have influenced them (Bishop, Donald Hall, Hecht, Hollander, Donald Justice, X. J. Kennedy, Stanley Kunitz, James Merrill, Nemerov, L. E. Sissman, W. D. Snodgrass, Robert Penn Warren, Richard Wilbur); the poems chosen are not necessarily the best or most representative, but at least the whole gang's here. But the introduction to the book is another matter.

Robert Richman has been associated with *The New Criterion* since its first issue; the jacket copy on his anthology informs us that he serves as poetry editor for that journal; the ideological stance of *The New Criterion* is unabashedly conservative. In their premier issue, the editors argue that, "We are still living in the aftermath of the insidious assault on mind that was one of the most repulsive features of the radical movement of the Sixties," and, "Not since the 1930s have so many orthodox leftist pieties so casually insinuated themselves into both the creation and the criticism of literature, and remained so immune to resistance or exposure." They see themselves as providing "a dissenting critical voice."[7] Richman has an axe to grind, and grind it he does.

For starters, there's the title of his book: metered verse may well be an increasingly important direction of poetry, but *the* direction? Then his introduction begins: "TO THE GENERAL READER [Richman's capitals], who has all but given up on contemporary poetry as a source of pleasure, this book will come as something of a surprise. After two decades of obscure, linguistically flat poetry, there has been a decisive shift.... Narration, characterization, and perhaps most significantly, musicality are showing new vigor." He equates the "return to musicality" to "the use of metrical language" as though free verse cannot be, or has not been, musical. "The free verse orthodoxy," he argues, has corrupted "the entire conception of form," and the Dacey and Jauss anthology, *Strong Measures* "provides a showcase" for "hybrid verse, in which pretense of a traditional form is used without any of its technical attributes." The poets in his anthology, however, are united in the "consistent use of a metrical foot," and, to make sure that we know what feet may be substituted for iambic ones, he gives us, in a footnote, Saintsbury's list from 1910.

Richman's comments on meter are either misleading ("in some poems, meter functions as a metaphor") or utterly ridiculous ("the metrical footing is not something to be outstripped but to fall back on—a rhythmic consolation for the loss of awe and wonder in our time"), and it rapidly becomes apparent that Richman does not understand what meter is.[8] He demonstrates his inability to distinguish rhythmic free verse from metrical verse by including (as Robert McDowell points out in *The Hudson Review*[9]) a number of poems that are not metrical.

The year after Richman's anthology appeared, Frederick Feirstein's *Expansive Poetry: Essays on the New Narrative and the New Formalism* was published, and Richman's "general reader," hoping for a fair and comprehensive introduction to new formalism, would be disappointed; it is a quirky and uneven collection of reprinted articles with an introduction by Feirstein and Frederick Turner. The best piece is Timothy Steele's excellent article (originally published in 1985) which presents the arguments in defense of metrical verse which he would later expand in his book, *Missing Measures*. Dana Gioia's "The Dilemma of the Long Poem" and "Notes on the New Formalism," are included, but nothing of Brad Leithauser's. Throughout many of these essays, references are made and rebuttals are offered to critics of the new formalism, yet statements by those critics are rarely summarized in any depth, which creates the maddening effect of hearing only one side of an ongoing conversation. The names of many poets usually associated with the new formalism never appear in either the introduction or any of the essays. Eventually one begins to feel that one has wandered into a private club.

Paul Lake defends the new formalism against the charge of conservatism by quoting from metrical poems that have liberal content.[10] Wyatt Prunty attempts to advance the cause of metrical verse by attacking free verse in general and A. R. Ammons and Robert Creeley in particular.[11] And Robert McPhillips argues that the New Formalism (his capitals) is not derivative of, or similar to, the high formalism of the 1950s, which he characterizes as distant, ironic, abounding in classical allusions; "quite frequently," he says, "[the '50s formal poem] focuses upon a cultural artifact, usually a European one." The diction in a new formalist poem is, by contrast, "colloquial rather than elevated. If the poem concerns cultural objects, they are likely to be from popular culture and to be indigenously American." Conveniently missing from his consideration are any poets who would contradict his thesis, most notably J. D. McClatchy, Alfred Corn, William Logan, Melissa Green, Richard Kenney, Marilyn Hacker, and Vikram Seth.[12]

The last essay, "The Neural Lyre: Poetic Meter, The Brain, and Time," by Frederick Turner and Ernst Pöppel, deserves more response than space will allow me to give it here. The argument purports to be based upon scientific research; most poets and commentators on poetry will not be well enough informed on recent findings in the study of brain function to be able to assess the claims and so might be tempted to accept the whole on faith; I would caution against doing that. One paraphrases such an article at considerable peril, so here are some representative quotations:

> [M]etered poetry is a cultural universal, and its salient feature, the three-second present moment of the auditory information-processing system. By means of metrical variation, the musical and pictorial powers of the right brain are enlisted by meter to cooperate with the linguistic powers of the left.... Meter breaks the confinement of linguistic expression and appreciation within two small regions of the left temporal lobe and brings to bear the energies of the whole brain.

Turner and Pöppel's article is fascinating reading; their argument unwinds step by step in a perfectly logical and ingenious way; yet, somewhere down the path, one begins to feel uneasy. It may indeed be the case that all cultures produce metrical poetry. Anyone who has read much metered poetry—certainly anyone who has written it—would not be surprised to hear the claim that the human brain is (as current jargon has it) hard-wired for metrical perception and production. But when we arrive at such statements as "free verse . . . is nicely adapted to the needs of the bureaucratic and even the totalitarian state," whereas "an education in [metered] verse will tend to produce citizens capable of using their full brains coherently, able to produce rational thought and calculation with values and commitment," it doesn't matter how logical and ingenious the argument has been, we are clearly in the realm of rhetoric, not science.[13]

The best defense of metrical poetry is Timothy Steele's clear, scholarly, and utterly formidable *Missing Measures: Modern Poetry and the Revolt Against Meter* (1990). What Steele sets out to do is simple enough: explore "ideas and conditions that led to the development of verse without meter"[14]; by the time he has finished, he has taken us from Pound and Eliot through the Renaissance theorists all the way back to the Greek and Roman poets and has apparently cited everyone—from Aristotle to Doc Williams—who has ever had an opinion about metrical verse. His discussion of the impact of science on modern poetry is especially fascinating (no one who has read it could ever again blithely and unreflectively use the word "experimental" to describe a style of poetry). There is only one relevant topic missing from Steele's book, and it is understandable why he did not address it; had he examined the second revolt against meter—the one that took place in the 1960s—he could easily have spent several more years and doubled his page count. *Missing Measures* is written with an extraordinary thoroughness, and anyone interested in contemporary poetry should read it.

Steele makes many points directly applicable to the ongoing debate over meter, but two of them stand out: first, that "the English and American experimentalists identified the florid idiom characteristic of much Victorian verse with meter itself. As a result, they believed that in order to get rid of Victorian style they had also to get rid of meter,"[15] but there is nothing intrinsic to metrical writing that ties it to the Victorian or to any other specific idiom; second, that "the hope of the modern movement's leaders was that if they overthrew the traditional system of English metric, a new system would generate itself out of the ruins,"[16] but no such new metric system has evolved. In his conclusion, Steele argues in his typically careful but forceful way: "It is not correct to tell [young writers in university workshops] that meter is no longer viable. Nor is it correct to evade fundamental questions of versification by referring to 'structure' and 'form' without relating these terms to the concept of metrical arrangement."[17]

The new formalism has been attacked on both political and aesthetic grounds. The political criticisms have often been based not upon a careful reading of a broad range of new formalist poetry but rather prompted by statements made by Brad Leithauser or Robert Richman. In an article titled "The Yuppie Poet" published in the *Associated Writing Programs Newsletter* (May, 1985),[18] Ariel Dawson sees the new formalism as part of a broader resurgence of conservatism in America. She likens the growing interest in meter and traditional forms to "renewed interest in country clubs."

Ira Sadoff, in an article called "Neo-Formalism: A Dangerous Nostalgia" (*The American Poetry Review*, January/February, 1990), presents a sophisticated (as opposed to vulgar) Marxist argument against the new formalism. He gets off to a bad start, however, from which he never recovers: "Robert Richman's anthology, *The Direction of Poetry*, offers readers an opportunity to evaluate the neo-formalist esthetic. His selection of poems, underlying assumptions of his introduction, and the writings of others associated with the movement, all provide evidence of what neo-formalists value and produce." But the only aesthetic we can evaluate in Richman's introduction is Richman's, and there is no discernable aesthetic common to the poems. For Sadoff, the "others associated with the movement" are, apparently, Brad Leithauser, and, strangely enough, Helen Vendler, who is not, by any means, directly associated with the new formalism (what Sadoff has against her, so it seems, is that she has praised Leithauser's poetry).

From an amalgam of Richman, Leithauser, Vendler, and a few poems selected from Richman's anthology, Sadoff creates a straw man that he proceeds to belabour with more force than clarity: "The neo-formalists' esthetic trivializes form...when it dissociates meter from vision...." "Poems that privilege sound and meter are conservative, then, not so much because they privilege tradition, but because they decontextualize poetry.... The neo-formalists' perhaps unconscious exaltation of the iamb veils their attempt to privilege prevailing white Anglo-Saxon rhythms and culture.... [O]ur poetries are enriched by otherness, by many different kinds of music and varieties of meters. Their [the neo-formalists'] narrow-minded appreciation of cadence and music unconsciously creates a kind of cultural imperialism."[19]

One waits in vain for Sadoff to explain what "vision" or (in this context) "decontextualize" mean. How can one "unconsciously" choose to write iambic meter? What is a white Anglo-Saxon rhythm? Meter is not an equivalent term to musicality; meter refers to specific ways of counting syllables, stresses, and lines in poetry; if poets from other cultures, when they are writing in English, employ many different varieties of meters, I would be delighted had Sadoff listed some of them and demonstrated how they work. How can an appreciation of cadence and music create cultural imperialism? Don't cultures other than white Anglo-Saxon appreciate cadence and music? And if we are doing these nasty things unconsciously, how can we be expected to mend our ways?

Wayne Dodd attacks new formalism from the free verse aesthetic position. He has been the editor of the *Ohio Review*, and his essays have appeared in various journals, including his own, throughout the '80s; they have been collected in *Toward the End of the Century: Essays into Poetry* (1992). For Dodd, "the best contemporary poetry" is "almost all of it in free verse,"[20] for metered verse is "a poetry of fixity" whereas free verse is "a poetry of possibility."[21] He frequently refers to quantum theory, invokes Einstein, Planck, and Heisenberg nearly as often as he does Doc Williams, Robert Bly, or Galway Kinnell, and appears genuinely to believe that the words of a free verse poem—in "The dynamic of the page: the 'field' in which discovery is worked out"[22]—are directly analogous to subatomic particles, that modern physics has "robbed the phenomenal, the appearing world, of its solid, unquestioned external existence."[23] The notion of form—as something predetermined and imposed upon the poem—is, therefore, suspect: "...one of the poet's primary needs—even an ethical responsibility—is to allow the poem to hear and embody—to incarnate—the experience's truest music, the world's music. What greater enemy to such freedom than the 'idolatry' of some privileged forms?"[24]

With such a position there is no compromise; the new formalists are simply wrong—Dodd accuses them of "know-nothingism"—for they wish to return to the comfort of a time before modern physics destroyed our old notions of the universe. "Relativity. Uncertainty. Phenomenology," Dodd writes. "So far as I am aware, that is still the world we know, the world that responsible, serious, informed thought engages and expresses. To deny its reality, indeed its primacy, does not change those profound facts. And the longing for a simpler world, does not constitute a responsible alternative."[25]

But it is dangerous to generalize theories of modern physics beyond the areas in which they were originally applied—to treat them metaphorically, as Dodd does—and then to take those metaphors as literal descriptions of the world. Einstein's special theory of relativity does not imply that all things are relative, and Heisenberg's uncertainty principle does not imply that the outcome of every measurement is uncertain. It could well be that there is no certainty, but skeptical arguments date from antiquity and are not unique to modern physics. When you're building a bridge, Newtonian physics works just fine, and what has all this got to do with the structure of poetry anyway? And, no matter how important one's world view might be to one's own work, why try to impose it upon other poets?

Poet Richard Kenney finds the "form war" irritating. "Too tiny for a war," he says in an interview at the Iowa Writers' Workshop, "call it a police action. Generally speaking, the terms of the argument are construed out of a hopeless confusion of ethical with aesthetic thinking." He adds flatly and accurately: "No moderate yet universal argument against strict form seems possible."

Kenney continues:

> Is the "free" in "free verse" really the same as the one in "free country"? Or "free lunch"?... Is the conservation of prosodic forms more like the conservation of the Amazon rain forest, or the "conservative" position on abortion?... Is there a "Neo-Formalist Movement," apart from the retrospect of critical historians? If these "Neo-formalists" are imagined to be some conspiratorial squadron of goose-steppers or constipated gentlemen's clubbers who sip weak brandy and whisper how we've got to turn back the clock and write in meter again, then no thanks. But there's no such conspiracy. There have been and likely always will be poets who are inclined to old-fashioned pattern and sound effect. If there seem to be more of them publishing these days, does that constitute a "movement"? Am I one of them? I guess I must be. I don't mean to disavow anybody. I just don't feel "aligned."... It's ludicrous. Here in one corner, somebody's stabbing his forefinger at somebody else's chest, telling him how not to write, while up in the attic, somebody's writing the poem that will break everybody's heart. Is it free verse? Is it metered? I beg your pardon? Who in his right mind cares?[26]

2.

With the exception of the erudite Timothy Steele, many of the writers who have lined up on one side or the other of the debate between the proponents of free and formal verse don't know quite enough to be making authoritative pronouncements. Brad Leithauser, for instance, writing about the American poets born in the 1920s, argues "that they had the good fortune to begin their careers during the Forties and Fifties when an orthodoxy of formal verse [was] obtained. This period is often criticized as sterile...but surely it was advantageous for them to train in the same basic tools as the titans of English verse."[27] If there is a "dangerous nostalgia" exhibited by any of the new formalists, this is it.

It would be futile to argue that poets who were trained in meter did not benefit from the experience; of course they did (Berryman, for instance, could not have achieved some of his best effects in his *Dream Songs* without his thorough knowledge of meter), but the New Critical orthodoxy of the '40s and '50s did more than train one in meter; it defined the style, tone, subject matter, and diction of poetry so narrowly that the permissible would have fit inside a snuff box. "There were poets trained that way," Robert Lowell says in an interview, "writing in the style, writing rather complicated, difficult, laboured poems, and it was getting very dry. You felt you had to get away from that at all costs."[28] Lowell was not alone in his feelings: for every Richard Wilbur who continued to write in metered verse, there were a multitude—like James Wright, Philip Levine, or Adrienne Rich; like Lowell himself or Berryman—who had to get away at all costs and who converted, either partially or entirely, to free verse. They identified meter with writing in the New Critical style, much the way earlier poets at the turn of the century—as Timothy Steele demonstrates—had identified meter with "dated diction and subject matter."[29]

An enormously influential anthology—Berg and Mezey's *Naked Poetry: Recent American Poetry in Open Forms*—was published in 1969. The poets whose work was included had been lucky enough to have begun their careers in that golden age of orthodoxy so praised by Leithauser and must all have been told at one time or another by some eminent authority that what they were writing was not merely bad, but that it was not poetry at all—so it is not surprising that the personal statements they submitted along with their poems are alternately so truculent and so apologetic. They knew that what they were doing was not respected in academia; they had little hope that it ever would be. They were about to win the war, but they had no way of knowing that.

The *Naked* poets were writing at a time that brought everything into question—even the claims of rationality itself—for intellectuals who were not in open revolt were seen as tools of a rotten civilization which was conducting an obscene and stupid war against Vietnamese peasants. However wrong-headed the Romantic anti-intellectualism of the '60s might appear to us now, it was a perfectly understandable—almost inevitable— stance to take, and, although the poetry written by the *Naked* poets is still fresh and exciting, what they had to say about poetry (with the exception of Lowell's terse, clear statement) is mysterious, murky, and downright Zen-like in its refusal to be pinned down. Their poetry, they assert again and again, whether they call it "open" or "organic" or "free," is just as formal as anything written in meter, but when they try to say how it is formal, they never refer to anything as concrete as a text.

Organic poetry, Denise Levertov says, "is a method of apperception, i.e., of recognizing what we perceive, and is based on an intuition of an order, a form beyond forms, in which forms partake...."[30] Allen Ginsberg tells us "that tune and language are invoked shamanistically on the spot from the unconscious."[31] What is needed to transform an "unwritten hope" into a poem, W. S. Merwin says, "is not a manipulable, more or less predictably recurring pattern, but an unduplicatable resonance...."[32] Gary Snyder's poem goes "straight from the deep mind of the maker to the deep mind of the hearer."[33] Robert Bly is the most combative—and bombastic— of the lot; he equates formal structure with jail, attacks Olson for "love of technique" (Olson!—many things might be learned from Charles Olson, but technique is not one of them), and hurls at him one of the most damning epithets of the '60s: middle-class. "I refuse to say anything at all about prosody," Bly snarls. "What an ugly word it is!"[34] None of the *Naked* poets (again with the exception of Lowell) has anything to say about prosody; their statements concentrate on the subjective experience of writing poetry. They see the source of poetry as intuition, the practice of writing poetry not as an art or craft but as a spiritual—even mystical—discipline.

When the rebel, outsider, free verse poets became workshop leaders and tenured professors, they passed on to their students more than the style—or styles—of the writing that we call free verse; they passed on their deep-seated, nearly superstitious, distrust of prosody. Wayne Dodd is a perfect example. For Dodd, prosody is "the prosody of the democratic ideal, of physical exuberance, of optimism, of geographic largeness. The prosody of American names, of scope, of plenitude. The prosody of rivers and forests..."[35]—anything but what prosody actually is: the study—expounded in a clearly intelligible, non-mystical way—of how poetry is constructed. So, with little or no discussion of prosody, without even much discussion of its own origins or history, free verse has evolved to where it is today.

Despite the plethora of aesthetic positions and concomitant possible styles of contemporary poetry, many of the poems appearing in North American literary journals so strongly resemble each other as to constitute a dominant mode, a generic free verse that is not so much naked as denuded. With little attention to line breaks (certainly without the focused and sustained attention that characterized the good old Doc Williams style), without even much variation in line length, without (it goes without saying) meter, stripped of every poetic device associated with formal poetry (rhyme and slant rhyme, assonance, alliteration), often without even the faintest suggestion of rhythm, written in a flat, colloquial language and a severely limited vocabulary, the generic free verse poem is, when set in type, roughly two inches wide and rarely exceeds two pages in length; it is a short personal essay arbitrarily broken into lines, building toward an arresting image, or an epiphany, or a joke-like punch line—or at least to something that will provide a sense of closure. The generic free verse poem is what we have after twenty years of not studying prosody.

I may be exaggerating the situation, but not by much, and anyone who reads much contemporary poetry will know exactly what I am talking about. Leithauser is right; free verse is showing signs of exhaustion. Of course excellent free verse is still being written, but, upon those rare occasions when we see it, isn't it always something different from the dominant style? The free verse that crackles and leaps off the page—Amy Clampitt's baroque, densely knotted syntax and her rhythms often floating just at the edge of meter; Albert Goldbarth's long, blathery, digressive and discursive lines; Alice Fulton's brilliant, sassy word play and the increasing formality of her construction—isn't it always quite different from that deadly, dull, flat, exhausted dominant style of free verse?

The exhaustion of the dominant style is one of the primary reasons for the resurgence of formalism; the new formalist poets could well have said, echoing Lowell, "it was getting very dry. You felt you had to get away from that at all costs."

There is, finally, another matter that is not widely enough understood. Unfortunately for the polemicists on both sides of the fence, "metered" is not a term analogous to "pregnant"; that is, it does not describe a state in which one either is or isn't. If we imagine a continuum with verse that is clearly metrical on one end and verse that is clearly free on the other, we will be left with an area in the middle that is hard to define. If we are coming from the direction of metered verse, we approach the middle by allowing an increasing number of foot substitutions and variations in line length, if from the direction of free verse, by allowing an increasing number of metrical phrases; at the center of the continuum, it is impossible to tell whether we are looking at a metrical poem that has been loosened or a free verse one that has been tightened, and the exact point at which one draws the line between free and metered is somewhat arbitrary. Is "The Love Song of J. Alfred Prufrock" free verse or iambic pentameter? The answer to that question depends entirely upon where one draws the center line.

Let us consider an example of a kind that is likely to cause trouble:

> Everything looked authentic and frail.
> And the great clappers of rainfall
> made one fancy Noah's ark
> drydocked on the lawn, ready to sail.
>
> At the gate were cypress,
> the mangy cemetery sort, and beyond
> lay the aboretum of the Holy Land.
> On a quarter acre it flourished
>
> against the south cathedral choir.[36]

These lines of Henri Cole's, although highly rhythmical, are not written in meter. They are free verse —a free verse that hovers close to the center of the continuum, but free verse nonetheless. If we were to call them metrical, we would be stretching the term so far that it would lose all usefulness and we would become hopelessly bogged down —as so many recent commentators (like Robert Richman) have apparently been —in a confusion between meter and rhythm.

Meter —remember, it means "measure" —requires both a normal foot and a normal line; this poem establishes neither, and the rest of the poem confirms what we discover in the lines quoted: it appears to be more iambic than anything else, but there are so many anapestic feet that it never settles down to become entirely iambic; the four-beat line, employed distinctively at cadences, struggles to establish a norm but never quite wins out over the five-beat line; three and even two-beat lines appear from time to time. Are these flaws in the poem? No, of course not. To criticize Cole for them would be like objecting that he didn't score a touchdown when he was playing basketball.

What do we call poetry like this? Dana Gioia calls it "pseudo-formal" and, mistakenly, sees it as a recent development. "The metrical incompetence of pseudo-formal verse is the most cogent evidence of our literature's break with tradition and the lingering consequences," Gioia writes. "These poets are not without talent.... How then do these promising authors...not hear the confusing rhythms of their own verse?"[37] Well, perhaps because they have been reading Pound or Eliot, for, although it would later be supplanted by the Doc Williams style, this kind of verse was the bread and butter staple of free verse in the early years of the movement. (Eliot: "The ghost of some simple metre should lurk behind the arras in even the 'freest' verse: to advance menacingly as we doze, and withdraw as we rouse."[38]) If we don't wish to call it by the pejorative "pseudo-formal," we should find another term. I'll offer "semi-metrical."

There are many ways to go about writing semi-metrical verse; it is not any easier to write well than anything else, and bad poems written semimetrically are easy enough to find (Gioia gives examples of two of them), but semi-metrical verse can be beautifully written—T. S. Eliot wrote it beautifully—and if, as Leithauser argues, free verse needs "to gather to itself a broader collection of effects, a denser music,"[39] semi-metrical verse would seem an excellent place to begin.

It should be clear by now where I am headed, but I am certainly not the first—and I'm sure I won't be the last—to suggest that North American poets need to return to the serious study of prosody. In a remarkably clear-sighted article on the new formalism (1987), the poet David Wojahn argues that "young poets need more carefully to study form and meter, and to experiment with form and meter in their work, even if they plan eventually to write only free verse." One of the few points upon which I disagree with Timothy Steele is his claim that free verse "has no positive principles for its proponents to defend." The multiplicity of styles of free verse has, by now, evolved many positive principles, but they have not been clearly enough articulated, and I agree with Wojahn that there is "a special need for criticism regarding the prosody of free verse." Finally, one of Wojahn's suggestions strikes me as particularly useful: that we should abandon "our present two-party system in regard to our thinking about form." He argues that, by labeling "a writer either a free verse poet or a formalist poet," we are implying a misleading metrical party line. He would like to see "an exciting cross-fertilization between the possibilities of formal verse and those of free verse."[40]

3.

Whether we like it or not, the term "new formalism" appears to have, by now, established itself as a critical category. The recently published (1994) *Oxford Companion to Twentieth-Century Poetry in English* contains an entry under "new formalism"; there an unwary reader will learn that the new formalists "returned to traditional metres and forms and to narrative in order to give back to American poetry a clarity, a music, and an objectivity which might make it accessible to a general audience."[41] The implication is, of course, that clarity, music, and objectivity were not available in free verse. *The Oxford Companion* entry was written by Robert McPhillips, and he defines the new formalist aesthetic much the way he defined it in his article reprinted in *Expansive Poetry* — direct depiction of emotion, colloquial diction, ease with American popular culture — and then claims that "these qualities are best exemplified" in particular poems by Gioia, Steele, and Gjertrud Schnackenberg. Once again, poets are ignored who don't fit the thesis, but poets are also ignored who do fit it. If accessibility to a general audience is a criterion, why not include Vikram Seth who has, with *The Golden Gate*, already reached a wider audience than most poets — metered or free — ever dream of? And how could he not mention Brad Leithauser who, as a critic and gadfly for the emerging movement, had been as significant as Gioia? McPhillips defines a narrow new formalist aesthetic that is simply not applicable to many of the American poets currently writing in meter.

What I am afraid we are seeing is the evolution of an extreme position, a new formalism (most emphatically with capitals) that believes, based upon Turner and Pöppel's "scientific" evidence, that free verse is bad and metrical verse good, believes further (as Turner and Pöppel argue in a footnote)[42] that free verse "is not poetry," that would urge all of us, as Robert Richman does, to return to the rules Saintsbury set down in 1910. Combine those beliefs with the frequently heard cry for plain speech and easily accessible subject matter aimed at some hypothetical general audience and the result is what we're already beginning to see in many literary magazines: metrical poems so lacking in rhythmic counterpoint, so resolutely end-stopped, so loaded with full rhymes falling like sledgehammers at the ends of lines, that they are either painfully archaic or soporifically bland — poems so mediocre that they are scarcely distinguishable from greeting card verse.

But the new formalism may be defined narrowly, as Robert McPhillips does, or broadly — and more usefully — as do Mark Jarman and David Mason, the editors of *Rebel Angels: 25 Poets of the New Formalism* (1996). In their preface, they claim, quite rightly, that "the New Formalism as a movement has not been a narrow one" and that "there is more variety in their approach to form and subject than in some work of the previous generations."[43] To substantiate this claim, they have included in their excellent anthology a remarkably varied selection of poetry.

If we define new formalism in the broadest sense — as Jarman and Mason do — then the new formalists have already accomplished what at least some of them consciously set out to do: broadened the range of the possible. A measure of their success can be seen in the ever increasing number of young poets writing formal verse. But if the new formalists have also been instrumental in encouraging all young poets — whether they are writing formal verse or free — to turn again to the serious study of prosody, then they will indeed have genuinely achieved the "revolution... [, a] fundamental change... in the art of poetry as it is practiced in this country"[44] that Jarman and Mason attribute to them — and perhaps then it will be time to let the term "new formalist" go, and, as David Wojahn suggests, simply talk about poets and poetry.

Why shouldn't a young poet write a sonnet one day and a free verse poem the next (as, indeed, many of them are already doing) — or write semimetrically, or combine free and metered verse in the same poem as Pound did, or, indeed, write in any way at all? The enemy is not someone who writes differently from you. The enemy is the same old enemy who has always been around: someone who tries to tell you that there is only one way to write.

Works Cited

1. Some poets who would later be labeled new formalist actually began publishing in the late 1970s, most notably Marilyn Hacker (*Presentation Piece*, 1974, and *Separations*, 1976) and Timothy Steele (*Uncertainties and Rest*, 1979), but it was not until the 1980s that anyone suspected that the writing of formal verse by young poets might be anything more significant than an individual, isolated phenomenon.

2. Brad Leithauser. "Metrical Illiteracy," in *The New Criterion* (January 1983), 46.

3. Dana Gioia. "The Dilemma of the Long Poem," in *The Kenyon Review*, (spring 1983), vol. V, no. 2.

4. Philip Dacey, and David Jauss, eds. *Strong Measures: Contemporary American Poetry in Traditional Forms* (New York: Harper & Row, 1986), 1-16.

5. Brad Leithauser. "The Confinement of Free Verse," in *The New Criterion* (May 1987).

6. Dana Gioia. "Notes on the New Formalism," in *The Hudson Review* (autumn 1987).

7. "A Note on *The New Criterion*," in *The New Criterion* (September 1982), 1-5.

8. Robert Richman, ed. *The Direction of Poetry: An Anthology of Rhymed and Metered Verse Written in the English Language Since 1975* (Boston: Houghton Mifflin, 1988); all quotations in this and the preceding paragraph are from Richman's introduction, xiii-xxi.

9. Robert McDowell. "The Poetry Anthology," in *The Hudson Review*, vol. XLII, no. 4, winter 1990, 604. The non-metrical poems McDowell lists are "Peter Davison's 'Questions of Swimming, 1935,' Dana Gioia's 'California Hills in August,' Edward Hirsch's 'Fast Break,' Michael Blumenthal's 'Inventors,' and Donald Hall's two poems."

10. Paul Lake. "Toward a Liberal Poetics," in *Expansive Poetry: Essays on the New Narrative & the New Formalism*; Frederick Feirstein, ed. (Ashland, Oregon: Story Line Press, 1989), 113-123; first published in *The Threepenny Review*, vol. 8, no. 4 (winter 1988).

11. Wyatt Prunty. "Emaciated Poetry," in *Expansive Poetry*, op. cit., 176-194; first published in *The Sewanee Review* (winter 1985).

12. Robert McPhillips. "What's New About the New Formalism?" in *Expansive Poetry*, op. cit., 195-207; first published in *Crosscurrents, A Quarterly*, vol. 8, no. 2, (1988).

13. All quotations in this and the preceding paragraph are from Frederick Turner, and Ernst Pöppel. "The Neural Lyre: Poetic Meter, the Brain, and Time," in *Expansive Poetry*, op. cit., 209-254; also published in Frederick Turner's *Natural Classicism* (Paragon House, 1985).

14. Timothy Steele. *Missing Measures: Modern Poetry and the Revolt Against Meter* (Fayetteville and London: The University of Arkansas Press, 1990), 4.

15. Ibid., 7.

16. Ibid., 28.

17. Ibid., 291.

18. Ariel Dawson. "The Yuppie Poet," in *Associated Writing Programs Newsletter* (May 1985).

19. All Ira Sadoff quotations are from Sadoff's "Neo-Formalism: A Dangerous Nostalgia," in *The American Poetry Review* (January/February 1990).

20. Wayne Dodd. *Toward the End of the Century: Essays into Poetry* (Iowa City: University of Iowa Press, 1992), 79.

21. Ibid., 133.

22. Ibid., 59.

23. Ibid., 90.

24. Ibid., 57.

25. Ibid., 140.

26. All Richard Kenney quotations are from an interview published in *The Iowa Writers' Workshop Newsletter* (Spring/Summer 1990).

27. Brad Leithauser. "Metrical Illiteracy," op. cit., 44-45.

28. Robert Lowell quoted: Alvarez, A. "Robert Lowell in Conversation," reprinted in *Robert Lowell: Interviews and Memoirs*; Jeffrey Myers, ed. (Ann Arbor: University of Michigan Press, 1988), 79-83.

29. Timothy Steele. *Missing Measures: Modern Poetry and the Revolt Against Meter*, op. cit., 32-44.

30. Stephen Berg, and Robert Mezey, eds. *Naked Poetry: Recent American Poetry in Open Forms* (Indianapolis and New York: Bobbs-Merrill, 1969), 141.

31. Ibid., 221.

32. Ibid., 270-271.

33. Ibid., 357.

34. Ibid., 161-164.

35. Dodd, op. cit., 79.

36. Henri Cole. "The Biblical Garden at St. John the Divine in New York City," in *The Marble Queen* (New York: Atheneum, 1986), 19.

37. Dana Gioia. "Notes on the New Formalism," op. cit.

38. T. S. Eliot. *To Criticize the Critic* (New York: Farrar Straus, 1965), 187.

39. Leithauser, Brad; "The Confinement of Free Verse," op. cit., p. 14.

40. Wojahn, David; "'Yes, But...': Some Thoughts on the New Formalism," in *Crazyhorse* 32 (spring 1987), 64-81.

41. Ian Hamilton, ed. *The Oxford Companion to Twentieth-Century Poetry in English* (Oxford and New York: Oxford University Press, 1994), entry on "The New Formalism" by Robert McPhillips, 381-382.

42. Frederick Turner, and Ernst Pöppel. Footnote 25 to "The Neural Lyre: Poetic Meter, the Brain, and Time," in *Expansive Poetry*, op. cit., 54.

43. Mark Jarman, and David Mason. *Rebel Angels: 25 Poets of the New Formalism* (Ashland, Oregon: Story Line Press, 1996), xx.

44. Ibid., xv.

A Controversy Reignited: The Early 20th Century Vers Libre Debate as an Antecedent of New Formalist Criticism

Meg Schoerke

> But to return to the modern scene in literature, leaving the fallacies with which certain critics strive to diminish it, its virtues have been gleefully magnified and its flaws unfairly pilloried by the emotional parading and table-smashing that passes for criticism at the present time. You have certain critics who tell you that [contemporary poetry] is important only when it ironically celebrates the chaos of this age; that it must be a vigorous affirmation of the essential beauty and importance of living; that it must take root in the vast urges and local mannerisms of a country; that it should be the prophet of a new spiritual order.... Should you dare to contend that you see a bit of right and a great deal of wrong in these various credoes [*sic*] all camps will unite to scoff at you. An ill-tempered and crudely dogmatic flavor saturates the criticism of [poetry] at present. The scene narrows; almost no critic can spy more than two or three foremost poets...; critics become the mere official megaphones of a group or school; and one can foretell almost the exact manner in which a critic will praise the darlings of his magazine and denounce or disparage the rest of the field.
> — Maxwell Bodenheim, "The Modern Scene," 1923

Although perhaps as extreme as the criticism it denounces, Maxwell Bodenheim's description of the oppositional tendencies of early twentieth-century literary critics could serve equally well as a gauge of the poetry wars of the last fifteen years, in which poet-critics have often claimed qualities such as those Bodenheim enumerates as the essential provenance of either free verse or formal verse. But, "table-smashing" aside, the most striking feature of the current debate is that, apart from the charges of fascism that each side so freely aims at the other, contemporary arguments for and against free verse repeat almost exactly challenges first raised during the controversy over *vers libre* that flooded literary journals in the teens and early '20s. For, with the rise of modernism in poetry, objections to the new aesthetic invariably arose; what makes them distinctive is that almost all of the denunciations, however varied, are linked by critics to a primary and fundamental objection to free verse. Similarly, today's new formalists, although they attack contemporary poetry on a number of grounds, consistently refer their criticisms back to their fundamental objection to free verse. In doing so, they often echo specific arguments and strategies of argumentation adopted by their early twentieth-century counterparts, for both early and late century advocates of formal verse respond to the incendiary rhetoric of free verse proponents.

First, it is important to note that both the *vers libre* and new formalist controversies arose in a literary climate where free verse dominated American poetry and apologists for free verse attacked metrical verse as obsolete. As Annie Finch notes in *The Ghost of Meter*, around 1912 "many influences had been leading to free verse for a long time, but after they had converged, the first free verse movement developed and declined astonishingly quickly and was astonishingly widespread. Nonmetrical verse was as common in American poetry by the beginning of the twentieth-century as iambic pentameter had been in English and American poetry for the preceding three hundred and fifty years" (83). Moreover, as Finch points out, "the early free-verse movement bore many of the distinguishing marks of a fad" (92). Certainly, the sudden and overwhelming popularity—and subsequent banality—of the free verse that inundated literary journals so alarmed Ezra Pound and T. S. Eliot that they felt compelled to qualify their support of *vers libre*. Pound, in "A Retrospect," complains: "This school has since been 'joined' or 'followed' by numerous people who, whatever their merits, do not show any signs of agreement with the second specification ['To use absolutely no word that does not contribute to the presentation']. Indeed, *vers libre* has become as prolix and as verbose as any of the flaccid varieties that preceded it" (3). And Eliot, disparaging free verse manifestoes, declares that "*vers libre* has not even the excuse of a polemic; it is a battle-cry of freedom, and there is no freedom in art. And as the so-called *vers libre* which is good is anything but 'free,' it can be better defended under some other label" (229). Eliot here denounces populist champions of *vers libre*, who justified not only as a boon to the art but as evidence of America's democratic spirit the widespread experimentation with free verse among people who ordinarily would refrain from trying their hand at writing metered poetry. Arthur

Davison Ficke, for example, in a 1914 *Little Review* essay, "In Defense of Vers Libre," argues that:

> Certain devoted American friends of poetry have been trying for some time to encourage poetry in this country; and I think they are on the right track when they go about it by way of encouraging *vers libre*. No other method could so swiftly and surely multiply the number of our verse-writers. For the new medium presents no difficulties to anyone; even the tired business-man will find himself tempted to record his evening woes in singless song. True, not everyone will be able at first trial to produce *vers libre* of the quality that appears in the choruses of *Sampson Agonistes* [*sic*].... But some kind of *vers libre* can be turned out by anyone. (21)

Nonetheless, like Pound and Eliot, many poets and critics soon grew weary of the waves of interchangeable free verse poems saturating both little and mainstream magazines. Louis Untermeyer, in a 1922 *Nation* essay, "Return of the Vers Libretine," asserts that: "For six years—from 1914 to 1920, to be coldly statistical—vers libre was the fashion in these otherwise conservative States. Not only did the leaders of the style adapt their tropes and figures to this form but whole regiments of amateurs, imitators, and young men-about-literature cut their patterns along its attenuated lines" (686). Like Finch, he emphasizes the subsequent return to metrical writing by many poets—including Pound and Eliot—who had once enthusiastically embraced *vers libre*, and, after extolling the merits of form, he concludes with an analogy that challenges the painterly ambitions of the Imagists and implies that restriction in art is both necessary and desirable: "So we see one creator after another turn to a resisting form, to a medium that does not submit too easily.... The poet, in the end, learns to enjoy the edged limitations of his verse as keenly as the painter appreciates the sharp confines of his canvas" (687).

Although of much longer duration than the free verse movement of the teens and early '20s, the free verse movement of the 1960s and '70s also bore the signs of a fad, for, to update Untermeyer's assessment slightly, not only did established poets adopt the form, but whole regiments of amateurs, imitators and young women-and-men-about-literature—often under the auspices of university creative writing programs—cut their patterns, too, along its lines. But free verse proponents of the '60s and '70s proclaimed their "freedom from the bondage of meter" in rhetoric that bears a remarkable similarity to that of early twentieth-century poets and critics who defined free verse as liberating, referred to meter as a "straitjacket," and characterized anyone who wrote in traditional forms as essentially conservative. Here, for example, is Arthur Davison Ficke again:

> The properly qualified judge of poetry can have no doubts about *vers libre*; if he doubts it, he is no judge. He belongs to that class of hide-bound conservatives who are unwilling to discard the old merely because it is old. He does not yet understand that the newest is always the best. Worst of all, he does not appreciate the value of Freedom.... The old fixed verse-forms—such as the sonnet, blank verse, and all the other familiar metres—were...cramping to the free creating spirit of the poet.... To be honest, we must admit that there was something sickly and soul-destroying about the earlier verse-forms. (19)

Maxwell Bodenheim, also writing in 1914, entitles his essay, published in *The Little Review*, "The Decorative Straight-Jacket: Rhymed Verse." He argues that:

> Rhymed verse mutilates and cramps poetry. It is impossible for even the greatest poet completely to rise above its limitations. He may succeed in a measure, but that is due to his strength and not to the useless fetters he wears. But, say the defenders of the fetters, rhyme and meter are excellent disciplines. Does Poetry or does the Poet need to be disciplined? Are they cringing slaves who cannot be trusted to walk alone and unbound? (22)

I trust that, even though I won't quote from any comparable mid- and late-century reviews and manifestoes, the similarity of these examples to the charged rhetoric of many 1960s, '70s, and '80s free verse advocates is clear. In response to such rhetoric, in the 1980s defenders of formal verse offered counter-arguments that, both in content and tone, often resemble the counter-arguments developed by their precursors in the teens and early '20s. Just as advocates of free verse often tend to attribute not only aesthetic but moral value to the form, and insist that metrical verse breeds banality, conformism, and lack of thought, so too their opponents often ascribe aesthetic and moral beauty to metrical poetry and link banality, conformism, and lack of thought to free verse.

A number of critics from the teens stress their view that formal verse is more difficult to write than free verse and conclude that, because they practice "the easier form," free verse poets have succumbed to mental atrophy. Eunice Tietjens, in a 1914 *Little Review* essay entitled "The Spiritual Dangers of Writing Vers Libre," insists that:

> There seems to be a whole new set of dangers, especially virulent, that attend the writing of *vers libre* .... These dangers are inherent in the form and are directly traceable to it. For contrary to the general notion on the subject, it takes a better balanced intellect to write good *vers libre* than to write in the old verse forms. (26)

She specifies "the dangers of free verse" as, first, that of "being obvious"; second, "mental laziness" and the writer's ensuing "attempt to cover with words the fundamental paucity of the ideas"; third, "the danger of reducing the idea to a minimum and relying entirely on the sound and color of the words to carry the poem"; and finally, rank egotism (26-27). Similarly, Julius Pratt, writing three years later in *South Atlantic Quarterly*, suggests that the free verse movement "brought into the field...weak poets" whose mental incompetence he links with an inability to handle the demands of formal verse:

> To most poetry lovers...although [free verse] is a good addition to the recognized verse forms, it does not represent (as some claim) an "advanced artistry" over the older verse. Although most of the masters of free verse have shown themselves capable of writing good poetry in rime and meter, the new movement has also brought into the field of verse writing a considerable number of weak poets...who seem to have little genuine poetry in their thought, and apparently would be unable to express themselves under the technical burdens of meter and rime.
> ("Whitman and Masters," 225)

Like Pratt, Brad Leithauser, whose title of his 1981 essay "Metrical Illiteracy" implicitly connects a lack of metrical facility with ignorance, also indicts poets for what he believes are interrelated failings—lack of metrical skills and a self-serving professionalism grounded upon egotism: "A great many well-known poets simply have not worked in form and could not successfully if they tried. Ungainliness . . . would immediately show itself. Formlessness (ostensibly an avant-garde impulse) may, then, actually be kept alive by conservatism in its most basic sense—conservation of the self, the preservation of one's reputation in the poetry scene" (43). And

Frederick Feirstein, in "The Other Long Poem," suggests that "free verse forces the poet to rely on rhetorical devices that tend to create melodrama or to focus the reader on the poet's 'voice' instead of on the action — and so distances him perhaps altogether from involvement in the intended drama [of a long poem]" (11). He follows this assertion with an example of a contemporary poet, Bin Ramke, who admits that he has never been able to write a successful poem in rhyme and meter.

But even while pinning the blame largely on free verse for the charge of mediocrity which they level against the poetry of their contemporaries, present day and early twentieth-century advocates of form sometimes add the disclaimer that good free verse and good metrical poetry are both hard to write. Julius Pratt, in a 1917 review of Harriet Monroe's anthology, *The New Poetry*, notes that "good free verse requires quite as delicate an art as do rimed iambics" (274). Leithauser, in his 1987 essay, "The Confinement of Free Verse," emphasizes "the inherent difficulties of free verse" and takes Pratt's point one step further: "It is harder to write truly excellent free verse than excellent metrical verse" (9). He adopts this stance, however, as an indirect means of promoting meter:

> Once this truth is accepted, the extraordinarily anomalous condition of contemporary American poetry reveals itself. Nearly all of the verse now being composed in our country undertakes a severely taxing genre. From the evening workshop at the community adult-education center to the advanced writing seminar at the Ivy League university, most everyone has chosen to scale Parnassus from its most slippery and treacherous face. (9)

In contrast, Maxwell Bodenheim, in a 1922 defense of free verse published in *The Nation*, equalizes the level of difficulty of free verse and metrical writing as means of championing free verse against the glut of mediocre free verse poems — and nasty parodies of mediocre free verse poems — that prevailed in both the literary and mainstream magazines of the time:

> Probably the reason why so many poets fail at "free verse" is that the originality of their imaginations does not find itself equal to the labor of perfecting this individual form and what they achieve is merely a purposeless clash between form and content. It is deliciously easy to write a bad example of "free verse," and that is perhaps the reason why so many people have attempted it during the past

ten years, but it is also equally easy to fashion a jingle or
a trite love lyric in rhyme, as the pages of many an Ameri-
can magazine will testify. Excellent rhymed verse and
"free verse" both present equally formidable difficulties,
but these difficulties are of different kinds and they bar
the way to important but dissimilar attainments. (233)

Bodenheim's main point is an important one: excellent poetry depends
on the skill and talent of the poet, rather than on a particular verse form.
But Bodenheim, as I've already mentioned, co-opts this idea to serve his
larger purpose of proving the viability of free verse. Likewise, today's new
formalists, on the few occasions when they do acknowledge that specific
verse forms are, in and of themselves, neither essentially inferior nor supe-
rior to one another, do so to support arguments that favor metrical poetry.
Thus Dana Gioia begins his 1987 essay, "Notes on the New Formalism,"
with the caveat that:

Formal verse, like free verse, is neither intrinsically bad
nor good. The terms are strictly descriptive and not evalu-
ative. They define distinct sets of metrical technique
rather than rank the quality or nature of poetic perfor-
mance. Nor do these techniques automatically carry with
them social, political, or even, in most cases, aesthetic
values. (396)

And in his conclusion to the essay he emphasizes a similar point. But in the
body of the essay, Gioia maintains that many free verse poems may depend
upon a residual metrical base, and, on the other hand, that what he calls
"pseudo formalist poems"—poems that, at first glance, may seem to be writ-
ten in form—don't ultimately adhere to a metrical norm. Gioia uses these
examples to argue that "young poets have grown up in a literary culture so
removed from the predominantly oral traditions of metrical verse that they
can no longer hear it accurately. Their training in reading and writing has
been overwhelmingly visual not aural, and they have never learned to hear
the musical design a poem executes" (407). However much, in his introduc-
tion and conclusion, Gioia endorses both free verse and metrical composi-
tion as legitimate possibilities for poets, he nonetheless bases his judgments
of the poems he discusses in the essay primarily on metrical grounds.

Gioia concludes his essay with the hopeful suggestion that by the
end of the century the "narrow technical" debate over metrical versus
non-metrical verse will give way to more inclusive discussions "on form in

the wider, more elusive sense of poetic structure" (408). His wish echoes sentiments voiced by participants in the *vers libre* controversy who complained that the new poets were all too skilled at setting aside governing principles, but were making no attempt to build firm, new structures to take their place. In a 1916 *South Atlantic Quarterly* article, Edward Cox laments:

> Equally indicative of mental exhaustion and distemper is that indiscriminate sense of values which leads to proclaiming any whimsy, mutation of thought, or blush of feeling as soundings from the soul's immensity.... What sins they have to answer for in the shape of art that is spineless for want of ideas,... slovenly for want of patience to undergo the long years of hard apprenticeship, and dilettante for want of an acquaintance with what is solid and fundamental. (364)

For Cox, modern art—and modern poetry in particular—lacks any determinate structure and depends primarily on randomness; like many early twentieth-century apologists for formal verse, he suggests that modern art is solipsistic and undisciplined. Similarly, Julius Pratt, again in his 1917 review of *The New Poetry*, remarks that: "The period has been one of chaos. With the old laws largely discarded, new ones have been slow to shape themselves, with the result that there has been much ill-considered play of whim and caprice in the choice of both substance and form and much worship of the new merely because it is new"(271).

Seventy years later, using 1917 as a bench mark, Brad Leithauser makes a comparable argument:

> The problem of free verse in 1917, when Eliot wrote, and even more pressingly in 1987, is the necessity of discovering sufficient rewards to compensate for those lost with the abandonment of traditional prosodic devices. And in 1987 it grows evident that if free verse is ever to go forward and forge a body of work comparable to that cultivated under the iamb, it will require fresh tools. It must "make new" what was made new before.
>
> ("The Confinement of Free Verse," 10)

Equally, Timothy Steele, in his conclusion to *Missing Measures*, stresses that the moderns have not created any new laws with which to replace the old laws that they presumably discarded wholesale:

> [The] predicament [of the modern movement's leaders]
> was that of successful revolutionaries in any field: hav-
> ing claimed special liberties for themselves, they found it
> difficult to persuade their followers to adopt a more re-
> strained approach. They saw the kind of poetry they de-
> sired to avoid more clearly than the kind they wanted to
> write and, consequently, placed more emphasis on the
> destruction of the old than on the creation of the new. (281)

In *Missing Measures*, Steele offers extensive discussions that, among other factors, link the rise of free verse to the moderns' search for novelty at all costs and to the influence of Kantian aestheticism with its emphasis on pure subjectivity. But at least one critic of the teens — Edward Cox — not only attributes free verse to the modernist emphasis on individuality and the search for the new, but also to aestheticism, though he looks back not specifically to Kant, but only to Wilde and Pater:

> It seems then that individuality, intoxicated with its re-
> lease from the control of tradition, has lost all sense of
> bounds. Grown bolder it imagines that it can turn its
> back on man in the mass, and now speak in a mode in-
> telligible only to itself. Hence the passion to find an
> idiom never before used and hereafter to be entirely its
> own, and growing out of this a belief in its ability to
> voice the unutterable and to fix in a precision of line
> and phrase the minutest shade of variation. As guilty
> here I would mention especially that exotic school of
> artists who flourished in the 'nineties just past, namely,
> Oscar Wilde and his like. I would not exempt the great
> Pater himself. (363)

And, like many new formalists, particularly Steele, Gioia, and Leithauser, Cox also points out what he views as the essential conservatism of writers of *vers libre* when he asks: "Is there any attitude more conventional than that of trying to be unconventional?" (362).

Cox's strategy of turning the tables on free verse writers who pride themselves on their unconventionality also prefigures new formalist com-plaints that free verse, rather than being "radical," has become the norm, institutionalized in literary magazines and the academy. Although attacks on "academic" free verse may seem only to have been made possible by the rise of university creative writing programs, even during the *vers libre* debate critics chided free verse advocates for being academic. In *Poetry*, for example, Alice Corbin Henderson writes, in 1919: "In the last few years so much has been written in defense of radicalism in poetry, so much has been said of the hampering restrictions of what is regarded as conventional, conservative verse, that now perhaps it becomes necessary to defend the classics against what we may call the 'New Academism' of the Radicals!" (269). In both the early and late century controversies, free verse advocates and defenders of formal verse each strive to style themselves as cutting-edge dissenters, radical innovators battling an out-moded institution. The politics of the debate thus tend to become strangely neutral, for key words — "radical," "conventional," "conservative," "academic" — are often invoked more as blanket indicators of value than of a specific politics. Interchangeably, across the century champions of free verse and defenders of formal verse systematically equate "radicalism" with "goodness" and adopt "conventional," "conservative," and "academic" as terms of opprobrium. Regardless of their politics or the kind of verse they write, all participants in the debate wish to be thought of as radical and unacademic.

Along with charges of "conventionality" and "academism," during the teens advocates of formal verse also draw attention to what they view as the *vers librists'* excessive and childish focus on the self and consistently call free verse writers "egotistical" (and this, I believe, is the source of the title of the avant-garde magazine *The Egoist*, whose editors seem to be flaunting the accusation with pride). Even as early as 1914, in an essay optimistically entitled "The Return to Objectivism in Poetry," H. Houston Peckham attacks what he views as the excessive subjectivity of modern lyric poetry and, like many new formalists who object to the subjectivity of the contemporary lyric, blames academics, in part, for inculcating the aesthetic: "'If you would be a poet, young man,' says the professor of literature, 'be subjective, be egoistic. Talk constantly about yourself; for it is human nature to be more interested in one's self than in anybody or anything else, and the subject in which you are most interested you can make most interesting to others'" (45). His criticism is echoed three years later by Pratt, who observes that, unduly influenced by the example of Whitman, "in their efforts to give absolute personal impressions, [Imagist poets] are often egotistic and their writings bristle sometimes with the pronoun 'I'" ("Whitman and Masters," 223). Eunice Tietjens unwittingly offers the most amusing example of the accusation:

> Still another result of the complete loosening of the reins
> possible in *vers libre* is the immediate enlargement of the
> ego. It is not so easy to see why this should result, but it
> almost invariably does, and has since the days of
> Whitman.... The universe divides itself at once into two
> portions, of which the poet is by far the greater half. "I" —
> "I" — "I" they say, and again "I" — "I" — "I." And having
> said it they appear to be vastly relieved. The next step is
> to lay about them gallantly at every person or tendency
> that has ever annoyed them. "I have been abused," they
> say, "I have been neglected! I will get back at you!" (27)

Tietjens' complaints are reminiscent of new formalist attacks on the contemporary confessional lyric. Thus Leithauser describes a "typical bad poem of our time" as "thematically, a destructive blend of personal jadedness and self-congratulation" and associates these elements with what he calls the poems' "formlessness" ("The Confinement of Free Verse," 7). Feirstein follows his condemnation of free verse with an indictment of the solipsism and melodrama that he defines as essential attributes of confessional poetry (13). And Richard Moore laments: "No longer is the poet to make intelligible statements and discover fresh resemblances in the realm of common experience: the sole aim of the modern poem henceforth is to be self-expression. The words of the poem are to reflect the self — and only the self — of the poet, and the less they have to do with their ordinary prose meanings, the more torn from their usual contexts, the better" (42). Contemporary poetry, he argues, "is free in form and stereotyped in attitude" (44). For all of these critics, solipsism and *predictable, stereotyped attitudes* inevitably accompany free verse.

Finally, early and late century proponents of formal poetry, having linked free verse with solipsism, often turn, implicitly or explicitly, to condemning free verse on moral grounds. Pratt argues in 1917 that: "if the new poetry lowers the tone of our thinking, if it makes us forget that the highest beauty after all is moral beauty, its gifts to America will be more than counterbalanced by the stain it leaves on literature.... Philosophy, moral idealism, religion even, are not foreign to the beauty that may be enshrined in poetry" ("Whitman and Masters," 225). Likewise, Cox stresses, "[that] in bringing an indictment against [the] individualism and anarchy rampant in modern art, I do so from the fullness of conviction that art bears a definite relationship to our lives, that it has something to do with giving meaning to our experience, that it serves as a release for the impulse toward spiritual freedom" (361). As for new formalist analogues, Steele argues that the moderns' abandonment of meter has "[deprived] poetry of resources that enable it to examine human experience appealingly, distinctively, and meaningfully" (15). Robert McPhillips insists that "attention to form has allowed a significant number of younger poets to think and communicate clearly about their sense of what is of most human value—love, beauty, mortality" (207). And Frederick Turner and Ernst Pöppel, who, like several early twentieth-century defenders of formal verse, link meter with human biology,[1] remark that "metered poetry may play an important part in developing our more subtle understanding of time, and may thus act as a technique to concentrate and reinforce our uniquely human tendency to make sense of the world in terms of values like truth, beauty, and goodness" (251).

Now certainly all of these arguments regarding poetry's level of difficulty, its adherence to rules, its subjectivity or objectivity, and its morality—most of which originate in antiquity—have been applied in past centuries, in various debates about the nature of poetry. New formalist critics can be thought of as classicists who oppose the Romantic tendencies of much modern American poetry. But what's new about twentieth-century formalist criticism is that it applies classicist arguments specifically in order to defend metrical composition and to denigrate free verse. Thus many of the approaches common to new formalist criticism are not essentially "new," since they have precedents among the defenses of meter penned by early twentieth-century opponents of *vers libre*. In fact, the similarities between the past and present controversies are so marked that Steele, in *Missing Measures*, can offer as his primary objective the straightforward goal of examining "why modern poets, a great many of them at least, abandoned *metre officiel* in favor of free verse" (3-4). But he is also, and perhaps more pointedly, aiming to refute systematically the rationales for free verse promoted by the apologists of the 1960s, '70s, and '80s, for their arguments differ very little from those developed by champions of *vers libre*. What's new about the new formalist criticism, therefore, is its own historical context, for new formalists can try to support their contentions with a century's worth of evidence. It is crucial, however, to recognize not only that arguments in support of meter and rhyme have continued throughout the past

---

[1]For examples of early twentieth-century critics who base their defenses of meter and rhyme on biological grounds, see George Draper, "Vers Libre: Shown to Be a Biological Monstrosity" (*Vanity Fair*, Oct. 1919: 129-130) and Ludwig Lewisohn, "The Hour in Verse" (*The Nation* 116, no. 3014, 11 April 1923: 414).

85 years in the writings of poet-critics such as Yvor Winters, J. V. Cunningham, and Louise Bogan, but that the overall debate has been most heated at the beginning and at the end of the century.

Nevertheless, the question inevitably arises: will the controversy ever be laid to rest? new formalists, I suppose, would stress that, because the problems that plagued a great deal of early twentieth-century American free verse continue to trouble contemporary poetry, their claims are not only still relevant but perhaps even more necessary than were the comparable complaints raised by critics who objected to *vers libre*. As Steele notes: "For several generations we have been living with a phenomenon which I have elsewhere called recycled novelty. In ever-narrower ways, the procedures and ideas of the modern movement have been appropriated and deployed as if they were still brand-new and untried" (25). But it's just as important to acknowledge that arguments against the modern movement—and particularly against free verse—have also been recycled, so much so that, like the free verse revolutions, they have become an indelible—and equally predictable—feature in the history of twentieth-century American poetry.

Works Cited

Maxwell Bodenheim. "Concerning 'Free Verse,'" in *The Nation*, vol.115, no. 2983 (September 6, 1922), 233.

Bodenheim. "The Decorative Straight-Jacket: Rhymed Verse," in *The Little Review*, vol.1, no. 9 (December 1914), 22-23.

Bodenheim. "The Modern Scene," in *The Nation*, vol.116, no. 3014 (April 11, 1923), 412-413.

Edward Godfrey Cox. "The Distemper of Modern Art and its Remedy," in *South Atlantic Quarterly*, vol. 15, no. 4 (October 1916), 361-378.

George Draper. "Vers Libre: Shown to Be a Biological Monstrosity," in *Vanity Fair*, vol. 13, no. 2 (October 1919), 129-130.

T. S. Eliot. "Reflections on *Vers Libre*" (1917). Rpt. in *The Structure of Verse: Modern Essays on Prosody* (revised edition), Harvey Gross, ed. (New York: Ecco, 1979), 227-233.

Frederick Feirstein, ed. *Expansive Poetry: Essays on the New Narrative and the New Formalism*, (Ashland, Oregon: Story Line

Press, 1989).

Feirstein. "The Other Long Poem," in *Expansive Poetry*, 9-15.

Arthur Davison Ficke. "In Defense of Vers Libre," in *The Little Review*, vol. 1, no. 9 (December 1914), 19-22.

Annie Finch. *The Ghost of Meter: Culture and Prosody in American Free Verse*, (Ann Arbor: University of Michigan Press, 1993).

Dana Gioia. "Notes on the New Formalism," in *The Hudson Review*, vol. 40, no. 3 (autumn 1987), 396-408.

Alice Corbin Henderson. "Convention and Revolt." Revision of *Convention and Revolt in Poetry*, by John Livingston Lowes. *Poetry*, vol. 14, no. 5 (August 1919), 269-73.

Brad Leithauser. "The Confinement of Free Verse," in *The New Criterion*, vol. 5, no. 9 (May 1987), 4-14.

Leithauser. "Metrical Illiteracy," in *The New Criterion*, vol. 1, no. 5 (Jan. 1983), 41-46.

Ludwig Lewisohn. "The Hour in Verse," in *The Nation*, vol. 116, no. 3014 (April 11, 1923), 414.

Robert McPhillips. "What's New About the New Formalism?" Feirstein, *Expansive Poetry* 195-208.

Richard Moore. "From Tristam's Rhapsody: Tristam's Attack on Modern Poetry," Frederick Feirstein, ed., *Expansive Poetry* ,16-54.

H. Houston Peckham. "The Return to Objectivism in Poetry," in *South Atlantic Quarterly*, vol. 13, no. 1 (January 1914), 43-50.

Ezra Pound. "A Retrospect" (1918). *Literary Essays of Ezra Pound*, T. S. Eliot, ed. (New York: New Directions, 1935), 3-14.

Julius Pratt. "The New Poetry." Rev. of *The New Poetry: An Anthology*, Harriet Monroe and Alice Corbin Henderson, eds., *South Atlantic Quarterly*, vol. 16, no. 3 (July 3, 1917), 271-274.

Pratt. "Whitman and Masters: A Contrast," in *South Atlantic Quarterly*, vol. 16, no. 3 (July 3, 1917), 222-226.

Timothy Steele. *Missing Measures: Modern Poetry and the Revolt Against Meter* (Fayetteville: Univ. of Arkansas Press, 1990).

Eunice Tietjens. "The Spiritual Dangers of Writing Vers Libre," in *The Little Review*, vol. 1, no. 8 (Nov. 1914), 25-29.

Frederick Turner, and Ernst Pöppel. "The Neural Lyre: Poetic Meter, the Brain, and Time," Feirstein, ed., *Expansive Poetry*, 209-254.

Louis Untermeyer. "Return of the Vers Libretine," in *The Nation*, vol. 114, no. 297 (June 7, 1922), 686-687.

The Neural Lyre: Poetic Meter, The Brain, and Time

Frederick Turner and Ernst Pöppel

This essay brings together an old subject, a new body of knowledge, and a new scientific paradigm which have not previously been associated with one another. The subject is poetic meter, a universal human activity, which despite its universality and obvious importance in most human cultures, has received very little attention from humanists, except for the studies of a few literary prosodists, and virtually none at all from science. The new body of knowledge consists in the findings of that intense study of the human brain which has taken place in the last few decades; the new scientific paradigm has been developed by the International Society for the Study of Time. Its major postulates are: that an understanding of time is fundamental to an understanding of the real world; that time is not simple, but composite; that time is a hierarchy of more and more complex temporalities; that the more complex temporalities evolved as part of the general evolution of the universe, and in a sense the evolution of time *constitutes* the evolution of the universe; and that the hierarchical character of time as we know it reflects and embodies the various stages of its evolution.[1]

The radically interdisciplinary nature of this essay is not simply a consequence of the need to seek explanations across the boundaries of different fields. It represents also a commitment and a belief on the part of its authors. We are convinced not only that this type of study will cast light on its specific subject (poetic meter), but also that the scientific material will be reciprocally enhanced in value, taking its place within a framework which gives it greater predictive power; and we further believe that "understanding" itself consists in just such a union of detailed knowledge with global significance.

At this point it might be helpful to review the major characteristics of human cortical information-processing, as it has been provisionally determined by studies in perceptual psychology, brain-chemistry, psychology, brain evolution, brain development, ethology, and cultural anthropology. [2]

Individually, the characteristics of human brain-activity which are listed below are commonplace and uncontroversial for the most part; collectively, they constitute a new picture of the human mind. This new picture replaces older, simpler models of it, such as the unextended rational substance of Descartes, the association-matrix of Locke, the *tabula rasa* of Hume, the passive, reinforcement-driven animal of Skinner, and the genetically hard-wired robot of the sociobiologists, though it does include the elements which led those writers to construct their models.

Human information-processing is, on the crude level of individual neurons, *procrustean*. That is, it reduces the information it gets from the outside world to its own categories, and accepts reality's answers only if they directly address its own set of questions. In the macrocosm, our perception of electromagnetic radiation cuts out all but heat and the visible spectrum; in the microcosm, a given neuron in the visual cortex will fire only if certain characteristics—say, a moving vertical light contrast—are met by the retinal image, and will ignore all others. We possess, as it were, a certain domineering and arrogant quality in our dealings with sensory information, and our brain will "listen" only to replies to its own inquiries. In quantum physics the familiar procrustean questions—Waves or particles? Which slit did the photon pass through? Is this ray of light polarized north-south or east-west?—force reality into a certainty and definiteness which it did not naturally possess: and this insistence on unambiguity is rooted in our neurons themselves.

Thus we may say that human information processing is, secondly, *determinative*: that is, it insists on certainty and unambiguity, and is thus at war with the probabilistic and indeterminate nature of the most primitive and archaic components of the universe. This insistence on definiteness, however, is in a grand tradition: matter itself is a condition of energy which severely limits the probabilistic waywardness of its elementary particles; large clumps of organized matter, like crystals, have overcome much of the vagueness and unpredictability of their primary constituents (though they pay for their certainty by becoming liable to entropic decay). Indeed, the replication of living matter could be said to be another stage in the suppression of physical ambiguity, for it implies an exact continuity and stability of structure which survives even the matter of which it is composed. Thus the human neural insistence on determinateness is in line with a general tendency of nature, and is related to the syllogistic proposition that homeostatic systems tend to endure and survive.

Third, and in contrast to the "conservative" tendency we have just described, the human nervous system seems designed to register differences. It is *habituative*. That is, it tends to ignore repeated and expected stimuli, and respond only to the new and unexpected. Though it asks the questions, it is more interested in odd answers than ordinary ones. Temporally it hears changes and sees movements; spatially it sees contrasts and borderlines. Deprived of its saccades, the eye sees nothing, for it sees no differences.

Fourth, human nervous activity is fundamentally *synthetic* in its aim. It seeks gestalts even when they are not there: and there is a serious ontological question as to whether they do in fact come to exist when we find them there.

It is (5) *active* rather than passive: it constructs scenarios to be tested by reality, vigorously seeks confirmation of them, and painfully reconstructs them if they are deconfirmed. The brain is at least as much an organ of action as it is an organ of knowledge.

It is thus (6) *predictive*: the patterns it extrapolates or invents are patterns which involve specific expectations of what will happen next, and in the more distant future, expectations which await satisfaction and are tested by the senses. Dreaming—it would seem from the testimony of Shakespeare, Descartes, Kékulé, and Freud—is the formative stage of pattern-creation: out of dreams come *A Midsummer Night's Dream*, skeptical philosophy, the benzene ring, and a viable ego. So dominant is the human adaptation for predictive calculation that it might be said that the human senses exist as a check on our predictions rather than, as in most other animals, triggers for appropriate behavior.

The whole matter of prediction is very complex. One of us (Pöppel) has pointed out the relationship between prediction and memory; indeed, he says, the adaptive function of memory *is* prediction.[3] Memory, however, would be useless in an entirely random and indeterminate universe: therefore the very fact that the metabolically expensive neural machinery of memory evolved and proved adaptive is a kind of odd proof that the universe is at least locally predictable, to justify such an investment.

But, on the other hand, an entirely deterministic and predictable universe would have no use for memory, either. The *Umwelt* of the lower animals, as determined by their affectors and receptors, is so limited that, to the extent that organisms survive, such an *Umwelt* constitutes a predictable universe; therefore, they possess no memories but only fixed action patterns triggered by appropriate stimuli. Memory only makes sense in a world of many possible futures, a world not fully determined: otherwise we could be programmed to perform an automatic and invariable set of behaviors which would exactly fit our adaptive needs. All futures share a common past: and thus memory gives us a handle on any possible future.

It has been objected, however, that the universe is indeed deterministic and predictable, but so complex that no animal can exactly predict its behavior, and that the very complex nervous systems of the higher animals developed precisely in order to improve their predictive powers. Such an argument produces an interesting dialectic, which might be worth following. It could be replied to the objection that the nervous systems of human beings are many orders of magnitude more complex than the physical universe they are, it is claimed, designed to predict. There are billions of times more possible brain-states in a single human brain than there are particles in the physical cosmos: the relations of the brain's parts carry usable information, whereas the relations between particles in the physical world do not.

There might, however, be a rejoinder to *this* argument, in turn. Human brains are part of the universe, and they merely make the job of predicting it more difficult without altering, by their presence, its actual determinateness. The fact that a major function of human brains is to predict the complex behaviors of each other, in no way weakens the proposition that the world is predictable.

But even this argument can be countered. For it implicitly yields the point that the world is *in practice* unpredictable, because any mechanism complex enough to predict events outside itself would also be so complex as to pose an insuperable problem to another predicting-mechanism, unless that other mechanism were in turn more complex still. It would not, moreover, be able to predict its own behavior. If Apollo gives prophesies, we should perhaps believe him, because he knows the mysteries of things and all human thoughts. But if Zeus, who also knows what Apollo is thinking, and who thus knows what Apollo will do, makes a contrary prophesy, we should believe Zeus instead. But Zeus does not know what Zeus will do, so perhaps we should not even believe Zeus at all.

Our original objector might still be able to argue that the predictability of events is only theoretical, not practical. But this argument must fail, too; for when we are dealing with the whole universe, the practical *is* the theoretical: if something is practically impossible for the whole universe, that is a way of saying it is theoretically impossible.

Finally, our antagonist might fall back to the position that future events are *determined* but not *predictable*. But since predictability would be the only conceivable scientific *test* of determinateness, such a statement would be semantically empty. A system whose complexity is increasing faster than any theoretical prediction-system could operate would therefore not be fully determined. In such a universe free choice based on memory would be a powerful survival strategy.

The peculiar logical form of this digression—which uses the infinite regress as a way of proving a negative proposition by means of a *reductio ad absurdum*—illustrates the peculiar predicament that the human brain at once evolved to handle and at the same time helped to create for itself. The very structure of the thinking process itself reflects the increasing levels of complexity the brain was called upon to deal with.

Human information processing is, therefore, (7) *hierarchical* in its organization. In the columns of neurons in the sensory cortex a plausible reconstruction of the world is created by a hierarchy of cells, the ones at the base responding to very simple stimuli and passing on their findings to cells programmed to respond to successively more complex stimuli. Likewise, motor decisions are passed down a long command-chain of simpler and simpler neural servomechanisms.

The co-ordination of these hierarchical systems in which many kinds of disparate information must be integrated, some requiring more processing-time and some requiring less, requires a neural pulse within which all relevant information is brought together as a whole. For instance, in the visual system many levels of detail—frequency, color, and depth—must all be synchronized, or we would not be able to associate the various features of a visual scene.[4] Thus, brain processing is (8) essentially *rhythmic*. That these rhythms can be "driven" or reinforced by repeated photic or auditory stimuli, to produce peculiar subjective states, is already well known.

More controversial in detail, but in general widely accepted, is the proposition that the brain's activities are (9) *self-rewarding*. The brain possesses built-in sites for the reception of opioid peptides such as enkephalin—the endorphins—and also other pleasure-associated neurohumors such as the catecholamines. It also controls the manufacture and release of these chemicals, and it has been shown that behavior can be reinforced by their use as a reward. The brain, therefore, is able to *reward itself* for certain activities which are, presumably, preferred for their adaptive utility. Clearly if this system of self-reward is the major motivating agent of the brain, any external technique for calibrating and controlling it would result in an enormously enhanced mental efficiency: we would, so to speak, be able to harness all our intellectual and emotional resources to a given task. (Indeed, we will argue later that this is exactly what an esthetic education, including an early introduction to metered verse in the form of nursery rhymes, can do.) It is, we believe, precisely this autonomous and reflexive reward system which underlies the whole realm of human values, ultimate purposes, and ideals such as truth, beauty, and goodness.

Associated with the brain's capacity for self-reward is (10) that it is characteristically *reflexive*. It is within broad limits self-calibrating (partly because of the habituation response). And it seems, unlike a computer, to have a more or less general capacity to convert software into hardware— short-term memory into long-term memory, for example—and vice-versa, to examine by introspection its own operations, so that its hardware can become its input or even its program. In the brain the observer problem becomes most acute: in fact we might define consciousness itself *as* the continuous irresolvable disparity between the brain as observer of itself and the brain as the object of observation. The coincidence between the words for consciousness and conscience in many languages points, incidentally, to the relationship between self-awareness and self-reward.

The human nervous system, we know now, cannot be separated from the human cultural system it was designed to serve. Its operations are (11) essentially *social*. It is not only specific skills and communicative competencies that are learnt in a social context, but also the fundamental capacities of arousal, orientation, attention, and motivation. Clearly we possess genetic proclivities to learn speech, elementary mathematical calculation, and so on; but equally clearly we require a socio-cultural context to release that potential. On the other hand, human society itself can be profoundly changed by the development of new ways of using the brain: take, for instance, the enormous socio-cultural effects of the invention of the written word. In a sense, reading is a sort of new synthetic instinct, input which becomes a program and which in turn crystallizes into neural hardware, and which incorporates a cultural loop into the human nervous circuit. This "new instinct" in turn profoundly changes the environment within which young human brains are programmed. In the early stages of human evolution such new instincts (speech must have been one) had to wait for their full development while sexual selection established the necessary elaborate vocal circuitry in the cortex. Later on we were able to use our technology, which required much less time to develop, as a sort of supplementary external nervous system. A book is a sort of ROM chip we can plug into our heads.

One of the most exciting propositions of the new brain science is that human information processing is (12) *hemispherically specialized*. Here some important distinctions must be made. There are strong logical objections to the popular and prevailing view that the right brain is emotional while the left brain is rational, and that artistic capacities, being emotional, are located in the right brain. Both sides of the brain are capable of rational calculation: it is surely just as rational to "see" a geometric proof—which is the function of the right brain—as to analyze a logical proposition—which would be done on the left. And both sides of the brain respond to the presence of brain chemicals, and thus both must be said to be "emotional" in this crude sense. The right brain may be better able to recognize and report emotions, but this capacity is surely a cognitive one in itself, and does not necessarily imply a judgment about whether it *feels* emotions more or less than the left. Above all, art is quite as much a rational activity as it is an emotional one: so the location of art on the "emotional" right is surely the result of a misunderstanding of the nature of art. More plausible is the position of Jerre Levy, who characterizes the relationship between right and left as a complementarity of cognitive capacities.[5] She has stated in a brilliant aphorism that the left brain maps spatial information into a temporal order, while the right brain maps temporal information onto a spatial order. In a sense understanding largely *consists* in the translation of information to and fro between a temporal ordering and a spatial one—resulting in a sort of stereoscopic depth-cognition. In Levy's view, the two "brains" alternate in the treatment of information, according to a rhythm determined by the general brain state, and pass, each time, their accumulated findings on to each other. The fact that experienced musicians use their left brain just as much as their right in listening to music shows that their higher understanding of music is the result of the collaboration of both "brains," the music having been translated first from temporal sequence to spatial pattern, and then "read," as it were, back into a temporal movement. The neurobiologist Günther Baumgartner suggests that the fore-brain acts as the integrating agent between specialized left and right functions, and it is in this integrative process that we would locate the essentially creative capacities of the brain, whether artistic or scientific. The apparent superiority of the isolated right brain in emotional matters may well reflect simply the fact that emotions, like music, are temporal in nature and their articulation requires the sort of temporal-on-spatial mapping that is the specialty of the right.

Finally, human information-processing can be described as (13) *kalogenetic* (Turner), a word coined from the Greek *KALOS*, for beauty, goodness, rightness; and *GENESIS*: begetting, productive cause, origin, source.[6] Another word for this characteristic, coined in jest as an etymological chimera by Pöppel, is *monocausotaxophilia*, the love of single causes that explain everything. William James called it "the will to believe." Laughlin and d'Aquili use the term "the cognitive imperative," or the "What is it?" syndrome, while Zollinger has identified it in the scientific urge to confirm and affirm a given hypothesis, rather than to deconfirm it (as Karl Popper would have us do). Baumgartner's notion of the integrative function of the forebrain also partakes of the same idea. The human nervous system has a strong drive to construct affirmative, plausible, coherent, consistent, parsimonious, and predictively powerful models of the world, in which all events are explained by and take their place in a system which is at once rich in implications beyond its existing data and at the same time governed by as few principles or axioms as possible. The words that scientists use for such a system are "elegant," "powerful," and, often, "beautiful"; artists and philosophers use the same terms and also "appropriate," "fitting," "correct," "right," all of which can translate the Greek *KALOS*.

If this tendency *is* a true drive, then according to the theory of reinforcement, it is an activity for which the brain rewards itself; and if there were techniques by which the endogenous reward system could be stimulated and sensitized, then those techniques would enable us to greatly enhance the integrative powers of our minds.

❄ ❄ ❄

Any candidate for identification as such a technique would have to meet certain qualifications. First, it would probably be culturally universal, since it would be based on neural and biochemical features common to all human beings.[7] Second, it would be very archaic, identifiable as an element of the most ancient and the most primitive cultures. Third, it would be likely to be regarded by its indigenous practitioners as the locus of an almost magical inspiration and as a source of wisdom; it would have the reputation of having significantly contributed to the efficiency and adaptiveness of the societies in which it is practiced. Fourth, it would be associated with those social and cultural activities which demand the highest powers of original thought and complex calculation, such as education, the organization of large-scale projects like war and co-operative agriculture, and the rituals which digest for social uses the dangerous and valuable energies implicit in sexuality, birth, death, sickness, and the like.

Metered poetry, the use of rule-governed rhythmic measures in the production of a heightened and intensified form of linguistic expression, nicely fulfills these requirements. Jerome Rothenberg's collection of ancient and "primitive" poetry, *Technicians of the Sacred*,[8] contains poems or excerpts from poems from about eighty different cultures, past and present, in Africa, North and South America, Asia, and Oceania; W.K. Wimsatt's excellent collection of essays, *Versification: Major Language Types*, describes the metrical features of Chinese, Japanese, Hebrew, Greek, Latin, Slavic, Uralic, Germanic, Celtic, Italian, Spanish, French, Old English and Modern English, and apologizes (p. 17) for omitting the Vedic-Indic verse system, the Arabic, including Swahili, and the Persian.[9] Metered poetry is a highly complex activity which is culturally universal. One of us (Turner) has heard poetry recited by Ndembu spirit-doctors in Zambia and has, with the anthropologist Wulf Schiefenhövel, translated Eipo poetry from Central New Guinea.[10] He reports, as a poet, that the meter of Eipo poetry, when reproduced in English, has much the same emotional effect as it does in the original. Such a minute correspondence between poets in such widely different cultures surely points to an identical neurophysiological mechanism.

In nearly all cultures, metered poetry is used in the crucial religious and social (and often economic) rituals, and has the reputation of containing mysterious wisdom; the learning of major poetic texts is central to the process of education in nearly all literate traditions. Much work—farming, herding, hunting, war, ship-handling, even mining—has its own body of poetry and song.[11]

It may be objected, however, that we have simply lumped together many different uses of language under an artificial category of poetry. This objection is strongly negated by the fact that poets themselves, who ought to know, can recognize the work of their alien colleagues as poetry, despite cultural differences. But we do not have to rely only on the reports of qualified native informants. Objective and universal and specific traits can be identified across the whole range of poetic practice throughout the world and as far back into the past as we have records. From these universal characteristics we can construct a general definition of metered poetry which will hold good from the ancient Greeks to the Kwakiutl, and from Racine to Polynesia.

The fundamental unit of metered poetry is what we shall call the LINE. We distinguish it by capitalization from the normal use of the word, because some orthographic traditions do not conventionally write or print the LINE in a separate space as we do; and in other traditions there are examples of a long line divided by a caesura into two sections, which would, in terms of our classification, actually constitute a couplet of LINES. There are also examples of what we would call a single LINE divided in half on the page. The LINE is preceded and followed by a distinct pause (not necessarily a pause for breath), which, despite the presence of other pauses within the LINE, divides the verse into clearly identifiable pieces. Turner, for example, can readily recognize the LINE-divisions of poetry in languages he does not know, when it is read aloud. The LINE unit can contain from four to twenty syllables; but it usually contains between seven and seventeen in languages which do not use fixed lexical tones, or between four and eight syllables in tonal languages, like Chinese, in which the metrical syllable takes about twice as long to articulate. Most remarkable of all, this fundamental unit nearly always takes from two to four seconds to recite, with a strong peak in distribution between 2.5 and 3.5 seconds. A caesura will usually divide the LINES in the longer part of the range; sometimes (as with Greek and Latin epic dactylic hexameters), the unit will be four to six seconds long, but clearly divided by a caesura and constituting for our purposes two LINES.

Turner has recorded and measured Latin, Greek, English, Chinese, Japanese, and French poetry, and Pöppel has done so for German. Less systematic measurements, by syllable-count, have revealed fully consistent results for Ndembu (Zambia), Eipo (New Guinea), Spanish, Italian, Hungarian, Uralic, Slavic, and Celtic. An average syllable in a non-tonal language takes about ¼ second to articulate, and in a tonal language about ½ second, though recitation traditions vary in this respect. The Ndembu LINE averages ten syllables; Eipo poetry favors an eight- or twelve-syllable line; in Spanish the epic line of the *Poema de Mio Cid* is about fourteen syllables, but most other poetry is octosyllabic or hendecasyllabic (eight or eleven); the classic Italian line is the eleven-syllable *endecasillabo*; Hungarian uses lines between six and twelve syllables long, with a preference for eights and twelves; Slavic has octosyllabics and decasyllabics, with an epic long line of fifteen to sixteen syllables; Celtic has sevens, eights, nines, and some longer-lined meters.[12]

Among the traditions we have measured more closely, the results are as follows, giving a range of different meters:

Japanese

Epic meter (a seven-syllable LINE followed by a five-syllable one) (average)	3.25 secs.
Waka (average)	2.75 secs.
Tanka (recited much faster than the epic, as 3 LINES of 5, 12, and 14 syllables) (average)	2.70 secs.

Chinese

Four-syllable line	2.20 secs.
Five-syllable line	3.00 secs.
Seven-syllable line	3.80 secs.

English

Pentameter	3.30 secs.
Seven-syllable trochaic line	2.50 secs.
Stanzas using different line lengths	3.00 secs.
	3.10 secs.
Ballad meter (octosyllabic)	2.40 secs.

Ancient Greek

Dactylic hexameter (half-line)	2.80 secs.
Trochaic tetrameter (half-line)	2.90 secs.
Iambic trimeter[13]	4.40 secs.
Marching anapests	3.50 secs.
Anapestic tetrameter (half-line)	2.50 secs.

Latin

Alcaic strophe	3.90 secs.
Elegiac couplet	3.50 secs.
Dactylic hexameter (half-line)	2.80 secs.
Hendecasyllabic	3.80 secs.

French

Alexandrine (12-syllable)	3.80 secs.
Decasyllable with octosyllable (La Fontaine)	3.00 secs.

German

(Sample of 200 poems, collected by Pöppel)

LINE-length of under 2 seconds	3%
LINE-length of 2-3 seconds	73%
LINE-length of 3-4 seconds	7%
LINE-length between 4 and 5 seconds[14]	17%

This fundamental unit is nearly always a rhythmic, semantic, and syntactical unit, as well: a sentence, a colon, a clause, or a phrase; or a completed group of them. Thus other linguistic rhythms are entrained to the basic acoustic rhythm, producing that pleasing sensation of "fit" and inevitability which is part of the delight of the verse, and is so helpful to the memory. Generally a short line is used to deal with light subjects, while the long line is reserved for epic or tragic matters.

It is, we believe, highly significant that this analysis of the fundamental LINE in human verse gives little or no significance to breath, or "breath-units," as a determinant of the divisions of human meter. Thus our commonsense observation that breath in speech is largely under voluntary control, and that one could speak anything from one syllable to about forty in one breath, is vindicated. Systems of verse based on breath-units, such as "projective verse" and many other free-verse systems, therefore have no objective validity or physiological foundation.[15]

The second universal characteristic of human verse meter is that certain marked elements of the LINE or of groups of LINES remain constant throughout the poem, and thus serve as indicators of the repetition of a pattern. The 3-second cycle is not merely marked by a pause, but by distinct resemblances between the material in each cycle. Repetition is added to frequency to emphasize the rhythm.

These constant elements can take many forms. Simplest of all is a constant number of syllables per line, as in Hungarian folk poetry; but here the strict grammatical integrity of each line is insisted upon, as if to compensate for the absence of other markers. Some verse forms (for instance, that of the *Poema de Mio Cid*) have a fixed number of stressed syllables per line, with an unfixed number of unstressed syllables. Other meters (most

European ones, for example) use small patterns of syllables, distinguished by stress or length, to make feet, creating a line out of a fixed number of feet. Tonal languages, like Chinese, distinguish between syllables of an unchanging tone and syllables which change tone, and construct meters out of repeated patterns of changing and unchanging syllables. Celtic poetry uses prescribed *cadences*; Old English uses systematic alliteration. Many languages use some system of assonance, especially rhyme, which usually marks very strongly the ending of a line, and thus forms a strong contrast-spike to divide off one line from the next. Hebrew poetry uses semantic and syntactical parallels between its pairs of half-lines. Often many of these devices will be used at once, some prescribed by the conventions of the poetic form, others left to the discretion and inspiration of the poet. No verse convention prescribes *all* the characteristics of a line, so every poem contains an interplay between prescribed elements and free variation.[16]

Sometimes, as in the Spenserian stanza, or in the Greek or English ode, or in the invented stanzas of Donne or Yeats, a whole group of lines of different lengths will constitute a repeated element. When lines of different lengths are used together, as in Milton's *Lycidas*, the rhyme (which stresses the integrity of the line) and the foot are given especial emphasis to compensate for the variation in the fundamental pulse—as if to insist on the threshold dividing the carrier-wave from mere "noise." And in variable-lined verses there is usually a normal-length line which acts as an unconscious constant against which the exceptions are measured as such.

At this point, it should be indicated that some of the characteristics of metered poetry do not apply to songs and lyrics derived from a song tradition. Music has its own form of organization, which diminishes the importance of the line to the advantage of the musical phrase. But in those traditions where we can see poetry emerging from song, such as the Latin lyric, there is an interesting tendency, as the musical order is forgotten, toward the establishment of the characteristically poetic forms of organization: the regular line, with variations, the distinction between different types of syllable (long and short, stressed and unstressed, tonally changing or unchanging), and the rest. Thus the fact that songs do not conform to the limits of poetic meter is negative proof of the relation of language and meter.

The third universal characteristic of human metrical verse is *variation*, or, more precisely, a pseudolinguistic generativeness created by the imposition of rules, which makes possible significant perturbations of an expressive medium. Robert Frost put it very well, in a negative way, when he described poetry without meter as being like tennis without a net: the net introduces a restriction which is paradoxically fertile in the elaboration of groundstrokes which it demands, and significant in that it distinguishes legal from illegal shots.

Variation does not necessarily mean departure from the rules (Romantic and Modernist theories of art sometimes make this mistake). Variation does not occur *despite* the rules but *because* of them. Freedom never means a freedom *from* rules, but the freedom *of* rules. It is important here for us to distinguish our general position from that of sociobiological and other purists of the genetic-deterministic persuasion on one hand, and from the pure cultural relativists, behaviorists or otherwise, on the other. Genetic determinists would be likely to assume, once a human universal such as metrical verse is pointed out to them, that this behavior indicates the presence of a set of biological constraints which act as an outer envelope, restricting possible human behaviors within a given repertoire, large or small. Cultural relativists would tend to deny the existence of such a human universal, or would be inclined to dismiss it as an analogous response to similar problems or stimuli, or as an artificial product of the investigator's definitional vocabulary and research method.

We would adopt a third position, which is already hinted by our use of the word "pseudolinguistic." For us, the similarities between metered verse in different cultures are real and do indeed indicate a shared biological underpinning; but unlike the genetic determinists we do not regard this shared inheritance as a constraint, nor as an outer envelope restricting human behavior to a certain range. Rather, we would regard it as a set of rules which, though derived from the structure of the human auditory cortex and the brain in general, does not restrict, but enormously increases, the range of possible human behavior.

At first glance this position might appear paradoxical. How can the range of possibilities be *increased* by the imposition of rules governing their use? If rules are rules, then they must surely *deny* certain previously possible behaviors, and therefore decrease the total number of them.

The paradox is easily resolved. A mathematical analogy will help. Given four possible behaviors, A, B, C, and D, only four alternatives exist. If we now impose a rule, which is that these behaviors can only be performed two at a time, suddenly and strangely there are now not four but six alternatives: AB, BC, CD, AC, BD, AD. Of course, this is cheating, in a sense, because before we mentioned the rule we never hinted that behaviors might come in groups. It could be pointed out that if we are talking about *sets* of behaviors, in fact sixteen possibilities exist: the ten already mentioned, the four groups of three, the whole group together, and the null set. But this is precisely what the rule has done: it has created the *group* of behaviors as a significant entity, as a behavior in itself, and therefore expanded the repertoire from four to six. Furthermore, those six permitted combinations now stand in relation to ten non-permitted ones, and their correctness marks them out as valuable and special, as opposed to the "incorrect" permutations. Thus, the rule has introduced a) a greater repertoire of behaviors than was previously possible and b) a marker of significance and value. All game-rules work in this way, creating possible scenarios and desired goals out of thin air.

The linguistic rules of phonology, grammar, and the lexicon work in a generally similar way. Linguistic rules are, to an extent, arbitrary and culture-bound: but Chomsky has shown certain invariant characteristics in the way in which human languages use syntactical subordination, which are no doubt biological in origin (and probably related to the *hierarchical* nature of human brain process). Meter, with its cultural variations in LINE-length, shows a similar interplay of cultural and genetic forces, and, more important, it produces a similar *increase* in the repertoire of behavior and a similar capacity to create significance.

In fact it is this general strategy by which the DNA molecule of life and the nervous systems of the higher animals attained greater complexities than the physical universe out of which they evolved; by making *permutations* of elements significant through highly restrictive "rules," and therefore increasing, as it were, the "cardinality" of the number of bits of information that the organism could hold. We find, for example, a similar interplay between genetic and cultural factors in the human recognition of colors: a rather restricted set of anatomically-determined color sensitivities is combined by culture into a large, and often idiosyncratic repertoire of tints and shades, many of them with strong ideological significance. The range, variety, and combinations of colored pigmentation used in animal ritual behavior attests to a corresponding extension and valorization of color distinctions among the higher animals.

Thus metrical variation can be seen as a code, or communicative device, and the various elements of meter can be neatly described in terms of information theory. The three-second LINE is the communicative medium or "carrier-wave," which must be distinguishable from mere "noise" or the random transmissions around it, by the recurrence of a pause at the LINE-ending, by the many regular metrical features — syllable-count, stress, quantity, tone, systematic assonance, etc. — that we have described, and by the coincidence of semantic, syntactic, and rhythmic units with the LINE unit. Metrical variation is the "message" which is transmitted upon the communicative medium — like a radio-transmission, it consists of a systematic distortion of a regular medium or wave, which nevertheless remains within the regular parameters of the medium so that at all times the transmission is distinguishable from random noise.

The "message" that metrical variation conveys, however, is rather mysterious. If it is a code, what kind of code is it? Metrical scholars have attempted to discover exact relationships between individual metrical variations and the semantic content of poetry.[17] But their conclusions have been disappointingly vague or arbitrary, reminiscent, in fact, of musicological attempts to assign fixed meanings to different musical keys, signatures, and variations, so as to make a symphony describe a scene or conduct an argument. Here the analogy between metrical and linguistic significance breaks down. Certainly a connection between metrical (or musical) and linguistic meaning exists, and in some cultural traditions (English Augustan poetry and European Romantic music, for instance) artists have developed a self-conscious repertoire of metrical or musical codes to convey specific meanings. But other traditions do not possess such codifications, or else use the same specific devices to convey entirely different ideas.

The predicament of the critic, in fact, can be likened to that of a viewer of a visual artifact who is so convinced that what he is looking at is a page of writing that he does not realize that the artifact is actually a *picture*. Perhaps it is a picture of something he has never seen (or even noticed), and thus his mistake is a natural one. But the attempt to extract a sort of linguistic meaning out of the planes, lines, corners, masses, and angles of a picture would be frustratingly arbitrary — especially if he had a whole series of paintings of different subjects, in which the same visual elements were used for entirely different purposes; the same curve for a face, a hillside, and the sail of a ship. Linguistic meaning and pictorial meaning are based on codes so fundamentally different that no code-cracking algorithm that would work on one could possibly work on the other. Their mutual intelligibility cannot be sought in the direction of analysis, but only within the context of a synthetic whole which contains both of them.

What we are suggesting is that a linguistic type of analysis of meter, as of music (or painting, e.g., Chinese landscape painting), is likely to be fruitful *only* when the composer has arbitrarily *imposed* linguistic meaning on the elements of his composition; and that the meaning of metrical variation must be sought in a fashion much more like that of the recognition of a tune or the subject of a picture. That is, metrical variations are not significant in themselves, like sememes: but rather they form, together, a picture-like *Gestalt* which is a distinct representation of something that we can recognize; and thus, like pictorial representations, or music, they are much less culture-bound than linguistic codes. But here, excitingly, we encounter a paradox stemming from the gross structure of the human brain. Poetry, being an art of language, is presumably processed by the left temporal lobe of the brain. But meter, we are suggesting, carries meaning in a fashion much more like that of a picture or a melody, in which the meaning inheres more in the whole than in the parts. There is no "lexicon" of metrical forms: they are not *signs* but elements of an analogical structure. And this kind of understanding is known to take place on the *right* side of the brain. If this hypothesis is accurate, meter is, in part, a way of introducing right-brain processes into the left-brain activity of understanding language; and in another sense, it is a way of connecting our much more culture-bound (and perhaps evolutionarily later) linguistic capacities with the relatively more "hardwired" spatial pattern-recognition faculties we share with the higher mammals.

* * *

It is in the context of this hypothesis that we wish to introduce the major finding of this essay, which explains, we believe, the extraordinary prevalence of the three-second LINE in human poetry.

If we ask the question, "What does the ear hear?" the obvious answer is "sound." What is sound? Mechanical waves in the air or other medium. But this answer is not very illuminating. We can, for instance, perceive mechanical waves by the sense of touch: it would be as inaccurate to say that a deaf man "heard" a vibrating handrail with his fingers, as it would be to say a blind man "saw" a fire with the skin of his face. What characterizes hearing as such is not that it senses mechanical waves but that it senses the distinctions between mechanical waves; just as what characterizes sight is not the perception of electromagnetic waves but the perception of distinctions between electromagnetic waves.

For the sense of sight those distinctions (except for color) are spatial ones; but for the sense of hearing they are mainly temporal. To put it directly: what the sense of hearing hears is essentially *time*. The recognition of differences of pitch involves a very pure (and highly accurate) comparative measurement of different frequencies into which time is divided. The perception of timbre, tone, sound texture, and so on consists in the recognition of combinations of frequencies; and the sense of rhythm and tempo carries the recognition of frequency into the realm of longer periods of time.

The sense of hearing is not only a marvelously accurate instrument for detecting differences between temporal periods; it is also an active organizer, arranging those different periods within a hierarchy as definite as that of the seconds, minutes, and hours of a clock, but one in which the different periodicities are also uniquely valorized. In the realm of pitch the structure of that hierarchy is embodied in the laws of harmony, and is well known (although it has not often been recognized that "sound" and "time" are virtually the same thing). New discoveries by Ernst Pöppel's group in Munich have begun to open up the role of the auditory time-hierarchy in the structure and function of the brain. Out of this investigation is coming a comprehensive understanding of the general scheduling-organization of the human sensory-motor system, and a fresh approach to the production and understanding of language. We shall first briefly outline the auditory hierarchy.

Events separated by periods of time shorter than about three thousandths of a second (.003) are classified by the hearing system as simultaneous. If a brief sound of one pitch is played to one ear, and another of a different pitch is played to the other less than .003 seconds later, the subject will experience only one sound. If the sounds are a little more than .003 seconds apart, the subject will experience two sounds. However, he will not be able to tell which of the two sounds came first, nor will he until the gap between them is increased ten times. Thus the lowest category in the hierarchy of auditory time is *simultaneity*, and the second lowest is mere temporal *separation*, without a preferred order or time. The most primary temporal experience is timeless unity; next comes a spacelike recognition of difference—spacelike because, unlike temporal positions, spatial positions can be exchanged. One can go from New York to Berlin or from Berlin to New York; but one can only go from 1980 to 1983, not from 1983 to 1980. Likewise, the realm of "separation" is a non-deterministic, acausal one: events happen in it, perhaps in patterns or perhaps not, but they cannot be said to cause one another, because we cannot say which came first.

When two sounds are about three hundredths of a second apart, a subject can experience their *sequence*, accurately reporting which came first. This is the third category in the hierarchy of auditory time, subsuming separations and simultaneities and organizing them rationally with respect to each other. But at this stage the organism is still a passive recipient of stimuli; we can hear a sequence of two sounds one-tenth of a second apart, but there is nothing we can do in response to the first sound before the second sound comes along: we are helpless to alter what will befall us, if the interval between the alert and its sequel falls within this range. Unlike the world of temporal separation, which is in a sense a realm of chance and pattern, the world of sequence is a realm of fate and cause. Events follow each other, and their temporal connections can be recognized as necessary, if indeed they are; but there is nothing we can do about it.

Once the temporal interval is above about three-tenths of a second, however, we have entered a new temporal category, which we might call *response*. For three-tenths of a second (.3 sec.) is enough time for a human subject to react to an acoustic stimulus. If we play two sounds to our subject a second apart, the subject could in theory prepare to deal with the second sound in the time given him after hearing the first. The perceiver is no longer passive, and events can be treated by him as actions in *response* to which he can perform actions of his own and which he can modify before they happen if he understands their cause. For response to exist there must be simultaneities, a separation, and a further element which might be characterized as function or, in a primitive sense, purpose. The response to a given stimulus will differ according to the function of the responding organ and the purpose of the organism as a whole.

At several places in this analysis it has been pointed out that a given familiar temporal relation—chance, pattern, fate, cause, action, function, purpose—only becomes possible when there is enough time for it to exist in. The idea that an entity needs time to exist in has become commonplace recently: an electron, for instance, requires at least 10^{-20} seconds of time (its spin period) to exist in, just as surely as it requires 10^{-10} centimeters of space (its Compton wavelength). The corollary to this observation is that entities which consist only in spatio-temporal relations are not necessarily less real for that than material objects, for spatio-temporal relations are exactly what material objects consist of too. But though a given period of time may be sufficient for an example of given relation—chance, cause, function—to be recognized in, it is not enough for the concept of the relation to be formulated in. It takes much less time to recognize or speak a word once learned than it takes to learn the word in the first place. Many examples of the sequence or response relation between events must be compared before a causal or purposive order can be formulated and thus recognized in individual cases. But comparison requires discrete parcels of experience between which the comparison may be made, and since the entities being compared are themselves temporal in nature, these parcels of experience must consist in equal periods of time. In like fashion, the analysis of a picture (for transmission, reproduction, or identification of its details) might begin by dividing the picture up into "pixels" by means of a series of grids of various frequency; the highest-frequency grid representing the limit of the eye's activity, the lower ones increasingly concerned with complex relations between details. The next lowest time-division beyond the .3 second response-frequency must be sufficiently long to avoid falling into the range of the characteristic time-quanta required for the completion and recognition of the temporal relations to be compared. The comparison of experience takes more time than experience itself; the recognition of a melody takes more time than the hearing of the single notes.

This fundamental "parcel of experience" turns out to be about three seconds. The three-second period, roughly speaking, is the length of the human present moment. (At least it is for the auditory system, which possesses the sharpest temporal acuity of all the senses. The eye, for instance, is twice as slow as the ear in distinguishing temporal separation from simultaneity.) The philosophical notion of the "specious present" finds here its experimental embodiment.

A human speaker will pause for a few milliseconds every three seconds or so, and in that period decide on the precise syntax and lexicon of the next three seconds. A listener will absorb about three seconds of heard speech without pause or reflection, then stop listening briefly in order to integrate and make sense of what he has heard. (Speaker and hearer, however, are not necessarily "in phase" for this activity; this observation will be seen to be of importance later.)

To use a cybernetic metaphor, we possess an auditory information "buffer" whose capacity is three seconds' worth of information; at the end of three seconds the "buffer" is full, and it passes on its entire accumulated stock of information to the higher processing centers. In theory this stock could consist of about 1,000 simultaneities, 100 discrete temporal separations, and ten consecutive responses to stimuli. In practice the "buffer" has rather smaller capacity than this (about 60 separations); it seems to need a certain amount of "down-time."

It appears likely that another mechanism is involved here too. Different types of information take different amounts of time to be processed by the cortex. For instance, fine detail in the visual field takes more time to be identified by the cortex than coarse detail. (Indeed, the time taken to process detail seems to be used by the brain as a tag to label its visual frequency).[18] Some sort of pulse is necessary so that all the information of different kinds will arrive at the higher processing centers as a bundle, correctly labeled as belonging together, and at the same time; the sensory cortex "waits" for the "slowest" information to catch up with the "fastest" so that it can all be sent off at once. And this three-second period constitutes a "pulse."

Beyond the two horizons of this present moment exist the two periods which together constitute *duration*, which is the highest or "longest-frequency" integrative level of the human perception of time. Those two periods, the past and the future, memory and planning, are the widest arena of human thought (unless the religious or metaphysical category of "eternity" constitutes an even wider one). It is within the realm of duration that what we call freedom can exist, for it is within that realm that purposes and functions, the governors of response, can themselves be compared and selected. The differences between past and future, and the differences between possible futures, constitute the field of *value*, and the relations between low-frequency objects and the more primitive high-frequency objects of which they are composed constitute the field of *quality*.

It is tempting to relate this foregoing hierarchical taxonomy of temporal periodicities to the structure and evolution of the physical universe itself. The temporal category of *simultaneity* nicely corresponds to the atemporal *Umwelt* of the photon, which reigned supreme in the first microsecond of the Big Bang. The category of *separation* resembles the weak, acausal, stochastic, spacelike temporality of quantum physics, within which there is no preferred direction of time; a condition which must have prevailed shortly after the origin of the universe, and of which the quantum-mechanical organization of subatomic particles is a living fossil. The category of *sequence* matches the causal, deterministic, and entropic realm of classical hard science, whose subject came into being some time after the origin of the universe, once the primal explosion had cooled sufficiently to permit the existence of organized, discrete, and enduring matter. With the category of *response* we are clearly within the *Umwelt* of living matter, with its functions, purposes, and even its primitive and temporary teleology, which began about ten billion years after the Big Bang. Once we cross the horizon of the present we leave the world of animals and enter the realm of *duration*, which first came into being perhaps a million years ago (if it was roughly coeval with speech and with that development of the left brain which gave us the tenses of language). The evolution and hierarchical structure of the human hearing mechanism thus could be said to recapitulate the history and organization of the cosmos. The history of science has been the retracing of that path backwards by means of clocks of greater and greater acuity.

☙ ☙ ☙

Cosmological speculation aside, it should already be obvious that a remarkable and suggestive correlation exists between the temporal organization of poetic meter and the temporal function of the human hearing mechanism. Of general linguistic significance is the fact that the length of a syllable—about $1/3$ second—corresponds to the minimum period within which a *response* to an auditory stimulus can take place: this is common-sense, really, as speech must, to be efficient, be as fast as it can be, while, to be controllable, it must be slow enough for a speaker or hearer to react to a syllable before the next one comes along.

Of more specific significance for our subject is the very exact correlation between the three-second LINE and the three-second "auditory present." The average number of syllables per LINE in human poetry seems to be about ten; so human poetic meter embodies the two lowest frequency rhythms in the human auditory system.

The independence of poetic meter from the mechanism of breathing, which we have already noted, is thus explained by the fact that the master-rhythm of human meter is not pulmonary but neural: we must seek the origins of poetry not among the lower regions of the human organism, but among the higher. The frequent practice in reading "free verse" aloud, of breathing at the end of the line—even when the line is highly variable in length and often broken quite without regard to syntax—is therefore not only grammatically confusing but deeply unnatural; for it forces a pause where neural processing would not normally put it.

But at least there was a clear, if erroneous, rationale for the doctrine of meter as made up of "breath-units." Without this rationale, how do we explain the cultural universality of meter? *Why* does verse embody the three-second neural "present"? What functions could be served by this artificial and external mimicry of an endogenous brain rhythm? Given the fact, already stated, that poetry fulfills many of the superficial conditions demanded of a brain-efficiency reward control system, how might the three-second rhythm serve that function? And what is the role of the other components of meter—the rhythmic parallelism between the LINES, and the information-bearing variations upon that parallelism?

One further batch of data will help guide our hypothesizing: the subjective reports of poets and readers of poetry about the effects and powers of poetic meter. Although these reports would be inadequate and ambiguous as the sole support of an argument, they may point us in the right direction and confirm conclusions arrived at by other means.

A brief and incomplete summary of these reports, with a few citations, should suggest to a reader educated in literature the scope of their general agreement. Robert Graves speaks of the shiver and the coldness in the spine, the hair rising on the head and body, as does Emily Dickinson. A profound muscular relaxation yet an intense alertness and concentration is also recorded. The heart feels squeezed and the stomach cramped. There is a tendency toward laughter or tears, or both; the taking of deep breaths; and a slightly intoxicated feeling (Samuel Taylor Coleridge compared it to the effects of a moderate amount of strong spirits upon a conversation). At the same time there is a cataract or avalanche of vigorous thought, in which new connections are made; Shakespeare's Prospero describes the sensation as "beating mind" (the phrase is repeated three times in different places in the play). There is a sense of being on the edge of a precipice of insight—almost a vertigo—and the awareness of entirely new combinations of ideas taking concrete shape, together with feelings of strangeness and even terror. Some writers (Arnold, for instance) speak of an inner light or flame. Outside stimuli are often blanked out, so strong is the concentration. The imagery of the poem becomes so intense that it is almost like real sensory experience. Personal memories pleasant and unpleasant (and sometimes previously inaccessible) are strongly evoked; there is often an emotional re-experience of close personal ties, with family, friends, lovers, the dead. There is an intense valorization of the world and of human life, together with a strong sense of the reconciliation of opposites—joy and sorrow, life and death, good and evil, divine and human, reality and illusion, whole and part, comic and tragic, time and timelessness. The sensation is not a timeless one as such, but an experience of time so full of significance that stillness and sweeping motion are the same thing. There is a sense of power combined with effortlessness. The poet or reader rises above the world, as it were, on the "viewless wings of Poesy," and sees it all in its fullness and completeness, but without loss of the quiddity and clarity of its details. There is an awareness of one's own physical nature, of one's birth and death, and of a curious transcendence of them; and, often, a strong feeling of universal and particular love, and communal solidarity.

Of course, not all these subjective sensations necessarily occur together in the experience of poetry, nor do they usually take their most intense form; but a poet or frequent reader of poetry will probably recognize most of them.

To this list, moreover, should be added a further property of metered poetry, which goes beyond the immediate experience of it: that is, its memorability. Part of this property is undoubtedly a merely technical convenience: the knowledge of the number of syllables in a line and the rhyme, for instance, limits the number of words and phrases which are possible in a forgotten line and helps us to logically reconstruct it. But introspection will reveal a deeper quality to this memorability: somehow the rhythm of the words is remembered even when the words themselves are lost to us; but the rhythm helps us to recover the mental state in which we first heard or read the poem, and then the gates of memory are opened and the words come to us at once.

Equipped with the general contemporary conception of brain-processing with which this essay began, with the temporal analysis of meter and its correlation to the hearing-system, and with the subjective reports of participants in the art, we may now begin to construct a plausible hypothesis of what goes on in the brain during the experience of poetry.

Here we can draw upon a relatively new and speculative field of scientific inquiry, which has been variously termed "neuro-physiology," "biocybernetics," and "biopsychology," and is associated with the names of such researchers as E. Bourguignon, E.D. Chapple, E. Gellhorn, A. Neher, and R. Ornstein. Barbara Lex's essay "The Neurobiology of Ritual Trance,"[19] in which she summarizes and synthesizes much of their work, provides many of the materials by which we may build an explanatory bridge between the observed characteristics of human verse and the new findings of the Munich group about the hearing mechanism. Although Lex is concerned with the whole spectrum of methods by which altered states of consciousness may be attained—alcohol, hypnotic suggestion, breathing techniques, smoking, music, dancing, drugs, fasting, meditation, sensory deprivation, photic driving, and auditory driving—and her focus is on ritual rather than the art of poetry, her general argument fits well with our own findings.

Essentially her position is that the various techniques listed above, and generalized as "driving behaviors," are designed to add to the linear, analytic, and verbal resources of the left brain the more intuitive and holistic understanding of the right brain; to tune the central nervous system and alleviate accumulated stress; and to invoke to the aid of social solidarity and cultural values the powerful somatic and emotional force mediated by the sympathetic and parasympathetic nervous systems, and the ergotropic and trophotropic responses they control.[20] "Trophotropic" refers to the corresponding system of rest, body maintenance, and relaxation: decreased heart rate, a flow of blood to the internal organs, an increase in the activity of the digestive process, drowsiness, and a hormone balance consistent with sleep, inactivity, or trance.

It has been known for many years that rhythmic photic and auditory stimulation can evoke epileptic symptoms in seizure-prone individuals, and can produce powerful involuntary reactions even in normal persons. The rhythmic stimulus entrains and then amplifies natural brain rhythms, especially if it is tuned to an important frequency such as the ten-cycle-per-second alpha wave. It seems plausible to us that the three-second poetic LINE is similarly tuned to the three-second cycle of the auditory (and subjective-temporal) present. The metrical and assonantal devices of verse such as rhyme and stress, which create similarities between the LINES, emphasize the repetition. The curious subjective effects of metered verse—relaxation, a holistic sense of the world and so on—are no doubt attributable to a very mild pseudotrance state induced by the auditory driving effect of this repetition.

Auditory driving is known to affect the right brain much more powerfully than the left; thus, where ordinary unmetered prose comes to us in a "mono" mode, so to speak, affecting the left brain predominantly, metered language comes to us in a "stereo" mode, simultaneously calling on the verbal resources of the left and the rhythmic potentials of the right.[21]

Of course, the matter is not as simple as this, even at this level of discussion. The accurate scansion of poetry involves a complex analysis of *grammatical* and *lexical* stress, which must be continually integrated with a non-verbal right-brain understanding of *metrical* stress. The delightful way in which the rhythm of the sentence, as a semantic unit, counterpoints the rhythm of the meter in poetry, is thus explained as the result of a co-operation between left and right brain functions. The "stereo" effect of verse is not merely one of simultaneous stimulation of two different brain areas, but also the result of a necessary integrative collaboration and feedback between them. The linguistic capacities of the left brain, which, as Levy says, provide a temporal order for spatial information, are forced into a conversation with the rhythmic and musical capacities of the right, which provide a spatial order for temporal information.

But the driving rhythm of the three-second LINE is not just any rhythm. It is, as we have seen, tuned to the largest limited unit of auditory time, its specious present, within which causal sequences can be compared, and free decisions taken. A complete poem—which can be any length—is a duration, a realm of values, systematically divided into presents, which are the realm of action. It therefore summarizes our most sophisticated and most uniquely human integrations of time.

There is, perhaps, still another effect at work on the cortical level. The various divinatory practices of humankind (another cultural universal, perhaps) all involve a common element: a process of very complex calculation which seems quite irrelevant to the kind of information sought by the diviner. A reader of the Tarot will analyze elaborate combinations of cards, an *I Ching* reader will arrive at his hexagram through a difficult process of mathematical figuring, a reader of the horoscope will resort to remarkable computations of astronomical position and time. (The common use of the word "reader" in these contexts is suggestive.) The work of scanning metered verse, especially when combined with the activity of recognizing allusions and symbolisms, and the combination of them into the correct patterns, seems analogous to these divinatory practices. The function of this demanding process of calculation may be to occupy the linear and rational faculties of the brain with a task which entirely distracts them from the matter to be decided—a diagnosis, a marriage, the future of an individual. Once the "loud voice" of the reductive logical intelligence is thus stilled by distance, the quieter whispering of a holistic intuition, which can integrate much larger quantities of much poorer-quality information in more multifarious ways—though with a probability of accuracy which is correspondingly much lower—can then be heard. The technique is something like that of the experienced stargazer, who can sometimes make out a very faint star by focusing a little to one side of it, thereby bringing to bear on it an area of the retina which, though inferior in acuity, is more sensitive to light. The vatic, prophetic, or divinatory powers traditionally attributed to poetry may be partly explained by the use of this technique. If the analogy is slightly unflattering to the work of some professional analytic critics of poetry—reducing their work, as it does, to the status of an elaborate decoy for the more literalistic proclivities of the brain—there is the compensation that it is after all a very necessary activity, indeed indispensable precisely because of its irrelevance.

On the cortical level, then, poetic meter serves a number of functions generally aimed at tuning up and enhancing the performance of the brain, by bringing to bear other faculties than the linguistic, which we can relate to the summary of healthy brain characteristics at the beginning of this paper. By ruling out certain rhythmic possibilities, meter satisfies the brain's procrustean demand for unambiguity and clear distinctions. By combining elements of repetition and isochrony on one hand with variation on the other, it nicely fulfills the brain's habituative need for controlled novelty. By giving the brain a system of rhythmic organization as well as a circum-scribed set of semantic and syntactical possibilities, it encourages the brain in its synthetic and predictive activity of hypothesis-construction, and raises expectations which are pleasingly satisfied at once. In its content, poetry has often had a strongly prophetic character, an obvious indication of its predictive function; and the mythic elements of poetry afford more subtle models of the future by providing guides to conduct. Poetry presents to the brain a system which is temporally and rhythmically hierarchical, as well as linguistically so, and therefore matched to the hierarchical organization of the brain itself. It does much of the work that the brain must usually do for itself, in organizing information into rhythmic pulses, integrating dif-ferent types of information—rhythmic, grammatical, lexical, acoustic—into easily assimilable parcels and labeling their contents as belonging together. Like intravenous nourishment, the information enters our system instantly, without a lengthy process of digestion. The pleasure of metered verse evi-dently comes from its ability to stimulate the brain's capacities of self-re-ward, and the traditional concern of verse with the deepest human *values*— truth, goodness, and beauty—is clearly associated with its involvement with the brain's own motivational system. Poetry seems to be a device the brain can use in reflexively calibrating itself, turning its software into hardware and its hardware into software; and accordingly poetry is traditionally concerned, on its semantic level, with consciousness and conscience. As a quintessentially cultural activity, poetry has been central to social learning and the synchronization of social activities (the sea-shanty or work-song is only the crudest and most obvious example). Poetry, as we have seen, enforces cooperation between left-brain temporal organization and right-brain spatial organization and helps to bring about that integrated stereoscopic view that we call true understanding. And poetry is, *par excellence*, "Kalogenetic"—productive of beauty, or elegant, coherent, and predictively powerful models of the world.

It might be argued—and this is a traditional charge against poetry—that in doing all these things poetry deceives us, presenting to us an experience which, because it is so perfectly designed for the human brain, gives us a false impression of reality and separates us from the rough world in which we must survive. Much modern esthetic theory is in fact devoted to reversing this situation, and making poetry—and art in general—so disharmonious with our natural proclivities that it shocks us into awareness of the stark realities. Clearly a poetry which was too merely harmonious would be insipid—for it would disappoint the brain's habituative desire for novelty. But mere random change and the continuous disappointment of expectations is itself insipid; we are as capable of becoming habituated to meaningless flux as to mindless regularity.

Modernist esthetic theory may be ignoring the following possibility: that our species' special adaptation may in fact be to expect more order and meaning in the world than it can deliver; and that those expectations may constitute, paradoxically, an excellent survival strategy. We are strongly motivated to restore the equilibrium between reality and our expectations by altering reality so as to validate our models of it—to "make the world a better place," as we put it. The modernist attack on beauty in art would therefore constitute an attack on our very nature itself; and the modernist and post-modernist criticism of moral and philosophical idealism likewise flies in the face of the apparent facts about human neural organization. What William James called "the will to believe" is written in our genes; teleology is the best policy; and paradoxically, it is utopian to attempt to do battle against our natural idealism. Much more sensible to adjust reality to the ideal.

But our discussion of the effects of metered verse on the human brain has ignored, so far, the subcortical levels of brain activity. Let us substitute, as *pars pro toto*, "metered verse" for "rituals" in the following summary by Barbara Lex:

> The *raison d'être* of rituals is the readjustment of dyspha-
> sic biological and social rhythms by manipulation of neu-
> rophysiological structures under controlled conditions.
> Rituals properly executed promote a feeling of well-be-
> ing and relief, not only because prolonged or intense
> stresses are alleviated, but also because the driving tech-
> niques employed in rituals are designed to sensitize and
> "tune" the nervous system and thereby lessen inhibition
> of the right hemisphere and permit temporary right-hemi-
> sphere dominance, as well as mixed trophotropic-
> ergotropic excitation, to achieve synchronization of cor-
> tical rhythms in both hemispheres and evoke trophotro-
> pic rebound.[22]

Lex maintains that the "driving" techniques of rhythmic dances, chants, and so on can produce a simultaneous stimulation of both the ergotropic (arousal) and the trophotropic (rest) systems of the lower nervous system, producing subjective effects which she characterizes as follows: trance; ecstasy; meditative and dreamlike states; possession; the "exhilaration ac-companying risk taking"; a sense of community; sacredness; a "process of reviving the memory of a repressed unpleasant experience and expressing in speech and actions the emotions related to it, thereby relieving the per-sonality of its influence"; alternate laughing and crying; mystical experi-ence and religious conversion; experiences of unity, holism, and solidarity. Laughlin and d'Aquili add to these effects a sense of union with a greater power, an awareness that death is not to be feared, a feeling of harmony with the universe, and a mystical *"conjunctio oppositorum,"* or unity of the opposites. This list closely resembles our earlier enumeration of the experi-ence of good metered verse as described by literary people.

If Lex is right, we can add to the more specifically cortical effects of metered verse the more generalized functions of a major ritual driving tech-nique: the promotion of biophysiological stress-reduction (peace) and so-cial solidarity (love). Meter clearly synchronizes not only speaker with hearer, but hearers with each other, so that each person's three-second "present" is in phase with the others and a rhythmic community, which can become a performative community, is generated.

Laughlin and d'Aquili connect the mythical mode of narrative with the driving techniques of ritual, pointing out that mythical thought expresses the "cognitive imperative," as they call it, or the desire for an elegant and meaningful explanation of the world;[23] and McManus argues that such practices are essential in the full development and education of children.[24] (Again we might point out that the modernist praise of mythical thought is misplaced; for it values the irrational element it discerns in myth, whereas true mythical thought, as Levi-Strauss has shown, is deeply rational and has much in common with scientific hypothesis.)

The theory of the state-boundedness of memory might also explain the remarkable memorability of poetry. If meter evokes a peculiar brain state, and if each meter and each use of meter with its unique variations carries its own mood or brain-state signature, then it is not surprising that we can recall poetry so readily. The meter itself can evoke the brain-state in which we first heard the poem, and therefore make the verbal details immediately accessible to recall. Homer said that the muses were the daughters of memory, and this may be what he meant. By contrast, the modernist critic Chatman sneeringly dismisses the mnemonic function of metered poetry as being in common with that of advertising jingles. But if advertising jingles are left holding the field of human emotional persuasion, poetry has surely lost the battle—or the advertising jingles have become the only true poetry.

        ❈ ❈ ❈

To sum up the general argument of this essay: metered poetry is a cultural universal, and its salient feature, the three-second present moment of the auditory information-processing system. By means of metrical variation, the musical and pictorial powers of the right brain are enlisted by meter to cooperate with the linguistic powers of the left; and by auditory driving effects, the lower levels of the nervous system are stimulated in such a way as to reinforce the cognitive functions of the poem, to improve the memory, and to promote physiological and social harmony. Metered poetry may play an important part in developing our more subtle understandings of time, and may thus act as a technique to concentrate and reinforce our uniquely human tendency to make sense of the world in terms of values like truth, beauty, and goodness. Meter breaks the confinement of linguistic expression and appreciation within two small regions of the left temporal lobe and brings to bear the energies of the whole brain.[25]

The consequences of this new understanding of poetic meter are very wide-ranging. This understanding would endorse the classical conception of poetry, as designed to "instruct by delighting," as Sir Philip Sidney put it.[26] It would suggest strongly that "free verse," when uncoupled from any kind of metrical regularity, is likely to forego the benefits of bringing the whole brain to bear. It would also predict that free verse would tend to become associated with views of the world in which the tense-structure has become very rudimentary and the more complex values, being time-dependent, have disappeared. A bureaucratic social system, requiring specialists rather than generalists, would tend to discourage reinforcement techniques such as metered verse, because such techniques put the whole brain to use and encourage world-views that might transcend the limited values of the bureaucratic system; and by the same token it would encourage activities like free verse, which are highly specialized both neurologically and culturally. Prose, both because of its own syntactical rhythms and because of its traditional liberty of topic and vocabulary, is less highly specialized; though it is significant that bureaucratic prose tends toward being arrhythmic and toward specialized vocabulary. The effect of free verse is to break down the syntactical rhythms of prose without replacing them by meter, and the tendency of free verse has been toward a narrow range of vocabulary, topic, and genre—mostly lyric descriptions of private and personal impressions. Thus free verse, like existentialist philosophy, is nicely adapted to the needs of the bureaucratic and even the totalitarian state, because of its confinement of human concern within narrow specialized limits where it will not be politically threatening.

The implications for education are very important. If we wish to develop the full powers of the minds of the young, early and continuous exposure to the best metered verse would be essential; for higher human values, the cognitive abilities of generalization and pattern-recognition, the positive emotions such as love and peacefulness, and even a sophisticated sense of time and timing, are all developed by poetry. Furthermore, our ethnocentric bias may be partly overcome by the study of poetry in other languages, and the recognition of the underlying universals in poetic meter. Indeed, the pernicious custom of translating foreign metered verse originals into free verse may already have done some harm; it involves an essentially arrogant assumption of western modernist superiority over the general "vulgar" human love of regular verse.

It may well be that the rise of utilitarian education for the working and middle classes, together with a loss of traditional folk poetry, had a lot to do with the success of the political and economic tyranny in our times. The masses, starved of the beautiful and complex rhythms of poetry, were only too susceptible to the brutal and simplistic rhythms of the totalitarian slogan or advertising jingle. An education in verse will tend to produce citizens capable of using their full brains coherently, able to unite rational thought and calculation with values and commitment.

Works Cited

1. This body of theory is developed in J.T. Fraser, *Of Time, Passion and Knowledge* (Braziller, 1975), and in J.T. Fraser *et al.*, eds., *The Study of Time*, vols. I, II, and III (Springer-Vrlag, 1972, 1975, 1978).

2. The following summary of characteristic human information processing strategies owes much to these sources of information:

The proceedings of the Werner Reimers Stiftung *Biological Aspects of Esthetics* Group.

C. D. Laughlin, Jr., and E.G. d'Aquili. *Biogenetic Structuralism* (Columbia University Press, 1974).

E. G. d'Aquili, C.D. Laughlin, Jr., and J. McManus, eds. *The Spectrum of Ritual: A Biogenetic Structural Analysis* (Columbia University Press, 1979).

D. E. Berlyne and K.B. Madsen, eds. *Pleasure, Reward, Preference: Their Nature, Determinants, and Role in Behavior* (Academic Press, 1973).

A. Routtenberg, ed. *Biology of Reinforcement: Facets of Brain Stimulation Reward* (Academic Press, 1980).

J. Olds. *Drives and Reinforcements: Behavioral Studies of Hypothalamic Functions* (Raven Press, 1977).

C. Blakemore, *Mechanics of the Mind* (Cambridge University Press, 1977).

3. Ernst Pöppel. "Erlebte Zeit—und die Zeit uberhaupt," paper given at the Werner Reimbers Stiftung "Biological Aspects of Esthetics" conference, January, 1982.

4. Private communications, I. Rentschler, 1981 and 1982.

5. "Biological Aspects of Esthetics" meeting, January 1982.

6. Frederick Turner. "Verbal Creativity and the Meter of Love-Poetry," paper given at the "Biological Aspects of Esthetics" meeting, September 1980.

7. On cultural universals, see I. Eibl-Eibesfeldt, *Ethology* (Holt, Rinehart, 1970).

8. Jerome Rothenberg, *Technicians of the Sacred* (Doubleday Anchor, 1968).

9. W. K. Wimsatt. *Versification: Major Language Types* (New York University Press, 1972).

10. Presented at the "Biological Aspects of Esthetics" meeting, April, 1981.

11. For instance, in Yanomami contract-chants and Western advertising jingles.

12. W. K. Wimsatt. *Versification: Major Language Types* (1972).

13. This is a narrative meter, whose actual pauses do not necessarily fall upon the line-endings. In Aeschylus' *Agamemnon*, for example, an 11-line sample contained 15 pauses, and lasted 48 seconds. Thus in practice the LINE-length is about three seconds.

14. Probably reflects the statistical effect of lines with a strong caesura.

15. Charles Olson's *Projective Verse* (New York: Totem Press, 1959) is a good example of such free-verse theories.

16. W. K. Wimsatt. *Versification: Major Language Types* (1972).

17. There is an interesting account of various critical theories of meter in the introductory chapter of C. Chatman's *A Theory of Meter* (Mouton, 1965), but it is flawed by a bias against the possibility of biological foundations for metrical usage.

18. Private communication, I. Rentschler, 1981.

19. d'Aquili *et al.*, *The Spectrum of Ritual*, chap. 4, 117-51.

20. "Ergotropic" refers to the whole pattern of connected behaviors and states that characterize the aroused state of the body, including an increased heart rate and blood flow to the skeletal muscles, wakefulness, alertness, and a hormone balance consistent with "fight or flight" activities.

21. John Frederick Nims makes exactly this point in his *Western Wind: An Introduction to Poetry* (Random House, 1983), 258.

22. d'Aquili *et al.*, *The Spectrum of Ritual*, 144.

23. *Ibid.*, chap. 5, 152-82.

24. *Ibid.*, chap. 6, 183-215.

25. Charles O. Hartman, in his *Free Verse: An Essay on Prosody* (Princeton University Press, 1980), like many free-verse theorists, argues against the isochronic theory of meter. But his strictures apply to the lengths of syllables and feet, not to the LINE; and part of his argument is based on the fact that much free verse does not fit any temporal scheme. This would not be a problem for our argument, which does not consider such free verse to be poetry in the strict sense. His argument attempts to save free verse, and therefore defines verse in a hopelessly vague way; ours is content to abandon it *as verse* unless it consciously or unconsciously employs the human and universal grammar of meter. It may be an admirable kind of word play, and it might even be argued that it is a new art-form of our century. But it is not poetry; and if this sounds dogmatic, it should be remembered that dogmatism is only bad when it is wrong.

26. *The Defense of Poesy.*

Emaciated Poetry

Wyatt Prunty

I

Since the early 1960s American poetry has constituted something quite different from the high modernist work of Eliot, Tate, the early Lowell, and others. Two of the most prominent practitioners of this new poetry are Robert Creeley and R.R. Ammons. The first characteristic you notice about the change to which Creeley and Ammons have contributed is a shrinkage in margins that has produced a stylish, highly marketable thinness. For two decades one of the most publishable forms for poetry seems to have been the lyric broken into lines that would fit in a newspaper column. Editors are always cramped for room to include everything they would like to publish, but more than a question of space is involved here. At the same time its margins have narrowed, this poetry has been restricted in other ways. It is thin in more senses than one.

The publication of *Life Studies* in 1959 announced that something drastic in American poetry had happened. At a time when the influence of existentialism had led to a premium's being placed upon authenticity, Lowell deserted the traditionalism of T.S. Eliot for the immediacy of William Carlos Williams. A general change in poetry was under way. Haute bourgeois was out, déclassé in. The rigors of poetic form amounted, it was now thought, to an inauthentic treatment of experience that, understood existentially, had to stand outside conventions as a unique moment. The isolated poet now set traditional categories of thought aside; the scales were removed from the shaman's eyes, and the poems about one's return to origins (which, like victims, are always innocent and good) proliferated. Moments from one's formative childhood and from dreams were accompanied by primitive objects, stones, bones, caves, and other items that seemed irreducible and thus appeared as the indices of the unconscious, the essen-

First published in *The Sewanee Review*, Winter, 1985, Copyright © 1985 by Wyatt Prunty. Reprinted with permission of the author and publisher.

tial man. What could be less ordered therefore more existentially authentic than the unconscious? Like a caveman's experience it was free of the clutterings of intellect and culture that stood between the eye and its object. The primitive, representing the unconscious, became a means for projection downward to dramatize human meaning much as religious belief and the traditional use of allegory had been an upward projection for transcendent meaning.

A change in poetic style is always connected to a change in thought. I have argued elsewhere that just as existentialism reached full stride Lowell's personal experience seemed to parallel much that Sartre and others were saying. Lowell's disillusionment over the allied bombing of civilian targets during World War II, the loss of his parents, his own mental difficulties, his departure from the church, his divorce from Jean Stafford (who also was a Catholic), and his marriage to Elizabeth Hardwick (who was not religious)—all of these events contributed to a shift in Lowell's thinking which in turn was reflected by a change in his poetic style. From the 1940s until the end of his life Lowell was a highly celebrated poet, and the scaled-down poetry of *Life Studies* significantly affected other poets. What Lowell's example urged was that poets should cease using classical and Christian allusions to constitute meaning, especially through the use of allegory, and should turn instead to experience. Having left the church and faced his own dark world of the unconscious, Lowell began writing out of personal experience, his family's experience, and the history of New England. The Christian myth, a basis for timeless meaning, had been replaced by mundane history and personal dislocation.

The urgency, however, to make experience intelligible in a time-ridden era (whether one should use myth, as Eliot suggested, reason, as Yvor Winters urged, or Jungian depth imagery) did not change with the shift in style that Lowell and others undertook. On the surface the classroom virtues of irony, paradox, and ambiguity taught by Cleanth Brooks and other influential critics half a generation earlier seemed to have been set aside. Beneath that surface, in fact, the problems the Brooksian categories addressed did not disappear; and poetry continued to respond to them. Whether one was concerned with religious experience (as Eliot was), with "preternatural" experience (as Winters said at times he was), or with the unconscious mind, poetry's task continued to be that of ferreting order out of apparent disorder. What actually happened was that a poor man's version of irony, paradox, and ambiguity sprouted as part of an excessive reliance upon enjambment. An abbreviated version of the Brooksian virtues appeared as the result of the use of excessively short lines, and it did so in the poetry of those who had rejected the New Criticism. We are familiar with the Brooks version; here is a variation on it:

> As I sd to my
> friend, because I am
> always talking, — John, I
> sd, which was not his
> name, the darkness sur-
> rounds us, what
>
> can we do against
> it, or else, shall we &
> why not, buy a goddamn big car,
>
> drive, he sd, for
> christ's sake, look
> out where yr going.

This is Robert Creeley's "I Know a Man." It presents us with a speaker worrying about one's movement through the dark, the unintelligible. For Brooks and the New Critics words are linked with their particular bits of cultural baggage, and out of the various torsions that these words generate as a group a greater, more complex meaning is construed. Irony, paradox, and ambiguity are the results of a building up, of putting words in tension with one another. In contrast Creeley's wry method in "I Know a Man" is to break down. Ambiguity is created because the poem's foreshortened lines frustrate the reader's syntactical expectations. A mechanical substitution is offered for an intellectual problem. The lines are so short they cannot function as run-on lines, only as syntactical interruptions. The reader teeters between the end of one line and the beginning of another with the vague feeling that things are ambiguous, ironical, or paradoxical because the units of language to which he is accustomed have been interrupted. Rather than irony, paradox, and ambiguity existing as a nexus of meaning, one is given the *impression* of these elements. Being a physical disruption rather than an intellectual complication, the trick is similar to the surprise generated by the home movie that is reversed just after a child dives into a swimming pool.

Creeley's excessive line breaks leave the reader struggling to get through the poem. Line breaks separate subjects from their verbs, interrupt phrases, and split individual words into lesser parts. The reader's pace is slowed to such an extent that what would be recognized as commonplace when confronted at ordinary mental speed sounds oracular at this halting pace. Robert Creeley speaks with as much facility as anyone—when he is not reading a poem. Give him a poem, however, one of his poems, and he stammers as though so fraught with emotion he can barely get the words over his lower teeth. Someone only casually familiar with poetry may think he has heard a great primal truth pulled from so deep within that the poet is barely capable of utterance. Actually he has heard an affectation made possible by foreshortened lines.

Here is another poem by Creeley, "Quick-Step":

> More gaily, dance
> with such ladies make
> a circumstance of dancing.
>
> Let them lead
> around and around, all
> awkwardness apart.
>
> There is
> an easy grace gained
> from falling forward
>
> in time, in
> simple time to
> all their graces.

This poem might well never have been written had William Carlos Williams not already written "The Dance," particularly the phrase "they go round and / around." There are some nice moments in "Quick-Step," though it is at best a wistful lyric. It creates the clear impression, however, of being much more than wistful. As an individual's exaggeration in dress and movement will hold our attention and suspend our ordinary goings-about-our-business, the truncated lines in this poem work against the forward pressure of what the poem says as it moves at an exaggeratedly halting pace. We are briefly arrested, slowed, and charmed more by the slowing than by what we are told. A major element in Creeley's method is to call greater attention to what is visual in the poem than we would normally grant it. Stumbling over line-break after line-break, you tend only to picture things that have been named because so little is being said about them. In "Quick-Step" the act of dancing seems more vivid because so little else is there to compete with it, not even the momentum of the poem's own language.

Here is the same poem put into conventional lines:

> More gaily, dance with such ladies
> make a circumstance of dancing.
> Let them lead around and around,
> all awkwardness apart.
> There is an easy grace gained
> from falling forward in time,
> in simple time to all their graces.

Given breadth, the language in "Quick-Step" demonstrates the same accented-unaccented alternation that has been with us since "Beowulf." Yet Creeley's use of foreshortened lines means that he was not seeking this sort of rhythm when he wrote the poem. The lines Creeley settled upon are too short for rhythm to work. But it exists in the language, whether the poet hears it or not.

Though greater momentum is generated by the use of conventional line lengths in "Quick-Step," the poem still produces a very ordinary event. Nothing can be done about what Creeley's enjambed method of composition did to the poem's content, particularly its overreliance upon that which is visual. There is a question as to how one should read the poem at the end of the first line because punctuation is needed there. (Creeley would say the point is that punctuation should not be there. He is interrupting our syntactical expectations with the absence of punctuation as well as with line-breaks.) Generally, however, the reader can move through the regularized version of the poem at a speed close to that at which we normally think. Doing so demonstrates the poem's essential slightness, in content as well as form.

Written with the oracular effect that excessive enjambment creates as an organizing principle, "Quick-Step" presents us with a characteristic trick in the first line; "such ladies" pretends to a specificity that does not exist. In addition the final word in the poem, "graces," is made to carry more significance than it can bear. The preceding words "awkwardness," "grace," and "falling" do not create a context for the ladies' "graces" to close the poem with anything definite enough to be meaningful. One is reminded of a vague, unrealistic, and high-handed male attitude that recent feminists have been so quick to identify. Creeley's poem is an unfocused wish directed toward an indefinite object. It is sentimental.

Creeley's use of enjambment disguises much that is objectionable in the poem because his line-breaks disturb the reader with a serious problem—the reliability of language to provide both a rational and truthful approximation of what is real. Initially you may not feel that Creeley's poem is simplistic because Creeley has skewed his writing so that the *way* he says things becomes the object of contention rather than *what* he says. Often the way a poem says what it means is nearly as important as what it does say, but in such situations the manner of statement, or suggestion, does not take place of meaning. Creeley's willingness to expose himself to linguistic chance in his poetry is a source not of strength but of weakness. Too often what his truncated lines create is an unjustified multiplication of a passing wistful thought, an oracular leap from the commonplace to the commonplace squared. He is a master of the emaciated poem.

II

Amidst many variations there are two distinguishing marks in poetry written since the late fifties: assumed primitivism in style and content, and an overreliance on the image that results in abandoning poetry as an auditory art. Much of the attraction these characteristics hold for poets stems from their desire to ferret meanings from what they consider to be their unconscious. The influence of psychology has led us to a new sort of allegory (though there are other instances of the allegorical impulse, science fiction and children's literature for example). Poems now bridge the gap between the conscious and unconscious mind rather than that between a physical and metaphysical world. The world of dreams is generally a silent one, thus the exclusion of auditory concerns in poetry; it is primitive, and it is usually experienced visually—thus the excessive reliance upon imagery.

W.H. Auden's lines from "In Praise of Limestone" provide an appropriate comment here: "The poet, / Admired for his earnest habit of calling / The sun the sun, his mind Puzzle." Auden is acknowledging the openness and capacity for wonder that are essential if one is to write poetry, whether the poet is open to reason, belief, the unconscious, or all of these. He is not urging ignorance as the basis for authenticity, however. The worst result of the poetic shift being considered has been the shamanism of poets like Allen

Ginsberg, Robert Bly, and (too often) Robert Creeley. The best result of this shift has been the adjustments made by poets like Auden, who have stood ready on the one hand to exploit conventional poetic modes and ready on the other hand to accept the mind as "Puzzle" and to regard experience from a position outside accepted categories of thought, causality for example. Along with a number of others, Anthony Hecht, Howard Nemerov, and Richard Wilbur have been quite successful at practicing this kind of poetry.

Yvor Winters faulted Allen Tate for an excessive use of enjambment. Though he had accurately identified a departure from end-stopped lines that was soon to be taken to an extreme, Winters was too scrupulous where Tate was concerned. As with Robert Lowell's early work, Tate's poetry grew out of a sustained rhetoric that overran the boundaries of end-stopped lines as a natural result of its own momentum. The headlong pace of such rhetoric compounded meaning almost as quickly as a cluster of images might, though with one important difference. Where an image conveys a nexus of meaning immediately, as with Pound's "black bough" or Williams's "red wheel/barrow," the use of rhetoric in a poem requires time, as meaning is built synthetically from moment to moment.

Rather than seeing the truth as though it were projected on a screen, the way Milton's angels were supposed to have done, Tate, Lowell, and others generated meaning out of the ongoingness of their own language. In part we have a distinction between poetry that generates meaning synchronically, with imagery, and poetry that operates diachronically, with rhetoric. The latter uses images also, but they are only part of the recipe. The rest of the formula includes statements, questions, all sorts of syntactical units. It also exploits the rhythms inherent in our language in a way that is discussed most successfully with the aid of phonetics.

Another element in the synthetic poetry of Tate and Lowell should be mentioned. The emotional thrust of the headlong pace of such poetry contributes greatly to the way that it affects the reader. As Winters knew, the rhythm in a poem reinforces meaning on an emotional level. What Winters saw toward the end of his life, however, was the growth of a poetry devoid of rhythm. Thin, usually very brief poems populating the pages of various periodicals ignored the rhythmical possibilities in language, relying instead upon imagery. Their lines were too short for effective movement to be established, the voice having no chance to gain momentum. What these lines did establish was the dominance of enjambment. End-stopped lines were the norm that gave significance to the reservation Winters made about Tate's and, indirectly, Lowell's use of enjambment, as they have been an essential part of poetry for centuries. But with the general turn made by poets to foreshortened lines enjambment was taken to such an extreme that its use was no longer significant. The rhythm to which it contributed could no longer be heard.

The momentum of language enables a poem's ending to stand on the ground of immediate conviction. The systematic disruption of that momentum by line-breaks, however, can leave a poem standing on the ground of immediate doubt. For us doubt is a familiar condition. But is the disruption of language that occurs in the poems discussed here a significant expression of doubt, or is it simply the incongruent exertion of an individual will? Showing that there are gaps in language is meaningful only if one's over-all purpose is to close them in some way. Language is self-sealing, and to a remarkable degree naming gaps seems to close them. In contrast the excessive use of enjambment makes you feel there are empty spaces in language, but that feeling names nothing, discloses nothing. It is the result of contrivance rather than an honest attempt to articulate a linguistic shortfall and correct it.

Irony, paradox, and ambiguity are intellectual answers to various linguistic shortfalls. They do not provide a complete solution to the problem of meaning, but they contribute to one. And they do so, finally, in an additive manner. As modes of thought they depend upon the extensiveness of meaning contained in language. The overuse of enjambed foreshortened lines for syntactical disruption is a physical response not grounded in the extensiveness of meaning but dependent upon the reader's expectations and the writer's will, the momentary surprise created by that will. Both methods are skeptical responses to experience. But the Brooksian formula proceeds additively on the assumption that language works, that it grasps what is really before us. The second formula proceeds subalternately on the assumption that reasoned language is arbitrary and inauthentic.

Here is a poem by A.R. Ammons, "Loss":

> When the sun
> falls behind the sumac
> thicket the
> wild
> yellow daisies
> in diffuse evening shade

lose their
rigorous attention
and
half-wild with loss
turn
any way the wind does
and lift their
petals up
to float
off their stems
and go

Though it is quite different from the poetry of Eliot, Tate, and early Lowell, the method used in this poem is not new. On the one hand we are provided an example of the pathetic fallacy, a phrase invented by Ruskin; on the other hand "Loss" is reminiscent of what the Imagists were doing more than sixty years ago, and in some ways the Decadents before that. In a Paterian mood Lionel Johnson would say what he said when defining English decadence in *The Century Guild Hobby Horse*—that Ammons is trying "to catch the precise aspect of a thing, as you see or feel it." The most striking characteristic in Ammons's poetry is that he restricts himself to literal imagery almost all the way through a poem, reserving only one or two moments when he breaks out into figurative imagery. His previous restraint makes this shift all the more effective, though his reliance upon this method is one reason his poems are not successful when read aloud. In fact the shift from literal imagery to figurative imagery is a mode of thought that seems suited to painting, and Ammons has turned to painting in recent years. Poetry's affinity with painting is a matter of long standing. If we look no farther than the pre-Raphaelites, "Loss" reminds us of Dante Gabriel Rossetti's "The Woodspurge." In other ways, however, it is much closer to an imagist poem, particularly in avoiding conventional rhythms through using foreshortened enjambed lines.

As in Creeley's poems, the fragmentation of normal syntactical units in "Loss" gives priority to the poem's imagery. Greater amounts of time are created for smaller units of language as the reader is encouraged to meet experience visually with hierarchies, categories, or presuppositions set aside. "Loss" is primarily an artistic exercise in nominalism. Forcing us to focus on the particulars of nature more than on its patterns, the approach Ammons uses is skeptical, particularly because of its minimal expectations. As part of this skeptical or minimal point of view sentimentality creeps in, "daisies...half-wild with loss." In fact not much is being lost here. Though in part we are provided a play on the daisies' wildness mentioned earlier in the poem, the emotion of this statement outstrips its meaning.

Rather than finding a matrix for meaning in an image, "Loss" dramatizes the incoherence that will always result when we fix upon a thing subject to process. In this circumstance Ammons has dramatized a few moments in an isolated consciousness that happens to be looking at daisies. The poem generates a self-fulfilling prophecy for that consciousness: it uses imagery to give permanence within its own boundaries to daisies that, we are told, are nevertheless subject to time. A sense of loss is inevitable if not trustworthy.

Eliot's contention that the use of myth can make modern experience intelligible is based on assumptions about permanence similar to those made by Ammons and others where imagery is concerned. In both cases a spatial priority is established for what is being said, but with an important difference. We should not confuse the synchronic impulse to freeze predicaments spatially by using an image with a nevertheless similar tendency that occurs in the use of myth. Freezing a temporal predicament through the use of myth is a different matter because myths are stories and thus have duration: they carry histories. Images are often extensive, parts in networks of meaning, but characteristically their significance is not born of the past or of a supposed past. When an allusion is made to a myth, the reader familiar with that myth suddenly recalls a chain of events: time is gathered. When an image is used, relations rather than events are invoked. The projection of a temporal predicament into an atemporal image, which is the method Ammons and many others use, voids the problem of time rather than addressing it. The reader is offered a mechanical solution for an intellectual problem that is basic to our process-minded era. In "Loss" the disruption of our syntactical expectations through enjambment and the overreliance upon imagery operates on the basis of the same trick in timing that one finds in Creeley's "I Know a Man" and "Quick-Step." These poems are written to be read much the way Burma Shave signs were placed to greet travelers along the highways.

A wide range of excellent poetry has been written over the last thirty years, some of the best of it in free verse. In the restrictiveness of its short lines, however, the emaciated poem is not free but rigid. The lines are not long enough for rhythm to be established. I suspect that Creeley and Ammons would say that their thin poems are honest and authentic and that Eliot, Tate, and company wrote poetry that was self-consciously learned and bulky, thus posed and inauthentic. The question of authenticity, however, is predicated upon doubt, the same uncertainty about oneself and the world one inhabits that caused Robert Lowell's poetic shift. Though the most influential recent episode has been the existentialists' alertness to the absurd, there is nothing new about doubt in our thought. Using the cogito, we have turned our predicament into our method: uncertainty has become our most reliable means for certainty as we have learned to rely upon the self-sealing character of language, which by allowing us to name a problem allows us in some way to move beyond that problem. Since we begin with uncertainty rather than belief, we must emphasize existence rather than essence. Because of the self's precarious position, as an entity standing in a world of process which dissolves entities, misshapen exertions of the will are inevitable, the most common of these being a very old and familiar exertion—sentimentality.

III

Writing an emaciated poem is not the only way to slow a reader and emphasize images. Reversing the rhythm in a line or placing caesura in a line or both—these are common ways to achieve the same effect and to do so without creating an interrupted surface that distracts the reader from what is being said. Here is the first stanza of "Painting a Mountain Stream" by Howard Nemerov:

> Running and standing still at once
> is the whole truth. Raveled or combed,
> wrinkled or clear, it gets its force
> from losing force. Going it stays.

Opening with the bold statement of a paradox, rather than a vague feeling of contradiction created by truncated lines, this is an ambitious poem. It entails the mutual dependence of apparent opposites. We think of a stream as nominal; thus we try to paint it. The real nature of that stream, however, is its ongoingness, which defies being fixed in a painting within a frame. Nemerov's answer to the intellectual problem of forcing something that is diachronic into synchronic terms in order to understand it is to say "paint this rhythm, not this thing." In other words the narrow thingness of Dr. Williams's red wheelbarrow is quickly exhausted, and we must move up to a level of abstraction—namely to the process within which wheelbarrows, boughs, daisies, and streams exist, in order to understand what we see. Having made such a move, we are capable of making more satisfactory statements. Having made a statement, Nemerov succeeds where Ammons fails. As a quiet part of what he is telling us, Nemerov sets up metrical reversals: they appear throughout the second line, in the first half of the third line, and in the second half of the fourth line. Anyone who wishes can break this poem into truncated lines, but doing so is unnecessary and would be cumbersome. Nemerov has already satisfied his poem's need for reversals, and has done so in a way that directs you to the meaning he intends rather than distracting you with syntactical interruptions.

For those intent on other ways of creating pauses here is an even quieter use of the caesura, taken from Nemerov's "The Blue Swallows":

> Across the millstream below the bridge
> Seven blue swallows divide the air
> In shapes invisible and evanescent,
> Kaleidoscopic beyond the mind's
> Or memory's power to keep them there.

The first, second, and fourth lines have an extra unstressed syllable each, placed after the second foot as a vestigial caesura. An interruption or slowing occurs, but its force does not exceed the surprise created by what is being said. Line-breaks substituted for Nemerov's caesuras not only would sacrifice the convincingness created by the poem's rhythm: being heavy-handed, they would be the first step toward sentimentality, the emotional force given the statement exceeding the significance of that statement. "The Blue Swallows" ends with a Kantian answer to the sort of position Pater took in the "Conclusion" to *The Renaissance*—that nothing external to the mind has any meaning other than what is provided it by the mind, because meaning is completely subjective, even imprisoning. Rather than making experience the object of his poetry, as Creeley and Ammons do in a way resembling Pater and the Decadents, Nemerov has relation as his object. Acknowledging external patterns (and their vast multiplicity) as well as internal ones, Nemerov is concerned finally with appropriateness—the appropriate relation between mind and thing, or things. Consistent with this concern, his poem demonstrates an appropriate balance between perception and articulation.

With the exception of Lowell and Roethke, the most talented (if not as a group the most influential) poets writing since World War II have continued to write poetry that takes advantage of traditional modes, a poetry that is successful auditorially as well as visually. Consider Louise Bogan, Edgar Bowers, J.V. Cunningham, Anthony Hecht, John Hollander, A.D. Hope, Elizabeth Jennings, Donald Justice, Maxine Kumin, James Merrill, Howard Nemerov, Robert Pack, Mona Van Duyn, Derek Walcott, Margaret Walker, Richard Wilbur, Reed Whittemore, and Judith Wright. Rather than using one poetic technique to the exclusion of others, these poets have been quick to exploit a wide range of tools traditionally available to poetry—rhyme, assonance, consonance, rhythm regular enough to function as rhythm, lines long enough to allow that rhythm to work, images, even symbols. In addition, these poets have been likely to be interested more in ideas about relations than in the "precise aspect" or nominalistic detail of an isolated experience.

There are variations on the shift in poetry I have described. Some poets write lines not shortened but elongated to the point that one seems to be reading prose—for example Whitman's windy descendant Allen Ginsberg. The existence of "poetic prose" is one truism among many that have been used to break down the altogether real distinction between poetry and prose. The prose poem, the one-word poem (which is four words), the concrete poem, and the emaciated poem have all resulted from half-truths. Though most often the image has been the basis, first one then another characteristic of poetry has been taken, to the exclusion of the rest of what constitutes poetry, and expanded to make a poetics. Because the method is easy to use, its results are easy to find.

Linked with the role the image plays in these variations is a question of talent that partly originates in the influence painting has had on the poetry of this century. In its silence and spatial fixity painting is vastly different from poetry, which is auditory and, like music, exists first in time. Seeking a quantity of output that reminds one of manufacturing, many poets writing emaciated poems are geared to the visual in poetry because the image is easy to use, as a visit to the typical workshop will demonstrate. At the same time poets writing overly thin poems have failed to employ some of the most effective poetic tools the language provides. And their poetry has suffered accordingly. Everyone recognizes the limitations of a painter who is color-blind. What about a poet who is tone-deaf or who lacks a sense of rhythm? For too many poets publishing today, creating the kind of poetry that Nemerov, Wilbur, and the others have written is not a realistic possibility. These poets will argue that what they are doing is the authentic thing to do. For those who have no choice, of course it is.

Works Cited

Special acknowledgment: "I Know a Man" and "Quick-Step" from *The Collected Poems of Robert Creeley 1945–1975* are reproduced by permission of the publisher, the University of California Press. Copyright © 1962 by Robert Creeley.

"Loss" is reprinted from *The Collected Poems: 1951-1971*, by A.R. Ammons, by permission of W.W. Norton & Company, Inc. Copyright © 1977 by A.R. Ammons.

Return to Metaphor: From Deep Imagist to New Formalist

Paul Lake

There is such stylistic diversity among individual poets and schools of contemporary poets in America today that often profound changes occur in the ways poets practice their art without our either noticing them or realizing their extent or significance. In this essay I am going to explore one of those sudden geological shifts that have rearranged the poetic land-scape: the change over the last twenty-odd years in poets' conception and use of figurative language. Specifically, I will compare the way the so-called deep image poets of the sixties and seventies used metaphor to that of a younger group of American poets often called the new formalists. The most obvious—and most publicized—difference between the two groups is, of course, the fact that the new formalists have abandoned the free verse of the deep imagists, restoring such traditional poetic devices as meter, rhyme, and stanzas. But this change from free to formal verse is not merely a mat-ter of poetic fashion, nor is it necessarily the most significant difference between the two groups. Rather, the shift from free to formal verse is but one aspect of the change in the way that each group views such fundamen-tal things as the relationship of word to object, of reason to sensory experi-ence, and of self to the world—a change that appears most vividly in their widely divergent notions about the importance and function of metaphor. To understand these changes in poetic practice, it is best to begin by com-paring individual poems.

The first poem I would like to look at is a brief lyric entitled "At Zero" by Charles Wright from his volume *China Trace* (1975). I have chosen it partly for its brevity and partly because it exemplifies many of the most baffling qualities of the work of the deep image poets. As you read, pay particular attention to the poem's figurative language:

AT ZERO

In the cold kitchen of heaven,
Daylight spoons out its cream-of-wheat.

From *Southwest Review* 74 (1989): 515-29.

Beside the sidewalk, the shrubs
Hunch down, deep in their bibs.

The wind harps its same song
Through the steel tines of the trees.

The river lies still, the jewelled drill in its teeth.

I am glint on its fingernails.
I am ground grains on its wheel.

Even after several readings, a reader puzzles before the cool surface of
the poem. How do we orient ourselves among such strange and seemingly
inconsistent or contradictory figures of speech? What is the tone, for in-
stance, of the opening couplet about the kitchen of heaven—or, rather,
daylight—spooning out its cream-of-wheat? Surely it must be comic. But
the latter half of the poem sounds much graver. And what does it mean for
daylight to "spoon out its cream-of-wheat," anyway? Are we meant merely
to note that daylight is the color of cream-of-wheat? Or is it the act of
spooning that we are supposed to envision?

On a closer look, a reader might consider that the poem is an extended
metaphor: after all, the shrubs hunch down in their bibs (of snow), the
wind harps through "the steel tines of the trees." Is the poem saying that
the world is a place where everything is consuming the cream-of-wheat of
heaven...*i.e.*, daylight? If so, then why is the wind doing something musi-
cal such as harping? And why, in the fourth stanza, does the poet abandon
his eating metaphor to tell us that "The river lies still, the jewelled drill in
its teeth"? In what sense does a river have teeth—could it be ice? And
what kind of drill is in the teeth and why is it there? And why a "jeweled
drill"? Finally, in the last couplet ("I am glint on its fingernails. / I am
ground grains on its wheel"), what is the antecedent of the pronoun "its,"
and why have we abandoned figures such as tines and teeth and cream-of-
wheat to talk of fingernails and wheels? What, in fact, *has* both fingernails
and a wheel, and by what process has the mysteriously appearing "I" of the
poem become "ground grains"? Is the antecedent of "its" the river, the jew-
elled drill, the zero of the poem's title, or something else altogether?

Frankly, I can only guess at the answer to these questions. My best
guess is that the poem is, as its title suggests, about a winter day on which
the temperature is at zero. Perhaps the landscape the poem describes is an
"objective correlative" (to use a now unfashionable term) of the poet's in-

ternal state; the zero of the title might then represent a metaphorical zero of the spirit in the same sense in which Emily Dickinson speaks of a "zero at the bone" in one of her poems. The "I" of the poem, who becomes "ground grains on its [zero's?] wheel," perhaps experiences some sort of dissolution or disintegration. But even if I have divined some sense of the poem's meaning—and I'm not sure I have—I don't think I have satisfactorily come to grips with the poem's figurative language, which indeed may not be possible given its puzzling inconsistency. To understand better why the poem is written the way it is, it is helpful to look at the theories of the deep imagists and see what they and their critics have said about that group's unusual use of figurative language.

One such critic—Alan Williamson, in a sympathetic essay about the deep imagist school, "Language Against Itself: The Middle Generation of Contemporary Poets" (*American Poetry Since 1960*, 1973)—has included the following poets among its ranks: Gary Snyder, James Wright, Galway Kinnell, W. S. Merwin, and Robert Bly. (I would delete Snyder from the list, except perhaps in special cases, and add the name of Charles Wright.) What these poets have in common, argues Williamson, is a deep distrust of poetic discourse—indeed, of any discourse whatsoever: "For all these poets," he writes, "language is at least as much the enemy as the facilitator of essential creativity." If the figurative language in poems such as Wright's "At Zero" baffles us, it is because for these poets, there is an implicit aversion to all rhetorical devices which set an image in an "improving"—or even interpretive—perspective; the image is intended to flash, like a spontaneous mental picture, and is usually coterminous with the line. Indeed, the whole aesthetic of "rendering" is suspect for these poets; its itemizing style of descriptive writing seems cold and shopworn, its theory a rejection of the spontaneity and purely inward validity of feelings. Often, these poets deliberately reinstate the outlawed 19th Century vocabulary of feeling and awe: Wright (James, not Charles) is devoted to the words "lovely" and "strange," Kinnell to forbidden abstractions like "infinite," "reality," "nothingness."

A less sympathetic critic, Robert Pinsky, has also noted the special vocabulary of the deep image poets. Writing in his 1976 book *The Situation of Poetry*, Pinsky notes that the allegedly surrealist nature of much of the imagery of the deep imagists often "suggests, not a realm beyond surface reality, but a particular reality, hermetically primitive, based on a new poetic diction: 'breath,' 'snow,' 'future,' 'blood,' 'silence,' 'eats,' 'water' and most of all 'light' doing the wildly unexpected." He warns readers of "the horrible ease with which a stylish rhetoric can lead poetry unconsciously to abandon life itself" and, further, that a "narrow poetic diction" can lead to the narrow "view of reality and language that diction implies."

But the project of the deep image poets was not merely to restore "the outlawed 19th Century vocabulary of feeling and awe," as Williamson described; rather, they wanted nothing less than to complete successfully the Romantic attempt to close the gap between language and object, thus healing the breach between self and the world that that gap implies. James Atlas, in his essay "Diminishing Returns: The Writings of W. S. Merwin" (also in *American Poetry Since 1960*), notes that Merwin exhibits a "tacit longing to live among whatever he names, entering the world again in some other elemental form." Atlas further suggests that it is "an absence of distinction between words and things...that lies behind *The Moving Target*, where Merwin's belief is in the similitude, even synonymity, of image and object."

To live among the things one names is certainly an ambitious, if thoroughly misguided, project. Though one might *believe* in the "synonymity" of image and object, the breach remains, a permanent gulf; one might explore the ramifications and dimensions of it—and in fact much of the best contemporary poetry has done just that—but it is naive and self-defeating to act as if it doesn't exist. For as Pinsky again notes, "Every word is an abstraction, the opposite of a sensory particular; sentences are abstract arrangements, and the rhythms of verse like all rhythms are based upon the principle of recurrence, or form." The attempt to write as if there is no distance between a word and the thing it names is doomed to failure; the ambition to lose one's human identity in the process of writing—becoming instead an elemental form—is equally misguided and doomed to partial success, at best. Writing of Keats's "Ode to a Nightingale," a classic examination of this dilemma, Robert Pinsky has suggested (accurately, I think) that for the speaker of that poem—indeed for any of us—"To escape the loneliness of being the only creature who uses terms, who reflects, who speaks, who is conscious of time—the only creature who is *in* time as other than a succession of discrete instants—we would have to die." That is, our intellects, if not our actual bodies, would have to die, at least for the duration of the poem.

The new formalists, as I will try to show, are aware of the problematic nature of writing, but unlike the deep imagists, who try to wish it away, they consciously explore its paradoxes and mine its contradictions. The yield is often poetry of a high order, full of rich ambiguities and surprising insights. Figurative language becomes in their hands not a series of discrete flashes, or spontaneous mental pictures, to use Williamson's terms, but a means of asserting relationships and finding resemblances between things. The differences between Charles Wright's "At Zero" and the following poem from *Portraits and Elegies* (1986) by Gjertrud Schnackenberg on a similar subject and theme are striking.

THE PAPERWEIGHT

The scene within the paperweight is calm,
A small white house, a laughing man and wife,
Deep snow. I turn it over in my palm
And watch it snowing in another life,

Another world, and from this scene learn what
It is to stand apart: she serves him tea
Once and forever, dressed from head to foot
As she is always dressed. In this toy history

Sifts down through the glass like snow, and we
Wonder if her single deed tells much
Or little of the way she loves, and whether he
Sees shadows in the sky. Beyond our touch,

Beyond our lives, they laugh, and drink their tea.
We look at them just as the winter night
With its vast empty spaces bends to see
Our isolated little world of light,

Covered with snow, and snow in clouds above it,
And drifts and swirls too deep to understand.
Still, I must try to think a little of it,
With so much winter in my head and hand.

The situation the poem describes—a speaker holding in her hand the miniature world of a paperweight, static, sealed off, impenetrable—would seem to the deep imagists the very image of all that is wrong with the way we as poets and human beings confront the world; the separation of the speaker from the things she describes seems almost absolute—the unbreachable gulf that their neo-Romantic aesthetic attempts to close, just as her artfully rhymed quatrains represent the stylistically "closed" form that their more syntactically and rhythmically simple free verse was meant to blast open. The contrast with Wright's poem is dramatic.

But Schnackenberg is not an ingenuous poetic imitator naively handling the empty forms of a moribund tradition. After describing the house, the man and woman, the snow, and her act of turning the object over in her hand, she examines, by means of this emblematic object, "what / It is to stand apart." "History," she tells us in the following stanzas, "Sifts down through the glass like snow," and the speaker perhaps begins to see in the miniature woman's subservience to and separation from her male companion a metaphor for her own life. But however much the poet tries to interpret their actions, or lack of them, the man and woman in the paperweight become like so many things in the world, ultimately "Beyond our touch, / Beyond our lives."

Or do they? For no sooner does the speaker reach that conclusion than she finds herself paradoxically observed by "the winter night / With its vast empty spaces" looming over her own "isolated little world of light." Microcosm becomes a metaphor for macrocosm and the speaker, along with the reader, experiences a mild shock of recognition. The speaker's world, like that of the couple in the paperweight, is covered with snow and faces a more dangerous threat from the "snow in clouds above it"—the threat of simply being buried under a storm of the "minute particulars" of sensory experience. The "drifts and swirls too deep to understand" also discourage the speaker in her attempt to place herself in her world. But instead of wishing away the difficulty of her situation or attempting to lose her human identity and consciousness in a Romantic merging with the things and processes she describes, the poet admits the precariousness of her dilemma and asserts her will and human intelligence in order to literally come to terms with experience. In one of the poem's most telling lines, the speaker insists, "Still, I must try to think a little of it, / With so much winter in my head and hand." Unlike the deep imagists, the poet doesn't make the quixotic attempt to merge with winter, in any of its appearances; instead, she incorporates all three levels of it—the actual winter outside her house, the emblematic winter in her hand, and the metaphysical winter in her head—into the body of the poem.

Schnackenberg's accomplishment, however remarkable, would not satisfy the objectives of the deep imagists. For the poet's main job, according to Robert Bly in a preface to *Forty Poems Touching on Recent American History*, "is to penetrate that husk around the American psyche, and since that psyche is inside *him* too, the writing of political poetry is like the writing of personal poetry, a sudden drive by the poet inward." Whether writing public or personal poetry, it is not by looking outward to such things as paperweights and snow and winter that the poet will find adequate images and poetic figures to render experience, according to Bly and others, but by looking inward to the most primitive, inward reaches of his or her own psyche.

It's not hard to see why in practice this theory might produce a good deal of the confusion we see in the work of the deep imagists. The problem is obvious. Even granting the existence of a collective unconscious and the validity of much that goes on in the irrational world of dreams and their waking counterparts, revery and imagination, what happens to language, particularly figurative language, when we abandon the external world and its relationships and laws to find the supposedly deeper connections between things that exist in our psyches? What, other than each poet's personal psychological make-up — or mere bald assertion — determines the basis for comparing one thing to another and finding a likeness?

Once again the deep imagists attempt to resolve these difficulties with a familiar tactic: by merging—in this case, the primitive reaches of the human psyche with the external world of nature. Alan Williamson again makes a useful observation:

> The poets less concerned with the literally primitive are often preoccupied with the evocation of a Jungian collective unconscious through free-association. But in Snyder's view, the two back countries "meet, one step even farther on, as *one*"; and "to transcend the ego is to go beyond society as well."

The danger for the poet of such a view is again apparent: if one assumes the two back countries of psyche and wilderness do meet, then to write of one is automatically to write of the other; a poet need only look in his soul and write, to use an old formula, without reference to the world except as it has been expropriated and colored by his or her individual psyche. Free-association replaces metaphor, as Williamson himself admits. There is no need to discover resemblances and relationships between things; one need only assert them, associating images and ideas freely, according to the deeper logic — or illogic — of the unconscious.

I'll return to the subject of free-association shortly. First, I want to look at a poem by Robert Bly that puts deep imagist theory into practice and compare it to a poem by Charles Martin, a new formalist. Unlike the Charles Wright poem, which I deliberately chose for its awkwardness, Bly's poem has a number of appealing qualities, and I take it from the 1973 edition of *The Norton Anthology of Modern Poetry*:

WAKING FROM SLEEP

Inside the veins there are navies setting forth,
Tiny explosions at the waterlines,
And seagulls weaving in the wind of the salty blood.

It is morning. The country has slept the whole winter,
Window seats were covered with fur skins, the yard was full
Of stiff dogs, and hands that clumsily held heavy books.

Now we wake, and rise from bed and eat breakfast! —
Shouts rise from the harbor of the blood,

Mist, and masts rising, the knock of wooden tackle in the sunlight.

Now we sing, and do tiny dances on the kitchen floor.
Our whole body is like a harbor at dawn;
We know that our master has left us for the day.

The central metaphor of the poem, that our body is like a harbor, is fairly consistent. Both the body and a harbor contain salty liquid and share certain other associations: early morning stirrings of activity, various currents and motions, associations with "arteries." Both human bodies and harbors might be said to represent boundaries or to occupy borders — the first between matter and mind or spirit, the second between land and sea. The first physical stirrings of a waking body and the first glimmers of consciousness might aptly be compared to the stirrings of ships at their docks in the first light of early morning. The poem is suggestive and in some ways well done and appealing. If it had gone no farther than making the above suggestions, it might be more completely successful.

The first stanza, for instance, does not actually use the word *harbor*. It merely pictures navies setting forth inside the veins and the agitation of propellers that causes explosions at the waterlines. But right after the reader has envisioned a waterline, which is in fact a boundary between the worlds of water and air, the poet tells us that there are "seagulls weaving in the wind of the salty blood." So there's no waterline after all; seagulls fly inside of our veins in the unidiomatic and puzzling "wind of the salty blood."

The second stanza adds an additional metaphor: an enchanted northern country whose inhabitants have apparently "slept the whole winter" —

not reading books, but merely holding them clumsily in their hands while they slept. Where are these people in relationship to the "harbor of the blood," as the third stanza calls it now? And what is the relationship of the harbor metaphor to the northern country metaphor? In the third stanza, Bly introduces the first person plural pronoun: "Now we wake." Is he suggesting that we enter and emerge from this strange country whenever we sleep or awaken...and that we simultaneously have a harbor inside our body?

The fourth stanza continues to use first person plural pronouns: "Now we sing, and do tiny dances on the kitchen floor. / Our whole body is like a harbor at dawn." And for a minute the reader, confronted by this collective entity (*we* sing, *our* whole body), pictures a human body—from which a moment ago "shouts" and the "knock of wooden tackle" had arisen—dancing on the kitchen floor. A dancing harbor! No wonder we hear shouts and the knock of wooden tackle. Surely Bly didn't intend this comic mixture of metaphors, but the reader visualizes it, nevertheless. Bly's attempt to unite the two disparate metaphors with the multiple but ambiguous meanings of the word "master" in the final stanza doesn't come off. By the time a reader has finished the poem, he feels that the author is less interested in revealing the nature of waking from sleep to consciousness than he is in displaying the cleverness of his own imagination. The poet does not reveal an unexpected likeness, but a programmatic assertion of likeness to which the reader can either assent or refuse to assent, depending on how tolerant he is of the poet's procedures.

Charles Martin's "Metaphor of Grass in California," from his 1987 volume *Steal the Bacon*, uses its central figure more consistently. Notice how the extended metaphor appears and then logically develops in the poem.

METAPHOR OF GRASS IN CALIFORNIA

The seeds of certain grasses that once grew
Over the graves of those who fell at Troy
Were brought to California in the hooves
Of Spanish cattle. Trodden into the soil,

They liked it well enough to germinate,
Awakening into another scene
Of conquest: blade fell upon flashing blade
Until the native grasses fled the field,

And the native flowers bowed to their dominion.

Small clumps of them fought on as they retreated
Toward isolated ledges of serpentine,

Repellent to their conquerors...
                              In defeat,

They were like men who see their city taken,
And think of grass—how soon it will conceal
All of the scattered bodies of the slain;
As such men fall, these fell, but silently.

The poem is lucid and its figurative language needs little explication. One notes gratefully how quietly the native grass comes to stand for those other natives of North America, the Indians, and how the blades of the Spanish conquerors, like the blades of the Old World grasses, subdue the native species till they are finally driven back to a few scattered reservations. Martin further suggests that the seeds borne to the New World derived from grasses that once covered the graves of "those who fell at Troy," thus tying the scenes of conquest in the New World to a cycle of human violence that goes back as far as recorded history and beyond. In a much truer sense than was intended by the deep imagists in their theories, the two back countries of human psyche and American wilderness meet in Martin's poem: man's most deep-rooted unconscious drives—for power and for the continuation of his own genes—appear as part of a much wider natural process, one shared even by the grass. But grass, unlike men, falls silently in defeat, the poem reminds us, and the sufferings of grass blades are not recalled by survivors who have seen "their city taken." The back countries meet, but only human beings endure tragedy and write about it. Martin, unlike Bly, is not making assertions ungrounded in experience, but discovering relationships and making distinctions; his figurative language is an affirmation, not a denial, of his human intelligence.

Finally, I want to examine two poems that deal with just this topic: human intelligence, that aspect of our nature that separates us from the rest of the world. Man is the only animal able to contemplate its own death. This is no doubt the ultimate reason for our feeling of separation from nature. Though I might be accused of chauvinism by advocates of animal intelligence, I think it is fair to say that human beings are the only animals that have identities and are, therefore, the only ones to experience existence as a crisis. The two poems that I now want to look at—the first by Charles Wright, the second by Timothy Steele—both deal with the crisis of human identity that results from confronting our mortality. Each poet considers death in a different way, using figurative language in radically opposing fashions. Here's Charles Wright's poem:

MOVING ON

Once it was lamb's fleece and the fall.
Once it was wedge of the eyelid and eyelid down to
poison and sheer slumber,
The flesh made flesh and the word.

Now it's the crack in the porcelain stick,
And midnight splashed on the 1st rocks and gone,
The wafer of blood in its chalk robes,

The bright nail of the east I usher my body toward.

Brief as this poem is, it returns us to familiar territory: a series of startling figures is enumerated by the poet in nearly self-contained free verse lines uncluttered by complicated syntax or logical argument. Once again we find an ambiguous pronoun: the first line begins, "Once it was lamb's fleece and the fall." Since the pronoun *it*, which occurs more than once, has no antecedent noun in the poem, are we to assume that the poem poses a riddle and that we are to try to supply a suitable one? If that's the case, the poem might support any number of readings; we can easily fill in our own favorite capitalized abstraction—Life, Death, Youth, God, Time, Man's Nature, Self—and satisfy ourselves that we have come close to the poem's meaning. Or, what is more likely, does the pronoun refer to the title, "Moving On," a phrase that might suggest one or more of the following: travel, aging, the passage of time, the speaker's movement toward death?

There are other difficulties with the poem's figurative language, and even with its grammar (the second line might be read in several ways, all awkward and unidiomatic), but I want to consider the last two lines. For whatever "it" was in the opening line, in the penultimate line "it" is now "The wafer of blood in its chalk robes."

One might be able to imagine a "wafer of blood," or to speak symbolically of one. One might also be able to imagine chalk robes, though they sound horribly stiff and heavy and uncomfortable. But to imagine a wafer—of blood or of anything else—in chalk robes is impossible; one simply can't visualize it. The metaphor is mixed, irredeemably. Even if the metaphor is meant to suggest blood in the marrow of bones, we can't escape the absurdity of the visual image the poem evokes.

The final line—in which "it" is now "the bright nail of the east I usher my body toward"—has similar problems with its figurative language and some rather sinister implications worth examining. First, is the "bright nail" that the poet asks us to visualize a fingernail (and thus perhaps an image of the moon) or the pointed steel object driven by a hammer? Given the religious connotations of several words in the previous line, and of the word "usher" in this one, is the reader supposed to imagine that the speaker is ushering his body toward some kind of crucifixion? And if so, why is there only one nail—shouldn't a crucifixion require a greater number?

I don't think these are trivial questions to ask of the poem. However the images originated in the poet's psyche, now they are making a pattern called a poem and they ask for interpretation and understanding. One can, in fact, make a pattern of the images and figures, with some effort, and though a great deal of ambiguity and awkwardness remain, here's what I think the poem suggests.

Once "it"—probably consciousness—was "lamb's fleece"; that is, innocent, pure, of a single, uncorrupted nature—probably in childhood: "it" was "flesh made flesh and the word." That is, spirit, mind, and body were one and indivisible. Now "it" is "the crack in the porcelain stick"; that is, consciousness, self, is divided. Only in death, after the penetration of the body by "the bright nail of the east"—perhaps the sun—will the speaker find unity of being. Orthodox Christianity suggests that there will be a resurrection after death, but the poem—despite its allusions to wafers and robes—stops short of saying that. Even if the "bright nail of the east" is a star—perhaps the one over Bethlehem—what is sure in the poem is that the speaker ushers his body toward oblivion. The only solution to the problem of human existence is once again to merge—with nail or east or perhaps even God—attaining unity of being at the price of losing one's body and human identity.

Timothy Steele suggests another solution in his poem "Last Tango," a lyrical meditation on human identity (*Sapphics Against Anger*, 1986). The poem is also, by the way, a fine movie review of the Marlon Brando movie *Last Tango in Paris*.

LAST TANGO

It is disquieting, that film
In which the plagued protagonist
Won't tell his lover who he is.
It's not just that she turns on him
Or that his youth and age consist
Primarily of chances missed:
The most disturbing thing's that he,
Who loses all else, cannot lose
His own identity.

All life conspires to define us,
Weighing us down with who we are,
Too much drab pain. It is enough
To make one take sides with Plotinus:
Sweet Universal Avatar,
Make me pure spirit, an ensouled star —
Or something slightly less divine:
Rain on an awning, or wind rough
Among clothes on a line.

Of course, it wouldn't do to flee
All longings, griefs, despairs, and such.
Blisses anonymously pursued
Destroy us or, evasively,
Both yield to and resist our touch.
The Brando figure learns as much:
A wholly personal collapse
Succeeds his nameless interlude.
One thinks, though, that perhaps

In some less fallen world, an ease
Might grace our necessary fictions.
There our identities would be
Like — what? — like Haydn's symphonies,
Structures of balanced contradictions,
For all their evident restrictions,
Crazy with lightness and desire:
La Passione, Mercury,
Tempesta, Mourning, Fire.

In this poem, Steele, like Charles Wright, imagines for a moment the possibility of escaping the pain of human identity by obliterating consciousness and becoming "an ensouled star." But unlike Wright, Steele raises the possibility only to reject it. "It wouldn't do to flee" our human condition to become something such as "rain on an awning" or wind. All blisses and ecstacies, which remove us from our bodies and normal human consciousness, destroy us, the poet reminds us. Like Wright, Steele envisions a "less fallen world" in which an "ease" might lighten the burden of identity, but Steele recognizes the impossibility of achieving that condition except in the temporary "structures of balanced contradictions" of art, as the poem's concluding simile reminds us. We can't become one with a tempest or with fire, but we might find our human passions mirrored in the balanced contradictions of a Haydn symphony or in a poem. It is the poet's task, as the new formalists recognize, to create such balanced structures, using all of the resources available, including consistent figurative language.

When looking at poems, it is helpful to remember that the root meaning of the word *metaphor* is *transference* in the Greek, and that the purpose of metaphor is revelatory: to suggest unexpected qualities or relations of the things being implicitly compared. The chief job of a poet, according to critics from Aristotle down, is not to penetrate his own psyche, freely associating the images he finds there, as Robert Bly suggests, but to find unexpected resemblances. To do this, a poet needs to look at the world to discover what lies hidden. The human unconscious, collective or otherwise, is not a substitute for the world, and to use it as a repository of "deep" images to be shuffled according to whim or fancy is to shirk the poet's primary task.

Merging with unconscious nature is impossible short of death. The gap between words and the things they name can't be wished away or closed, but it can be explored and tested. Metaphor is the one loophole through which a poet can sometimes pull part of the world into language — or at least pull two parts of the world together till the knot of language slips and things slide back into thingness again, leaving the reader holding the empty string of sounds and abstract patterns we call a sentence. Form — by which I mean the architecture of meter and rhyme and stanza — is one more piece of string for catching resemblances. The poets with the most string, it seems to me, stand the best chance of tying the biggest knots.

Metrical Illiteracy

Brad Leithauser

American verse is probably passing through a peculiar period when the word *disturbing* can, unadorned, serve as commendation on a dust jacket. The willing reader, or at least the willing reader of advertisements and blurbs for books of contemporary poetry, is offered *disturbing collections* and *disturbing new voices* and *disturbing sensibilities*.

To this particular reader of poetry, the word seems ironically appropriate. For while the books themselves are apt to prove not so much *disturbing* in any tonic, regenerative sense as simply *dismaying*, the state of contemporary verse as a whole does seem disturbing in the prime, portentous connotations of the word—worrisome, unsettling, even destructive.

Anyone generalizing about contemporary American poetry must first acknowledge that given its diffuse, factionalized condition any conclusions must be presented with hesitation. For diffusion more than any unifying trait defines its fundamental nature, and indeed at once provides the generalizer with one impregnably safe generalization: American poetry has never passed through such a scattered era. This diffusion may be a result of the deaths in the last few decades of so many of its ablest practitioners and guides (Eliot, Frost, Roethke, Bishop, Berryman—and these but begin the unhappy list), or perhaps it is tied to the larger directionlessness that seems presently to haunt so many of the arts.

Hesitantly, then, I would suggest that a second generalization might safely be tendered: there is a widespread perception that we are not living in a golden age of poetry, and that mediocrity prevails in the periodicals and on the bookstore shelves. It is this near-unanimous consensus that is of interest here rather than the mediocrity itself, for mediocre poems have always preponderated in the periodicals and on the bookstore shelves, and always will. In many of the anthologies of ten and twenty years ago one met boisterous assertions that American poetry was passing through a great age (a greatness variously led, depending on the anthologist's predilections, by the Beats or the New York School or the Whomevers). This is a claim

From *The New Criterion* 1.5 (Jan. 1983): 41-46.

less frequently or easily made now, I suspect, when our vitality rather than our greatness will likely be cited. Of course this consensus concerning the mediocrity of contemporary poetry is superficial and fragile. On closer examination, one would find little agreement about which constitute the few good, needle-bright poems, and which the haystack of bad ones. Still, this consensus offers its revealing and rather humorous picture—that of hundreds and hundreds of bad poets saying, "There are hundreds and hundreds of bad poets out there."

A third generalization is that very few young writers have worked diligently in poetic form. Such a commonplace is this that it's apt to obscure a rather remarkable fact. Never before in the long line of English verse have we seen the ascendancy of generations of poets who have at no time in their careers worked seriously with form. There are sometimes compelling artistic reasons for abandoning form, a few of which I will touch on, but most lying outside the focus of this article. Nonetheless, this abandonment represents a fundamental schism, something far more significantly divisive than any mere shift in formal fads or tastes. Throughout history, traditional forms and conventions have of course suffered their eclipses; the search for new methods and the impatience with tired ones (what Keats called "dead leaves in the bay wreath crown") have generated much of the brilliance and excitement of English literature. Take for example that robust Italian music box the sonnet (from "sonnetto," little song or sound). After displaying an overtaking brilliance under Shakespeare, Donne, Milton, Herbert, it was essentially set aside for more than a century; was born again, singing new melodies, with Wordsworth and the Romantics; underwent a great many freshening changes only to find itself, with Cummings and Pound a hundred years later, successfully sporting thee's and hath's and other locutions that Wordsworth himself on a good day probably would have eschewed as old-fashioned. A sonnet in the level, colloquial voice of Elizabeth Bishop may seem hundreds of years advanced over the rounded, often florid intonings of Edna St. Vincent Millay (though both women's working lives overlapped), and the former's work may even be seen as something of a repudiation of the latter's. Yet this process of repudiation, the fertile ferment of quiet revolution, is all taking place within the larger domain of English formal poetry. Two poets working in form, whatever the distaste they harbor for each other's verse, will probably share a kinship which a formal poet and an exclusively free-form poet will not know.

A fourth and final generalization is that while the poetry market in this era of blockbuster books is pitifully small, and a hardcover printing may run less than a thousand copies for even a prize-winning poet of some "fame" (a word that usually trumpets with bombastic humor when applied to any inhabitant of the contemporary American poetry scene), there are far more poets out there, and far more poems being produced, than ever before. One hears that an open manuscript competition like that for the Yale or Whitman Prize may draw a couple of thousand submissions — more submissions than the winning manuscript will sell books. More colleges are teaching poetry writing than ever before; more students are graduating from such classes and colleges in treadmill search of other such classes to teach.

Obviously these four conditions — diffusion, perceived mediocrity, the eschewal of form by the young, and an ever expanding number of poets — will greatly overlap. Take for example the last of these, poetry's burgeoning population. In a mock-scholarly way, one might even chart (much as an ecologist charts the population of birds or fish based on data about weather, predators, etc.) how the first three conditions might affect the number of people who choose to write poetry. For example, we would expect diffusion and population to exist in direct correlation: the more poets we have, the less we can logically expect unanimity or the hegemony of a single poetic school; conversely, the more diffusion, the greater the chance that new people will encounter some inspiring style or subject matter that nudges them into writing verse. The perception of mediocrity, too, can lead to rising numbers; for while great art can spark that liberating love which says I want to create, mediocre art may foster an equally propulsive I can do that just as well. Mediocrity often betokens opportunity. Similarly, once most of the demands of form have been scuttled by the young — once the notion is lost that poetry is a craft which, like carpentry, requires a long apprenticeship merely to assimilate its tools — there's no reason for anyone experiencing a potent joy or grievance, the stirrings of a cry from the heart, to feel excluded from Parnassus.

Actually, the rising number of poets, while it may create headaches for the poetry editors of magazines receiving perhaps a thousand submissions a week, would seem a healthy phenomenon for at least three reasons. First, it may help us regain some of the ground poetry has lost within the popular culture and thereby offer poets a re-burnished self-esteem, so that even if as civic beings they do not, with Shelley, believe themselves the unacknowledged legislators of the world, they might fancy themselves a small but clarion-voiced group of lobbyists (like the Audubon Society). A second benefit is that mediocre or even bad poetry can have a salutary effect on very young (especially precollege) potential poets, a group for whom the sort of poetry they're exposed to may be less important than the mere fact of their being exposed to poetry at all. This is a group in whom one cannot reasonably hope to instill a discerning love of what's good, but one can perhaps engender an embracing excitement about poetry that will in time lead to critical refinement. Third, a larger number of poets would seem to increase the likelihood (as in that familiar, though here perhaps unflattering, image favored by students of statistics: monkeys pecking randomly at typewriters) of durable, rewarding poems being written.

The diffusion of poetry, too, presents theoretical advantages. It would seem to increase the chance of a poet's finding useful models and a natural voice. A dominant poetic form or group of forms (rhymed pentameter, say) can squelch a great many poets not temperamentally suited to such strictures. One might reply that genius finds its own forms and surmounts the obstacles of pervading fashion—one might even erect a plausible definition of genius on such a premise—but surely not all great poems are written by geniuses and many great poems will be lost when a charmingly wayward muse is hitched up (by a sort of arranged marriage) to an autocratic prosody. Diffusion would seem to offer a utopian community where everyone practices what he or she does best.

In any case, diffusion would appear to be an inevitable and a lasting condition of the American poetry scene. Fashions will rise and fall, but it's extremely difficult to picture all of our wildly disparate schools and tastes again converging. It is as if after the big bang of modernism and its aftereffects the drifting bodies have finally moved too far apart, lack sufficient mass and centripetal gravity, ever to regather again around the core of a ruling orthodoxy.

Diffusion also seems inevitable for a second, extremely cynical, reason. A great many well-known poets simply have not worked in form and could not successfully if they tried. Ungainliness—a simple lack of professionalism—would immediately show itself. Formlessness (ostensibly an avant-garde impulse) may, then, actually be kept alive by conservatism in its most basic sense—conservation of the self, the preservation of one's reputation in the poetry scene.

What is so surprising about this diffusion, whether viewed as ultimately benign or merely inevitable, is how narrow on examination it turns out to be, especially as manifested in our college writing programs. Rarely is it Chaucer or Milton or Pope or Dickinson or Tennyson to whom such classes turn, but almost always a host of mediocrities risen since World War II, most of them theoretically progeny of William Carlos Williams (insofar as he can be read, falsely, as an endorser of plain-spoken disorder). While diffusion ideally ensures individuality, we find instead dozens and dozens of interchangeable tenured Blakes, visionaries without vision, who, having set up campus satraps, are continually venturing forth for drearily unproductive workshops, symposia, conferences. So goes the business of teaching poetry....

Admittedly, the poetry teacher occupies a problematic position, for the writing of poetry, despite the exploding population of poets, represents an increasingly "unnatural" practice. There was a time when poets might naturally, as a part of their culture, be steeped in verse, a time when anonymous ballads could flourish and perhaps even help a society find and define itself. In recent years, a number of poets and critics (notably Randall Jarrell, Richard Wilbur, W. H. Auden, George Steiner) have written fine, elegiac pieces about this decline, whose implications are enormous, minatory, and obscure. It is clear, however, that today, when that steeping process is no longer naturally imposed, young people who wish not merely to read but actually to absorb someone like Pope, so that lines will volley unexpectedly to mind, must perform an arduous, solitary task. According to a romantic view of poets (and when poets are thought of at all it is usually romantically), this task will be accomplished almost effortlessly, as the young poet, driven by a voracious love of poesy, engorges every stanza and line he can put his hands upon. It probably is love, as much as anything, that motivates the apprentice poet, but the romantic view fails to consider that an elementary mastery of this particular craft requires work of a decidedly onerous variety. The young poet who has spent an afternoon seriously grappling for the first time with, say, the cruxes and quibbles of the Shakespeare sonnets is apt to wind up feeling that, like his counterpart the apprentice carpenter, he has splinters in his fingers and sawdust in his lungs.

Ours is a clangorous and increasingly violent age, and the art of poetry, in all its subtleties and near-fatal unsexiness, is easily lost in the din and jostle. It will take years for any young poet who has spent his share of time at the movies, where knifings and garrotings and chain-saw eviscerations are served up with such ferociously unblinking exactitude, or at rock concerts where the very walls are set to shuddering, to appreciate the delicate but prodigious violence packed into a sonnet like Milton's "On the Late Massacre in Piedmont," with that central image of horror: "...and in their ancient fold / Slain by the bloody Piedmontese, that rolled / Mother with infant down the rocks." (Palgrave in his *Golden Treasury* called this "the most mighty Sonnet in any language known to the Editor.") And years to understand how a sonnet like Frost's "Design" is both presenting a wittily terrifying view of destiny and prosodically raising the stakes, doing Milton one better, by not only meeting all rigid constrictions of the Miltonic sonnet form but imposing a further obstacle, the use of one of the same rhyme-sounds ("ite") in both the sestet and octet:

> I found a dimpled spider, fat and white,
> On a white heal-all, holding up a moth
> Like a white piece of rigid satin cloth —
> Assorted characters of death and blight
> Mixed ready to begin the morning right,
> Like the ingredients of a witches' broth —
> A snow-drop spider, a flower like froth,
> And dead wings carried like a paper kite.
>
> What had that flower to do with being white,
> The wayside blue and innocent heal-all?
> What brought the kindred spider to that height,
> Then steered the white moth thither in the night?
> What but design of darkness to appall? —
> If design govern in a thing so small.

With a lucid, colloquial diction ("plain American which cats and dogs can read," in Marianne Moore's phrase), Frost has gone fourteen lines with hardly a break in the pentameter and with the employment of but three rhyme-sounds. Actually, at one point Frost contemplated writing this much-revised sonnet with even fewer rhyme-sounds. Given his awesome technical proficiency, he probably could have accomplished this, but perhaps to the detriment of the poem's music and emotional impact. Here is another fruitful tension — that between visceral force which ever seeks to loosen formal constraints and the technician's perverse urge to tighten them — whose appreciation requires years of study.

Even if the culture itself does not steep the young poet in poetry, he or she may be fortunate enough to grow to poetic adulthood in an era when form flourishes. Perhaps one of the reasons why so much accomplishment has come from American poets born in the 1920s (Anthony Hecht, Donald

Justice, James Merrill, W.D. Snodgrass, Richard Wilbur, James Wright—
and again this but begins the list) is that they had the good fortune to begin
their careers during the Forties and Fifties, when an orthodoxy of formal
verse [was] obtained. This period is often criticized as sterile, and doubt-
less in some of their work formalism has stunted the soul of a potentially
fine lyric, but surely it was advantageous for them to train in the same
basic tools as the titans of English verse. These are a generation of poets
who have "gone to school." One cannot read a poem like Richard Wilbur's
"A World Without Objects Is a Sensible Emptiness," written while he was
still some years short of thirty, without reflecting that here is someone who
purely in terms of craftsmanship has mastered a great deal. In twenty-
eight lines he manages articulately to state a philosophical position on the
dilemma of the spirit/body conflict; to enlist in support the prose of Tho-
mas Traherne, the seventeenth century poet and theologian from whose
Centuries of Meditation he draws the title; to cast a fresh and lively language
into the matrix of one of the hoariest poetic forms in English verse, the
ABAB quatrain. In the first fourteen lines he portrays the spirit's inclina-
tion toward the deserts of ascetic withdrawal; at the midpoint, the fifteenth
line, the tone shifts from description to exhortation, the verbs from
declaratives to imperatives; and in the closing eleven he openly urges the
spirit to "turn back," to enter the world fully:

> Turn, O turn
> From the fine sleights of the sand, from the long empty oven
> Where flames in flamings burn
>
> Back to the trees arrayed
> In bursts of glare, to the halo-dialing run
> Of the country creeks, and the hills' bracken tiaras made
> Gold in the sunken sun,
>
> Wisely watch for the sight
> Of the supernova burgeoning over the barn,
> Lampshine blurred in the steam of beasts, the spirit's right
> Oasis, light incarnate.

Note how the form is jerked deftly awry by the swallowed rhyme of "barn"
/ "incarnate." How the cool scientific nuances of "supernova" brilliantly
contrast with the hinted reference to that ancient image of the star over
Bethlehem; how directly yet subtly "wisely" evokes the Three Wise Men;
how the reference to Christ's birth—the Incarnation that is our most po-

tent and poignant image of the Spirit's embrace of the Material—at once broadens the poem's argument and concords so sweetly with the philosophy of Traherne himself. Wilbur has not only gone to school, he has proven himself a star pupil, and this training gives his work an amplitude very few living poets can match. (One might lightly, affectionately note that while the slight misquoting of Traherne in Wilbur's title is probably an act of poetic license, it may show that at that school which he attended Wilbur did not study transcription.)

Yet the poet who has not gone to school suffers more than a narrowing of the breadth of his own verse. His critical faculties are truncated. A crucial understanding of the past is lost. Under normal circumstances, the poet can offer a unique critical vantage. He is apt to understand better even than a far more erudite scholar a poem's construction. The poet empathetically senses which line in a wobbly heroic couplet has engendered the other; understands why a particular stanzaic pattern may have been selected, and even which stanza might have been the germ whence the pattern grew; knows firsthand how the paucity of English rhymes (especially for such much-used words as "self," "God," "truth") may unwittingly bend the flow and sense of a lyric; distinguishes between cases where "cheating" on formal requirements derives from felt necessity, and where from a deliberate, fine rebelliousness. Of course the poet has this special insight only if he has worked with these forms himself. Poets tend to resent, often rightfully, being reviewed by non-poet critics, who may not fully compass the actual ways a poem is constructed; but having once sacrificed a first-hand knowledge of poetic form, these poets themselves are, when passing judgment on the formal masters of the past, in precisely the same position as the non-poet critics they resent. The poet has lost that craftsman-to-craftsman affinity which is his special contribution to the ongoing evaluation and reappraisal of English-language verse. This loss seems especially grave when considered against the much diminished role verse now plays in the lives of the general populace, whose poetic tastes and sympathies might once have been expected to perform a preserving, archival function. If today poets themselves do not maintain an intimacy with formal technique, who can we expect will do so?

The exploding population of poets, the dizzying diffusion, the sense of open opportunities—clearly these conditions will little profit us so long as a belief persists that a person who is not a decent prosodist can be decent poet. Or so long as we fail to recognize that metrical illiteracy is, for the poet, functional illiteracy. To write a competent Miltonic sonnet—not even a good one, but merely one which satisfies formal requirements without relying on padding or wrenched syntax or archaic inversions—is a surprisingly difficult undertaking. Surely all poets ought to know this, even if not all critics do.

What's New About the New Formalism?

Robert McPhillips

The reflorescence of formal poetry in the United States in the 1980s has caught the comfortably-tenured corps of the "free verse revolution" by surprise. Predictably, many of these middle-aged poet-professors have launched blanket attacks on this diverse new movement, attempting to reduce it to something at best trivial, at worst downright dangerous. Such critical assaults have labeled these new formal poems as the products of "yuppie" poets for whom a poem is mere artifice, something to be valued as a material object; or, more perniciously, as the product of a neo-conservative *Zeitgeist*. There is, they further claim, nothing "new" about these poems at all. Rather than being perceived as innovative, these new formal poems of the '80s are dismissed as derivative, as retreats to the allegedly stale and stodgily "academic" formal poetry of the '50s against whose strictures the Beat, Confessional and Deep Image poets emerged. Such claims are simply untrue.

While there were many anthologies that showcased the formalist poets of the '50s, the most influential in establishing the identity of the movement was *New Poets of England and America* (1957), edited by Donald Hall, Robert Pack, and Louis Simpson, and given its imprimatur by Robert Frost's introduction. It was this volume that first collected the group one now identifies as the '50s formalist poets, a group that includes Edgar Bowers, Anthony Hecht, John Hollander, Donald Justice, Robert Lowell, William Meredith, James Merrill, Howard Moss, Howard Nemerov, Adrienne Rich, Louis Simpson, William Jay Smith, W.D. Snodgrass and Richard Wilbur. When one contemplates the American poets gathered in this seminal anthology, a certain composite poem emerges that defines their shared aesthetic assumptions. This collective poem is characteristically ironic, emphasizing the poet's distance from his subject. Quite frequently, it focuses upon a cultural artifact, usually a European one. Similarly, it routinely abounds in classical allusions and sometimes boasts a foreign-

First published in *Crosscurrents*, *A Quarterly*, vol. 8, no. 2, 1988. Copyright © by Robert McPhillips. Reprinted with permission of the author and publisher.

language title reflecting a cultural pedigree often backed up by an ornately baroque diction. It rarely displays strong emotions directly, even—indeed, most conspicuously—if it is a love poem. In short, the '50s formal poem is elegant and learned and makes little attempt to communicate with readers who are otherwise.

The most ostentatiously academic of the '50s formalists is John Hollander, a poet whose artistic development has been crippled by his abundant intellect. In his early poems printed in *New Poets*, one witnesses his penchant for the elitism of high culture. Two of the four poems representing Hollander's early work contain titles in French and Latin: "*Paysage Moralisé*" and "*Horas Tempestatis Quoque Enumero:* The Sundial." The former places the mythical figures of Daphnis and Chloe in its "moralized landscape," Chloe's resistance to Daphnis's erotic advances yielding the poem's concluding epigrammatic moral:

> Under a soupy tree
> Mopes Daphnis, joined by all
> The brown surrounding landscape:
> Even in Arcady
> Ego needs must spoil
> Such a beautiful friendship.

Hollander's use here of myth and the abstract, the pseudo-Freudian lingo, ironically juxtaposed to cliché, distances the poet from the potentially personal subject of erotic frustration, unrequited love.

"*Horas Tempestatis Quoque Enumero:* The Sundial" is a perfect example of the '50s formal poem that uses elevated diction to leisurely and elaborately describe an art object, in this case a sundial with a Latin inscription. Hollander's refusal to provide a translation of this inscription in his title (which could be rendered "I Too Reckon Up the Hours of the Season") suggests both the assumptions he makes about his audience and the heightened approach he will take to his subject. His description of a rainstorm in the third of the poem's long, baroquely elegant stanzas serves as a particularly extreme example of Hollander's ornate rhetoric:

> The sundial and birdbath (which is which now?) run
> Over into the lawn, and bubbling puddles
> Drop down the steps. Neglected, by a wall,
> Two marble *putti* weep as they are bathed,
> Still leering through the rusty stains about
> Their mouths. The ruin and the summerhouse

Are empty, but through the trumpeting downpour, somewhere,
Inside the long windows, Leopoldine is playing
Her *Gradus and Parnassum*, while nearby
A Chinese philosopher on a silk screen shrinks
From the thunder he has always held to be
The ultimate disorder, as the wind
Wrinkles a painted heron on the bank
    Barely suggested behind him.

While one responds to the lushness of Hollander's language and the effortless music of some of the lines, one is put off by the aloof description, as if objects existed merely to be translated into, well, "poetry." Only in the second half of this stanza, almost halfway through the poem, does one sense a human drama being introduced, albeit obliquely, and only then at the seeming excuse to write elegantly. The mellifluously named Leopoldine, struggling at her piano exercises, remains part of Hollander's flowing catalogue of cultural artifacts, as if there were no distinction between her and her *Gradus ad Parnassum*, or the silk screen of the Chinese philosopher behind her. The human significance of this scene is postponed until the poem's final two stanzas, set at some point in the future. But this drama comes so late, and is itself so obscure, that it fails to redeem one's suspicion that, for all his technical skill, much of Hollander's writing is elegant but empty.

From the beginning, Anthony Hecht has shown an awareness of the tragic nature of human life. "The Vow," the first of his poems in the *New Poets* volume, is a powerful presentation of a father's vow to a miscarried fetus to love the children he and his wife have in the future all the more because of this loss. Nevertheless, Hecht began as, and continues to be, a highly *literary* poet. From the onset, one of Hecht's primary concerns has been to display how urbane, how highly cultured American literature has become since the days of Eliot and James.

This theme is central to Hecht's often-anthologized "La Condition Botanique." Once again the title of a major poem by a '50s academic formalist is in French. The poem is a lengthy, ornate, but brilliantly sustained description of the Brooklyn Botanical Garden. Yet, like Hollander, Hecht is leisurely and indirect in his approach to his true subject. By way of introduction, Hecht digresses, describing European landscapes before finally, in his third stanza, proceeding with his description of the garden. Hecht's intention here is to claim for American culture a site of aesthetic refuge analogous to the Ischian health spa he describes in his first stanza. But Hecht's heightened poetic diction emphasizes that his poem is meant to be itself such a cultural oasis. One sees this immediately in the diction and baroque form of Hecht's opening stanza.

> Romans, rheumatic, gouty, came
> To bathe in Ischian springs where water steamed,
> Puffed and enlarged their bold imperial thoughts, and which
> Later Madame Curie declared to be so rich
> In radioactive content as she deemed
> Should win them everlasting fame.

One is most immediately impressed here by Hecht's heavy consonance ("Romans, rheumatic, gouty, came" reads almost like Hopkins) and smooth assonance, the ease with which he manipulates a complex verse form and set rhyme scheme, and the range of the stanza's cultural references. The language is lush and the allusions sophisticated. But one can't imagine a person speaking these lines or singing them. "La Condition Botanique" is a literary *tour de force*, an elegant verbal construct that recreates, with Biblical, classical and literary allusions—the poem merits no fewer than sixteen footnotes in *The Norton Anthology of Modern Poetry*—a landscape of aesthetic perfection far removed from the ordinary world, from the Brooklyn outside the haven of the botanical garden.

Even Richard Wilbur, one of our finest living poets, is drawn to indirection, exotic words and cultural elitism. Hence his poem on crickets is not entitled "Crickets" or "Cicadas" but "Cigales." And he cannot resist writing "A Baroque Wall-Fountain in the Villa Sciara," a poem whose title tells its story. These poems are hardly without their virtues. But it is worth noting that they are the virtues of a genteel cultural elite, their breeding ground the English Departments of the '50s with their Fulbright overseas scholarships and their zealous approbation of wit, irony, and complexity, the legacy of the New Critics.

These are not the values and virtues of the '80s formalist poets who are as likely to be found in the business world as they are in the university, and whose inspiration derives not from the academy but from the quotidian world and the desire to write about emotion directly and memorably. As yet, there is no anthology similar to that of *New Poets of England and America* to give the new formalists a representative group identity.* Still, a survey of dozens of volumes of poetry published in the last decade or so by younger poets experimenting with traditional forms does allow for significant generalizations.

---

*Editor's note: *A Formal Feeling Comes* and *Rebel Angels* have since appeared.

Characteristically, the diction of the new formalist poem is colloquial rather than elevated. If the poem concerns cultural objects, they are likely to be from popular culture and to be indigenously American. This is not to say that they aspire to the flat, affectless realism of the practitioners—Frederick Barthelme, Ann Beattie, the late Raymond Carver, et al.—of minimalist fiction. In general, the new formalists differ from the academic formalists in the ease with which they accept their own cultural tradition as firmly established—for which, of course, they are indebted to their more self-consciously cultural formalist predecessors. Hence, in the poems of such numerous and widely diverse poets as Dick Allen, Tom Disch, Frederick Feirstein, Dana Gioia, Emily Grosholz, Rachel Hadas, Paul Lake, Brad Leithauser, Charles Martin, Molly Peacock, Robert Phillips, Mary Jo Salter, Gjertrud Schnackenberg, Robert Shaw, Timothy Steele, and Henry Taylor, we find a variety of subjects quite distinct from those of the poems in *New Poets of England and America*. These subjects range from a Joycean account of a day in the life of an ordinary New Yorker to encounters with flying saucers, from the jazz musician Bix Beiderbecke to the twentieth-century saint Simone Weil, from masturbation to marriage, from the streets of Brooklyn and Buffalo to the farms of rural Virginia and the parched hills of California, from the fiction of Chandler and Cheever to the films of Bertolucci and Godard. There are also a more significant number of women poets in the '80s writing formal poems directly addressing distinctly female experience—sexuality, abortion, child-rearing—than was true of the '50s when the notable exception was Adrienne Rich, ironically one of the few poets from that group to make a fully successful shift from formal to free verse.

If the lives and culture that these poems derive from are less elevated than their '50s counterparts, rooted unself-consciously in the middle class rather than in a real or aspired to aristocracy, these are hardly brand-name poems in the way that Frederick Barthelme and Bret Easton Ellis's stories and novels are, reducing the quality of human life to the surface level of the detritus of the shopping malls and fast food chains, the chic nightclubs and MTV, that have become the tacky furniture of much of our contemporary existence. When Dana Gioia invokes an unnamed Beach Boys song in his autobiographical lyric "Cruising with the Beach boys" [*sic*], the occasion of the poet's hearing a song on the radio while on a business trip in an unfamiliar landscape prompts him to reflect on his late adolescence in Southern California and to reexperience the sense of vulnerability and self-pity he thought he had outgrown. One cannot imagine Hecht, Hollander or Wilbur ever daring to face such direct and potentially sentimental emotion in their poems.

Timothy Steele seems the most closely derivative from the academic formalists. Tellingly, however, it is less from the overly-baroque and erudite elements in that poetry than from the more modest, benignly pastoral side of Wilbur that he springs. In his *Sapphics Against Anger* (1986), Steele is not below naming a meditative poem "Chanson Philosophique" or writing on Biblical or historical subjects, as in "In the King's Rooms" and "1816." But neither is he above celebrating the ethnic vitality of the streets of Los Angeles ("Near Olympic") nor the exuberance of roller skaters at a California beach ("At Will Rogers Beach").

In "Timothy," Steele translates a kind of grass bearing his name into an emblem of himself, uniquely personalizing a poem of pastoral description. "Timothy," strongly reminiscent of two early Frost poems, "Mowing" and "The Tuft of Flowers," describes the harvesting of the grass for hay with the poet-harvester modestly taking "pleasure in the thought / The fresh hay's name was mine as well." The "soothing, rhythmic ache" of cutting the grass with a scythe becomes analogous to the poet's own labor at writing a poem, an idea elaborated on in the poem's final two quatrains:

> Pumping a handpump's iron arm,
> I washed myself as best I could,
> Then watched the acres of the farm
> Draw lengthening shadows from the wood
>
> Across the grass, which seemed a thing
> In which the lonely and concealed
> Had risen from its sorrowing
> And flourished in the open field.

There is little of the strain here of a metaphysical conceit, or the ornateness of diction of heaviness of wit characteristic of so much '50s formalism. Steele's strict adherence to metrics and rhyme (he is as much derived from Yvor Winters as from Wilbur) distinguishes his verse from most of his contemporaries; yet the simplicity of his language and the easy musical flow of his lines detract attention from the artifice of his rhyme pattern. Steele, as craftsman, "washe[s]" himself after the "sorrowing" of his labor, leaving the reader with an effortless poem that gracefully reveals what was previously "lonely and concealed" "in the open field" of his paradoxically metrically closed poem. Steele has, then, written a decidedly literary poem, recalling a tradition from Marvell to Wordsworth to Frost and Wilbur, without being in the least academic.

Charles Martin is a more eclectic poet. The poems from his two books, *Room for Error* (1978) and *Steal the Bacon* (1987), are set in Brooklyn, Buffalo, and Vermont, and his subjects encompass everything from graffiti to Latin American politics to Dracula, from *Robinson Crusoe* to flying saucers. Martin's Brooklyn poems—"Sharks at the New York Aquarium" and "Poem in Brooklyn," for example—differ radically from Hecht's "La Condition Botanique." The former, a sonnet, focuses on the aquarium at Coney Island with an economy of words rarely encountered in Hecht. Similarly, it is not told from the perspective of a cultured aesthete but from that of a speaker possessed of childlike wonder when confronted with the spectacle of the "simple lives" of the nonetheless exotic fish. Yet Martin's persona remains firmly rooted in the real world of Brooklyn, where he finds himself, at the poem's conclusion, "again, outside the tank, / Uneasily wrapped in our atmosphere!," one in which "children almost never tap on the glass."

But this sense of childlike wonder yields almost to one of religious yearning in "Taken Up," the final poem in Martin's unduly neglected first volume. This poem postulates a group of people "tired of earth" who long for some means of transcendence. They find this in the form of a flying saucer, a "disc descended, / That glowing wheel of lights whose coming ended / All waiting and watching...." In the poem's—and the volume's—final stanzas of rhymed tercets, Martin freshly presents an image of the desire to seek an entirely new culture, a desire for the possible transformations of the future rather than a nostalgic yearning for the classical European cultural past. The people gathered on a hill to greet the saucer respond thus to the aliens on board:

> Light was their speech, spanning mind to mind:
> *We came here not believing what we find —*
> *Can it be your desire to leave behind*
>
> *The earth, which even these angels bless,*
> *Exchanging amplitude for emptiness?*
> And in a single voice they answered *Yes,*
>
> Discord of human melodies all bent
> To the unearthly strain of their assent.
> *Come then*, the Strangers said, and those who were taken went.

Having paid tribute, earlier in this volume, to the Latin poet Calvus, as well as to Melville, Dante, Robert Duncan, Milton Avery, Theodore

Roethke, and Godard, Martin here seemingly tips his hat to Steven Spielberg. But what is more notable is Martin's unusual ability to write in clear, unadorned language, making each of his subjects memorable through his graceful, unobtrusive use of rhyme. In "Taken Up," Martin extends the range of contemporary poetry to include the resources of science fiction, as have Dick Allen and Frederick Turner. He does so in such a quiet yet skillful manner, mingling awe and muted humor—reminiscent, perhaps, in an odd way of some of Emily Dickinson's oblique and irreverently theological meditations on death—as to transform it into a distinctly contemporary form of religious verse.

Dana Gioia's first collection of poetry, *Daily Horoscope* (1986), could, in itself, constitute the central document establishing the most pertinent distinctions between the '50s and the new formalists of the '80s. Gioia has perfected a quiet, colloquial, genuinely human voice in his personal lyrics that is alien to the irony of the academic formalists and the frequent hysteria of the Confessional poets.

This intimate voice underlies Gioia's elegiac and decorously poised love poems as well as his numerous poems which eschew the personal, poems that range in subject matter from jazz to pornography, from the lives of the great composers to that of businessmen after work. The landscapes vary widely—and are quite distinct from the landscapes of the earlier formalist poets: Southern California, Westchester County, the expansive parking lot of a suburban corporation. They extend as well, in Stevens's phrase, to "an Italy of the mind" rather than of the guidebooks, not to that symbol of the pinnacle of European culture but the impoverished country from which the poet's family emigrated to the United States.

Some of Gioia's best poems remain uncollected.* In "Equations of the Light," published in *The New Yorker* in 1986, seven blank verse quatrains recreate the unexpected excitement and transience of a love affair. In this lyric notable for its intricate narrative structure, the poet contrasts the quotidian demands of life with the brief luminous moments afforded by an unexpected encounter:

> Turning the corner, we discovered it
> just as the old wrought-iron lamps went on—
> a quiet, tree-lined street, only one block long,
> resting between the noisy avenues.

---

*Editor's note: *The Gods of Winter* (1991) has since appeared.

> The street lamps splashed the shadow of the leaves
> across the whitewashed brick, and each tall window
> glowing through the ivy-decked facade,
> promised lives as perfect as the light.

These lines are as elegant as any by Hecht or Wilbur, but their elegance doesn't rely on elevated diction, literary allusions, or an exotic setting. Instead, the poem achieves its effect upon the reader through its reenactment of the poet's and his companion's experience of encountering this idyllic street with its promise of perfection wholly unawares. Likewise, it conveys the physical beauty of that street captured at just that magical moment which "lingered like a ghost," transforming it into the ideal objective correlative for this evanescently passionate meeting.

But to say that Gioia's language is plain is not to say that the emotion he evokes is simple. After feeling so at home in this discovered environment that the poet feels "we could have opened any door / entered any room the evening offered," he goes to question such certainty:

> Or were we so deluded by the strange
> equations of the light, the vagrant wind
> searching the trees, we believed this brief
> conjunction of our separate lives was real?

Whereas a poet like John Ashbery might push such a question so far as to disintegrate whatever image of epiphanic beauty his poem seemed to be building toward, or a Hollander use it to distance himself ironically from speaking directly about love, Gioia makes such a question an integral part of what constitutes both the beauty and fragility of love.

In these brief remarks I have tried to examine, in broad terms, what is *new* about the poems of the new formalists by examining the differences between the formalists who emerged after the Second World War and those who, in the late '70s and early '80s, have tried to regain for poetry some of the ground lost to it—not merely rhyme and meter, but more importantly a sense of common human experience as opposed to solipsistically unique "experiences"—by the free verse poets who understandably rebelled against what they perceived to be the overly academic, ironic, refined formal poems of the '50s.

Attention to form has allowed a significant number of younger poets to think and communicate clearly about their sense of what is of most human value—love, beauty, mortality. They address themselves primarily neither to the academy nor to other poets. Instead, they seem interested in reestablishing an audience of common readers, transcending sexual or ideological allegiances, tapping into a potential openness to the verities and music available exclusively in the aesthetic realm of poetry. The new formalists speak clearly and eloquently about our shared human experience. But at their best they do more. In the words of Dana Gioia, they remind us that even in the course of everyday life there come rare moments of luminosity when:

> ...only briefly then,
> You touch, you see, you press against
> The surface of impenetrable things.

"Counting Syllables on Her Fingers"
Introduction and Statements from
A Formal Feeling Comes: *Poems in Form by Contemporary Women*

ANNIE FINCH
Introduction

A Formal Feeling Comes: Poems in Form by Contemporary Women reflects a
surprising development in contemporary women's poetry in the United
States: a wide-spread turn—or return—to "formal" poetics. Readers who
have been following the discussion of the "New Formalism" over the last
decade may not expect to find such a diversity of writers and themes in a
book of formal poems; the poems collected here contradict the popular as-
sumption that formal poetics correspond to reactionary politics and elitist
aesthetics. This does not mean, however, that literary and cultural politics
have not affected women's use of poetic form. For serious twentieth-cen-
tury women poets, traditional poetic form is a troubled legacy. The lineage
of women poets in English is largely a formal one, but since the modernist
period, many have had reason to be ambivalent about form.

Women poets found themselves in a double bind during the reign of
modernism, in spite of the fact that their predecessors—from Lydia
Sigourney to Louise Imogen Guiney—had developed a popular mode of
female poetry during the course of the nineteenth century. While a line of
male poetic experimenters including Smart, Blake, Whitman, and Hopkins
inspired the modernist revolution for male poets, women's poetry had long
tended to favor accessibility and community-building over radical innova-
tion. Even Dickinson's innovative poems remain within traditional formal
limits much more than those of, for example, her contemporary, Whitman.

As one critic characterizes the female poet's predicament, "a modern
woman poet could not be a woman poet without reaching for a tradition
that would violate the unconventionality of modernism and seem politi-
cally regressive."[1] In the early twentieth century, the price of participation
in the new movement was the repression or abandonment of the women's
poetic tradition.

"Of sugar and spice and everything nice, / That is what bad poetry is made of," quipped William Carlos Williams in ironically perfect rhyme. Like other key modernist writers, Williams linked the major line of women's poetry with traditional verse forms and with inferior writing. Ezra Pound is unlikely to have been thinking of formal verse when he declared, "Poetry speaks phallic direction," and James Joyce meant to praise the metrically revolutionary *The Waste Land* when he observed that it "ends [the] idea of poetry for ladies." Elsewhere Pound remarked that he wanted "to write 'poetry' that a grown man could read without groans of ennui, or without having to have it cooed in his ear by a flapper."[2] Female modernists distanced themselves from the mode of more traditional women poets. Privately, H.D. is reported to have "considered herself and [Marianne] Moore far superior to other women poets such as Elinor Wylie, Edna St. Vincent Millay, or Sara Teasdale."[3]

Teasdale, Alice Dunbar-Nelson, Millay, Wylie, Louise Bogan, and others carried on the mainstream tradition nonetheless, continuing to write in traditional forms even after the modernist revolt. Although by mid-century almost all of the women poets of the nineteenth and early twentieth centuries had fallen out of print—and most certainly out of fashion—the legacy would continue, haltingly and often in secret. While Sylvia Plath was determined not to "write simple lyrics like Millay," Anne Sexton and Tillie Olsen guiltily confessed to each other their private love for the work of Millay and Teasdale.[4]

The poets in this anthology are reclaiming a formal inheritance more openly than women have done in many decades, and their work demonstrates that the long tradition of women's formal poetry is evolving once again. When I began to collect the poems for this anthology, I had no idea of the variety and extent of formalism among women poets. These poems have been gathered from all over the poetic map. With the exception of Marilyn Hacker, whose direct influence can be seen in the work of a number of the poets included here, there has been no particular central model for a return to conspicuously formal poetry. Far from being a poetic movement in the usual senses, the kind of "New Formalism" represented in this book has had an almost unconscious, grass-roots development.

Defining "formal" poetry broadly as poetry that foregrounds the artificial and rhetorical nature of poetic language by means of conspicuously repeated patterns, I have chosen a continuum of formal poems, from regular rhyme and meter through accentual verse through nonmetrical rhyming poems to repetitive chants. Each of the poems included here involves conspicuous repetition, of vowels and consonants (rhyme), rhythmic patterns (meter), phrases (refrain or anaphora) or larger poetic patterns (stanza form). Many of the poems also engage the traditions that have developed around these root-techniques in English-language poetry.

A Formal Feeling Comes includes examples of the most important prosodic forms in English—iambic and triple meters in a variety of line lengths, both rhymed and unrhymed; various quatrain rhyme patterns including the Italian (abba) and English (abab); other stanza patterns such as the hymn stanza, terza rima, rhyme royal, and Sapphic stanza; and forms such as the villanelle, sestina, ballade, Petrarchan and Shakespearean sonnet, crown of sonnets, blues, chant, haiku, and pantoum. I have also included several poems in original or "nonce" forms ranging from punpoems to oral literature-based chants.[5]

Some forms—for example, the sonnet—remain problematic to contemporary women poets. Most women poets have shied away from the sonnet for decades, perhaps sensing that, as Rachel Blau Du Plessis puts it, "The sonnet is a genre already historically filled with voiceless, beautiful female figures in object position"—Millay and Barrett Browning notwithstanding.[6] Many of the poets here use the sonnet form as they have inherited it, sometimes with ironic subject matter, while others change its form: some poets keep rhyme without meter, and others use subtle or rearranged rhyme schemes that are easier to miss in their "sonnets."

The contributors' statements on poetics provide clues about the reasons for these different approaches and the appeal of form for various poets. A number of contributors, sensitive to the gender implications of form, write in historically powerful poetic forms in order to transform them and claim some of their strength. Rita Dove, for example, describes her chosen form (the sonnet) as "stultifying," but hears voices in it that are "sing[ing] in their chains." Others, like Molly Peacock, find themselves freed, imaginatively or emotionally, by the aesthetic constraints of form which make feelings "safe to explore." Some relish the intellectual challenge of a rhyme scheme, while others describe the physical pleasure they experience among the rhythms of a metrical line and associate the beat of meter with the rhythms of the body. The passion for form unites these many and diverse poets. As Marilyn Hacker writes, "When I see a young (or not-so-young) writer counting syllables on her fingers, or marking stresses for a poem she's writing, or one she's reading, I'm pretty sure we'll have something in common, whatever our other differences may be."

As this book shows, women are taking on the risks of form in new ways. At their best, these poets combine the intellectual strength, emotional freedom, and self-knowledge women have gained during the twentieth century with the poetic discipline and technique that have long been the female poet's province. These poems point the way to a true linking of the strengths of the old with the strengths of the new: not a nostalgic return to the old forms but an unprecedented relationship with their infinite challenges.

Works Cited

1. Suzanne Clar. "The Unwanted Discourse: Sentimental Community, Modernist Women, and the Case of Millay," *Genre* 20: 2 (1987),145.

2. Quoted in David Perkins. *A History of Modern Poetry* (Cambridge: Harvard UP, 1976), 298. The quotes from Joyce and Williams, and Pound's quote on phallic direction, are collected in Sandra M. Gilbert and Susan Gubar, *No Man's Land: The Place of the Woman Writer in the Twentieth Century, vol. 1: The War of the Words* (New Haven: Yale UP, 1987), 155-56.

3. Barbara Guest. *Herself Defined: The Poet H.D. and Her World* (London: Collins, 1985), 133.

4. Plath is quoted in Gilbert and Gubar 204. The Sexton anecdote is in Diane Middlebrook, *Anne Sexton: A Biography* (Boston: Houghton Mifflin, 1991), 196.

5. I also urge those interested in chant forms to read the title poems from Joy Harjo's *She Had Some Horses* (Thunder's Mouth Press) and Pat Parker's *Movement in Black* (Eighth Mountain Press).

6. Rachel Blau Du Plessis, "Thinking About Annie Finch, On Female Power and the Sonnet," *(How)ever* VI: 3 (summer 1991) 16.

JULIA ALVAREZ
Housekeeping Cages

Sometimes people ask me why I wrote a series of poems about housekeeping if I'm a feminist. Don't I want women to be liberated from the oppressive roles they were condemned to live? I don't see housekeeping that way. They were the crafts we women had, sewing, embroidering, cooking, spinning, sweeping, even the lowly dusting. And as Dylan Thomas said, we sang in our chains like the sea. Isn't it already thinking from the point of view of the oppressor to say to ourselves, what we did was nothing?

You use what you have, you learn to work the structure to create what you need. I don't feel that writing in traditional forms is giving up power, going over to the enemy. The word belongs to no one, the houses built of words belong to no one. We have to take them back from those who think they own them.

Sometimes I get in a mood. I tell myself I am taken over. I am writing under somebody else's thumb and tongue. See, English was not my first language. It was, in fact, a colonizing language to my Spanish Caribbean. But then Spanish was also a colonizer's language; after all, Spain colonized Quisqueya. There's no getting free. We are always writing in a form imposed on us. But then, I'm Scheherazade in the Sultan's room. I use structures to survive and triumph! To say what's important to me as a woman and as a Latina.

I think of form as territory that has been colonized but that you can free. See, I feel subversive in formal verse. A voice is going to inhabit that form that was barred from entering it before! That's what I tried, in the "33" poems, to use my woman's voice in a sonnet as I would use it sitting in the kitchen with a close friend, talking womanstuff. In school, I was always trying to inhabit those forms as the male writers had. To pitch my voice to "Of man's first disobedience, and the fruit . . . ." If it didn't hit the key of "Sing in me, Muse, and through me tell the story," how could it be important poetry? The only kind.

While I was in graduate school some of the women in the program started a Women's Writing Collective in Syracuse. We were musing each other into unknown writing territory. One woman advised me to listen to my own voice, deep inside, and put that down on paper. But what I heard when I listened were voices that said things like, "Don't put so much salt on the lettuce, you'll wilt the salad!" I'd never heard that in a poem. So how could it be poetry? Then, with the "33" sonnet sequence, I said, I'm going to go in there and I'm going to sound like myself. I took on the whole kaboodle. I was going into form, sonnets no less. Wow.

What I wanted from the sonnet was the tradition that it offered as well as the structure. The sonnet tradition was one in which women were caged in golden cages of beloved, in perfumed gas chambers of stereotype. I wanted to go in that heavily mined and male labyrinth with the string of my own voice. I wanted to explore it and explode it too. I call my sonnets free verse sonnets. They have ten syllables per line, and the lines are in a loose iambic pentameter. But they are heavily enjambed and the rhymes are often slant rhymes, and the rhyme scheme is peculiar to each sonnet. One friend read them and said, "I didn't know they were sonnets. They sounded like you talking!"

By learning to work the sonnet structure and yet remaining true to my own voice, I made myself at home in that form. When I was done with it, it was a totally different form from the one I learned in school. I have used other traditional forms. In my poem about sweeping, since you sweep with the broom and you dance—it's a coupling—I used rhyming couplets. I wrote a poem of advice mothers give to their daughters in a villanelle, because it's such a nagging form. But mostly the sonnet is the form I've worked with. It's the classic form in which we women were trapped, love objects, and I was trapped inside that voice and paradigm, and I wanted to work my way out of it.

My idea of traditional forms is that as women much of our heritage is trapped in them. But the cage can turn into a house if you housekeep it the right way. You housekeep it by working the words just so.

KELLY CHERRY
A Flashlight or Map

Poetic forms, established or nonce, are like maps of places no one's ever been. They lead the writer into uncharted territory; they show the writer where to go, even though they cannot know the way. This paradox is what keeps poetic form eternally interesting. If the writer knew in advance what she would find on her journey through the poem, she would not bother to make it. But she doesn't know; she never knows; she knows only that the form is there like a flashlight or map and that she will see what the form reveals and go where the form takes her. She knows, too, that the form will take her somewhere, will show her a place never before seen or seen so clearly.

I began writing in forms after I had found, in my opinion anyway, my own voice. I was sitting in on a class taught by that exemplary gentleman Allen Tate. He was fastidious in his personal habits and fastidious about poetic forms too, a stickler for the rules: no rhyming a plural with a singular; no shifting of stress for the sake of scansion, and on and on. My first poems in form seemed to me to be a regression; I felt I had learned to walk, even run, and now could barely crawl, tripping over my painfully counted metrical feet as I toddled and lurched through sonnets and villanelles.

But of course, within a couple of years I could see that encountering Allen Tate was one of the truly lucky events of my literary life. I was working in forms all during the time when most young writers were not. It was certainly not all that I was doing in my writing, but it was one of the things I was doing—working in forms.

I find now that I like to use strong rhymes. I like monosyllabic rhymes. I like using the ordinary rhymes others may tend to avoid. These rhymes suit me; so, for that matter, do quatrains. I am very fond of quatrains and blank verse. I like simple words or perhaps I should say accurate words, which, if not always, often, it seems to me, turn out to be simple words. I like a complexity that grows out of thought and feeling and imagery and is not embossed on language baroquely.

There is too much showmanship around, too much that is not an honest attempt to make that journey into the poem that is also a journey into the self.

But to make that journey—that is a great thing to do, it really is. It is something to live your life for.

RITA DOVE
An Intact World

Sonnet literally means "little song." The sonnet is a *heile Welt*, an intact world where everything is in sync, from the stars down to the tiniest mite on a blade of grass. And if the "true" sonnet reflects the music of the spheres, it then follows that any variation from the strictly Petrarchan or Shakespearean form represents a world gone awry.

Or does it? Can't form also be a talisman against disintegration? The sonnet defends itself against the vicissitudes of fortune by its charmed structure, its beautiful bubble. All the while, though, chaos is lurking outside the gate.

The ancient story of Demeter and Persephone is a modern dilemma as well: there is a point where the mother can no longer protect her children, and both mother and child must come to terms with this. In her grief, Demeter defies the law of nature by neglecting her agricultural duties so that the crops die. In varying degrees she is admonished or pitied by the other gods for the depth of her grief. She refuses to accept her fate; she strikes out against the Law; and it is this neglect that triggers Olympus to reach compromise with Hades. Demeter may still defy natural law when she grieves every Fall and Winter; but she must act "normal" for the rest of the year.

Sonnets seemed the proper mode for this work-in-progress—and not only in homage and as counterpoint to Rilke's *Sonnets to Orpheus*. Much has been said about the many ways to "violate" the sonnet in the service of American speech or modern love or whatever; I will simply say that I like how the sonnet comforts even while its prim borders (but what a pretty fence!) are stultifying; one is constantly bumping up against the Law. The Demeter/Persephone cycle of betrayal/regeneration seems ideally suited for this form, since all three—mother-goddess, daughter, and poet—are struggling to sing in their chains.

SUZANNE J. DOYLE
When the Ballerina Doesn't Point Her Toes

The other night I attended a performance of the San Francisco Ballet and saw a new dance choreographed by Val Caniparoli. It was a light-hearted piece about love that involved lots of pairing and unpairing of partners, and it actually got some laughs, which is rare at the ballet. As soon as the male lead lifted the ballerina from the floor her toes sprang up at right angles to her legs. Not surprisingly, when the ballerina doesn't point her toes on stage she looks funny. Why? Because it defies our formal expectations and thereby creates a tension which, in this case, we dispel by laughing. And those ballerina's toes just happen to illustrate what I consider one of the greatest advantages of working in poetic form: you have a norm, artificial as it may be, from which to deviate for dramatic effect. I love to deviate.

But not so often as to lose the definition of the metric line. Even free verse can't escape the underlying rhythm of the English language, alternating unstressed-stressed syllables called iambs — which also happen to echo the beat of the heart. It is a rhythm I never tire of hearing, reassuring in its predictability, yet as infinitely capable of variation as the human voices it informs: "The barge she sat in, like a burnish'd throne"; "I'll have a beer, a burger, and some fries." And while, of course, there is nothing inherently better about poems written in formal measures, it seems foolish to me for a poet to ignore the proven power of this rhythmical pattern in the language. Like ballet dancing without toe shoes, it can be done, and done beautifully, but there are some heights you just can't reach, some lines you just can't realize without the shoes. I love those heights; I love those lines.

EMILY GROSHOLZ
Art and Science

In the decade after I turned sixteen, I covered a couple of meters of paper with poetic five-finger exercises. (The proof is in three or four cartons stashed out of sight in my office.) Without any reliable topics or firm experience, I nonetheless dimly felt that I was working on the "music" of my poems, and that establishing a musical line was somehow essential to my project. When I was in my late twenties, my friend Catherine Iino made two invaluable remarks about my writing in the midst of a poetry group discussion. She observed that it wasn't really necessary to capitalize the beginning of every line of a poem; and that I usually wrote blank verse. I was quite surprised to discover that what my ear had been unconsciously listening to for all those years, and what my hand had finally learned how to produce, was iambic pentameter. But there it was, reams of it.

In her review of my first book, *The River Painter* (University of Illinois, 1984), Mary Kinzie also noticed this feature, or peculiarity, of my writing; she further pointed out its inherent weakness (formal monotony) and made me for the first time conscious of a device that I had been using to relieve the monotony, the interspersing of trimeter lines. Her remarks are, as always, worth quoting:

Emily Grosholz is effortless in the iambic mode. Even in seemingly unmetrical, or at least unsymmetrical lines, the processional gait of blank verse is the audible norm.... She sprinkles trimeter lines among the pentameters, a technique that detains—holds back—the magniloquent blank-verse effect. These reduced lines also permit her to catch her breath, focus on the truest syllable expression, which may be briefer than the decasyllabic line, before launching out again in iambic pentameter, fully armed to wrest large experience from the even larger and more forbidding blank-verse tradition. Staying actions like the reduced trimeter line are doubly helpful for poets like Grosholz, who can do the pentameter in their sleep and hence fall too easily back into heavily stichic passages where the lines are end-stopped, unvaried by caesuras, and metrically regular, varying only in the use of pyrrhics (unstressed feet).

(*American Poetry Review*, March/April 1984: 42)

Once I'd read this articulation of my own practice, I started to count feet as I wrote, trying to use the trimeter lines with greater care in the context of blank verse, and by and large suppressing the tetrameter lines I'd let in before because I wasn't really keeping track. Many of what I think are the most successful poems in my latest book, *Eden* (Johns Hopkins University Press, 1992), are written in this metrical mode that I, stricken by the computer age, can't help calling my default mode. And the reason is that these poems were written in the face of imperious experience: I had to get them down, and get them down fast in the interstices of my overstuffed life. So I used the formal devices I knew would work for me.

All the same, I have from time to time played with other formal devices, and hope in the future to employ them at leisure, if I ever have any again. I've tried writing short line verse, which is usually not so much dimeter or trimeter in some particular foot, but rather accentual verse with two or three beats. And, in my opinion, my accentual verse so far is a bit shaky. I've also made attempts at rhyming schemes, most notably in my sonnets. But the rhyme is almost always slant, and I have never perfectly honored the scheme; indeed, often I was never quite sure which one I'd picked. Congruity of sound is an important dimension of the music of my poems, but it is more likely to be managed by assonance and consonance, slant-rhyme, and internal rhyme than by full end rhyme. In this I am a child of my half-century.

Lately I've noticed two tendencies in my writing, which strain away from iambic pentameter. On the one hand, I've been saying famous tetrameter poems over and over to myself ("Loveliest of trees, the cherry now," "Whose woods these are, I think I know," "Oh God, our help in ages past") in an attempt to secure that slightly shorter line-length, which lends itself to poems of special elegance and concision. On the other hand, I've been tending more and more to begin all or most lines with a stressed syllable: this could be just a truncated iamb, with the light first syllable left off, or pushed back up to the preceding line. Or it could be the first step in exploring the possibilities of trochaic feet. Who knows, perhaps after a while I'll move on to dactyls. In any case, the art and science of metrics has proved itself a source of illumination, occasional tears, and amusement in my career as a poet, and I look forward to the next stage of discovery.

MARILYN HACKER
Meditating Formally

The choice and use of a fixed or structured form—whether I learned it or invented it—has always been, for me, one of the primary pleasures of writing poetry. I have no political or aesthetic rationale for it, except that I like it. The intersection of that very sensory/sensual satisfaction, related to music, related to walking, breathing, all the rhythmic bodily motions, and the emotional or intellectual difficulty, complexity, of the narrative, lyric or meditative treatment of certain subjects creates a tension that is, for me, a mental equivalent of those physical states where pleasure approaches pain, or pain, pleasure—whether the activity involved is sex or hiking. I've never formally meditated, but I suspect the process is similar to what I've just described, indeed, as "meditating formally." Here, though, the focus of heightened awareness is language, and the multiple purposes of meaning, music and modulation it serves. I experience the same heightened interest and involvement as a reader of metrically structured poetry: an initial and a continued impetus for writing that way myself.

When I see a young (or not-so-young) writer counting syllables on her fingers, or marking stresses for a poem she's writing, or one she's reading, I'm pretty sure we'll have something in common, whatever our other differences may be.

RACHEL HADAS
The Skills of the Stow-Away

I began writing imitative poems by the time I was nine or ten—I can remember, with embarrassment, a balladish piece about wee bairns being put to bed. By thirteen, like countless other young people, I was aping e.e. cummings; around the same time there was also a fake-medieval ballad about the Crucifixion, and, a little later, scores of Shakespearean sonnets, some in more or less Elizabethan guise, some in accents closer to Meredith's *Modern Love*. Nothing is quite as world-weary as a fifteen-year-old.

A year or so later, at the end of high school and the beginning of college, I was starting to write poems I now regard as juvenilia but not absolute pastiche: "Super Nivem," "The Fall of Troy," "After the Cave," and—after my father's death—"That Time, This Place," and "Daddy." The best of these poems (many of which are collected in my first book, *Starting from Troy*) feel less like imitations than like imaginative syntheses of my reading and experience. I had no one model for any of them, and superficially speaking I made up my forms (the three-line stanzas of "Super Nivem" or the syllabics of "Ode") as I went along. But iambic pentameter was ringing in my ears, together with dactylic hexameter, Sapphics, Alcaics: I had four years of Latin (the best of it studying Vergil) in high school and started Greek in college.

The point is not that at a given hour I said, "I'll write like Tibullus/ Propertius/Catullus/Archilochus"—though translating the odd fragment didn't hurt. But I understood fairly early on that originality, in poetry, is a highly relative term. All writing is rewriting—something like this was my first crude formulation of the idea John Hollander puts much more elegantly: writing, far from being easier than reading (as beginning poets often think), is instead a difficult *form* of reading. Thus in a course on Roman elegy I came across the Greek term *paraclausithyron*, a generic term for a lament sung before the locked door of the beloved. Of course I made the term mine by writing my own *paraclausithyron*, with a certain suite in Harvard's Adams House in mind.

Wherever poems come from and wherever it is they fly off to, the young poet, and then the not-so-young poet, needs some of the skills of the stow-away: to climb aboard the vehicle, to make use of it to get you where you want to go. Is the vehicle formal verse technique? I'd rather call it all the poems ever written before—and having said that I realize I'm echoing a favorite passage of mine from Robert Frost, so—moving from aeronautics to meteorology—I'll let him have the last word:

> No one given to looking underground in spring can have failed to notice how a bean starts its growth from the seed. Now the manner of a poet's germination is less like that of a bean in the ground than of a water-spout at sea. He [sic] has to begin as a cloud of all the other poets he ever read. That can't be helped. And first the cloud reaches down toward the water from above and then the water reaches up toward the cloud from below and finally cloud and water join together to roll as one pillar between heaven and earth. The base of water he picks up from below is of course all the life he ever lived outside of books.

PHILLIS LEVIN
Embracing Fate

When I entered my freshman year of college I showed an alarmingly large manuscript of poems to one of the poets offering a workshop that semester. He weighed the manuscript in his hands, and then began to browse through page after page, skipping around and quoting lines he found especially felicitous or clumsy. He seemed to be looking for something in particular that he could not find. After a pause he asked me to show him a poem written in the first person that was not in rhyme and meter. Until that moment it had not occurred to me that since the age of twelve I had been writing with an unconscious system. I wrote many poems in free verse, and many more in blank verse or deploying both rhyme and meter, but most of my work in free verse was in the third person, and everything in the first person was in meter. So there was nothing—not one poem—I could show him that was free of measure and also in the first person.

The polarization of first person poems in measure and third person poems in free verse (some in rhyme and meter) was not a conscious choice. I needed to speak in the first person from a more formalized space, perhaps to give myself the distance necessary to overcome my introversion. Perhaps I needed—and continue to need—formal elements in order to create a ritualized experience that would allow me to exist in the bounds of the poem (a field of play) instead of the bounds of life, to enter an altered state, a heightened relation to the temporal. It was embarrassing to the other students that I didn't know I wasn't supposed to be doing this. How had I managed to avoid entering the modern world—that is, the mid-seventies—when it was especially out of fashion to read anything that wasn't contemporary or to write in a style alluding in any way to the subjects and forms of a literary tradition, i.e., to write under the influence of anything other than one's own immediate personal history? It had never occurred to me that I had to make a choice, yet somehow I was beginning to feel pressured, as if there were an allegiance I had failed to make and a loyalty I should have separated myself from.

Not until I was twenty-five did I allow myself to return to experimenting with meter, off-rhyme and rhyme. This change was precipitated by a conversation with a British critic who had read my poems and remarked on their internal music, and how he felt that I was resisting my own musicality, not allowing it to develop. Yes, I had internalized the subtle censorship of the 1970's, and now I had to return to the source and learn how to write the poems my ear wanted to hear while making a sense that was not obscure and hermetic, as was my earliest work. Writing almost exclusively in free verse for five years had separated me from what had come too easily, and thus when I began to work again with meter and rhyme my poems showed a confluence of more forces and possibilities, a familiarity with the contemporary idiom combined with a greater understanding of texture and prosody.

For me embracing form is a form of embracing fate, of simultaneously accepting and resisting, absorbing and shaping the forces of language and life, the interplay of the arbitrary and the given with the shaped and the chosen. So if, for example, my poem "Dark Horse" is halting in cadence, fluid and then awkward, one will feel and hear and see the meaning that is not stated, one will be involved through the prosody in my portrait of this horse, who embodied beauty, mystery, form, delicacy, vulnerability, and nobility. It is not necessary to know that I was thinking of Poland when writing this poem, that I had befriended a Polish painter who had spent hours talking of his country's complex history and its tragic position in 1984 before the fall of Communism; that I had seen this horse before and after this conversation, and that the horse began to embody a country, whose fate was that of a dark horse. But I felt I had to create in the poem an internal music that would be a simulacrum of the heavy and light, the gentle and the harsh, the fast and the slow. I searched for patterns of sound that would suggest the intrinsic relationship of the auditory and the visual, that would transform the coincidences of sound into an inevitable, evocative meaning. In the last line of the fourth stanza, "Dry leaves sighing through wind and tears," I attempted to bind these correspondences as tightly as possible in order to create a synesthetic effect. And so the word "sighing" carries in it the long "i" and the long "e" that occur first in the word "dry," then in the word "leaves," vowels that recur as echoes in "wind" and "tears." There are other presences at work here, as well, including an allusion to Auden's "The Fall of Rome" and Hardy's "During Wind and Rain," two poems that opened the possibility of intensifying both density and clarity. Perhaps my relationship to form and rhythm is a constant struggle to come as close as possible to the impossible. I suppose I am looking for wholeness and completion, or at least the patterns that call into being an image of wholeness and completion.

MARILYN NELSON
Sense of Discovery

Frankly, I find it easier to write in form than to write in free verse. There's a sense of closure, of completeness, in form which doesn't exist in free verse, and a tremendous sense of discovery in finding a rhyme or slant-rhyme. For slant-rhyme, I find that if I listen to the "weight" of the vowels, then balanced vowel sounds of equivalent "weights," the poem—I don't know how to say this—feels satisfying. The use of form seems to me to be more appropriate for poems about the historical past, and the rhythmical, "dancy" music for the poem about a dance ("Diverne's Waltz") seems . . . well, it just feels right. As for the sonnets: I've been experimenting with sonnets for some time, and enjoy working within that small tight space. I do not especially advocate formalist verse, though it does, I think, offer more "memorability" than free verse, and a strong sense of being part of a long tradition.

MOLLY PEACOCK
One Green, One Blue: One Point About Formal Verse Writing and Another About Women Writing Formal Verse

The dazzling confusion of style and substance, like a brilliant feather one cannot say for sure is absolutely green or absolutely blue, is what we refer to when we say that form creates content in a poem and content form.

But this forgets the initial palette of the creator of the poem, who knows (or hopes she knows) how much green and how much blue are required for the mix. Common wisdom says that the poet must choose the suitable form for the subject, where the mind and the language are at one. It says appropriateness is all: the form must be capable of the same gesture as the feeling. Supporting this is the brilliance of finished poems, their iridescence far removed from the initial palette the poet composed, where the blue was distinctly blue, the green distinctly green, and the leap of the imagination still.

I feel the initial choice, the conscious choice, of one traditional verse form over another, is not always the choice to match the feeling, but rather a choice to contain, to control, or otherwise make the feeling safe to explore. Take Elizabeth Bishop's late poem "Pink Dog," for example. Here are the first four stanzas, which occur during Mardi gras:

PINK DOG

Rio de Janeiro

The sun is blazing and the sky is blue.
Umbrellas clothe the beach in every hue.
Naked, you trot across the avenue.

Oh, never have I seen a dog so bare!
Naked and pink, without a single hair...
Startled, the passersby draw back and stare.

Of course they're mortally afraid of rabies.
You are not mad; you have a case of scabies
but look intelligent. Where are your babies?

(A nursing mother, by those hanging teats.)
In what slum have you hidden them, poor bitch,
while you go begging, living by your wits?

Why on earth would she choose to use rhymed triplets? What a bumpy, comic way in which to lavish solicitude on a hairless bitch out without her babies during carnival in Rio. But the enormity of the subject for Bishop — a mother dog who has abandoned her children to enter the mad world of carnival just as Elizabeth Bishop's own mother abandoned her and was consigned to a mental institution — is not at all comic. The depth of feeling does not match the form; it is much larger than tercets tripping samba-like along. The feeling is the opposite of comic: it is huge, and tragically overriding; it shadowed her entire life, reaching wherever in the hemispheres she tried to escape it. The form, almost the opposite of the feeling, makes the feeling explorable; it is the anchor of the opposite which makes the feeling approachable and which allows the humor and the light touch that give the poem its brilliance.

The tension of the lightness of the triplets, the clap-clap-clap of the rhymes festive and absurd as mardi gras, against the depth of the poet's complex feelings about the disoriented animal, give the poem that iridescent confusion of form and content. The triple rhymes create the emotion, while the emotion creates the demand for the triple rhymes in such balance that no other choice would be right. Indeed, in final products no other choice is "right." But the initial choice, to contain, to order, to form, to combat the overwhelming darkness of that abandonment, almost opposes the very feeling it is chosen to express, and therefore it makes a safe vehicle for expression. The verse form almost becomes the arms of comfort in which to express the enormity of emotion. This is how the huge inverted world of carnival, like the huge inverted world of Bishop's mother's absence, can be both invoked and tolerated—and made to seem seamless.

To me, formal verse makes impossible emotions possible. Look at the contrast between the children's laughter and the dark tower of night in Barbara Howes' poem "Early Supper," based on the triolet. Barbara Howes uses the highly repetitive triolet as a stanza form, building up the enormity of night in apposition to the contained repetition of the incredibly strict stanza structure. The containment of this strictness implies a terrifying chaos right from the beginning when the poem talks about children's laughter: "Laughter of children brings / The kitchen down with laughter. / While the old kettle sings / Laughter of children brings...." The children's laughter exists in an atmosphere of threat, simply because the verse form that boxes the threat is so small, ornate, and delicately hinged. Thus when the children are put to bed and the dark tower of night is introduced, the threat is openly acknowledged, and finally the poem makes sense. Here is the last of its three stanzas in full:

> They trail upstairs to bed,
>   And night is a dark tower.
> The kettle calls: instead
> They trail upstairs to bed,
> Leaving warmth, the coppery-red
>   Mood of their carnival hour.
> They trail upstairs to bed,
>   And night is a dark tower.

At the opening one almost resists it—what is this silly poem about kettles and laughter? Too, one almost resists the Bishop poem in its opening—do we have to read about this silly dog?—because the containment has yet to reveal its purpose, or what it contains (terror, of course).

That observation could quickly lead to the fallacy of the verse form as a container or the *outside* of something, and therefore, as an outside, something superficial, not deep, merely technical. But when I speak of containment, I am speaking about not being overwhelmed; I am not speaking about tying something up in a package to be shelved. I am indicating a poetic method of coping with the vastness of emotion that makes the poem worth writing in the first place. If you think of form as the outside of an Inside, that is only half the truth. Verse form is also inside the Inside. It acts as a skeleton as well as a skin. It is a body. Verse form literally embodies the emotion of the poem, in the sense that embodiment both *is* and *contains* the life it is the body of. The need to embody the dangerous is both a need to surround it *and* then to live it. Therefore the initial choice is to contain and the subsequent writing allows the danger to live as made possible by the containment.

❖ ❖ ❖ ❖

How I happened to permit myself to tackle a vast male tradition and also be so playful with it is due, in part, to my female models. I very much wanted to write "real" poetry and to me that usually meant Shakespeare or the Romantics and that always meant emotional. So part of my initial goal was very male-modeled, and naive, too, born of the values engendered by my teachers and of the colossal ambition these values encouraged. I loved the density of the formal enterprise, but the other part of my goal, to express emotion as directly as I could, caused me to shy away from the tyranny of perfection because, for me, emotion had to come first. The reason I loved the formal density is that with each poem I wrote I had to conquer the colossal fear of saying what I felt I could not say. At first it was the fear; of the sexually explicit, or the fear of revealing my father's alcoholism, then my position as adult hostage to this early abuse. Finally I realized every subject I was drawn to made me afraid. This continues in my life, and the poem "Devolution" is an example. It's frightening to me to discuss holy communion as the eating of God. I feared throughout the poem that I was transgressing if I discussed my childish idea that eating the host meant eating a part of Jesus—

His esophagus? His eyeball? His penis? Elizabeth Bishop's stylistic "imperfections" inspired me. If a rhyme scheme didn't suit her, she dropped it; if she felt like rhyming a syllable with a whole word she playfully hyphenated the word into two lines, and so do I, internalizing her example in "Devolution."

I was delighted once to hear a (probably apocryphal) story that Marianne Moore used colored pencils to keep her sound patterns in place as she wrote. That is the kind of thing I do when I work with learning-disabled children, and the kind of very simple system I need for myself. The story permitted me to draw charts of poems, laying them out spatially so that I could concentrate on the emotional complexities without losing the "grid" of the format. I did this in "ChrisEaster," which was very painful to write. Even the broken rhyme scheme I used (a mutilated abab) had to be charted separately before I began the poem. Otherwise, I couldn't have gotten through it.

I always look to female models, "minor" though they are thought to be. One important one is Elinor Wylie's sonnet sequence "Wild Peaches." I felt instantly on reading it that Wylie had started out to write one sonnet and had overrun it into more because she was out of lines but not out of things to say. "Good Girl" takes a bit of Wylie's advice. It's what I would call a heroic sonnet, but "Good Girl" came out unintentionally four lines over because I had more to say — I couldn't contain myself. Through "Wild Peaches" Elinor Wylie released me from the tyranny of fourteen lines, but not the guidance, safety, and mirroring of emotion that form offers. That's just what "Good Girl" is about; by running over I stopped myself from being a good girl to the sonnet.

I began to think of writing poetry as doing needlework: embroidering anything ambitious, however, even your stitches, requires you to negotiate tons of mistakes. For instance, "Anger Sweetened" appears to be a perfect sonnet, but my rhyme scheme got away from me. (It goes abbbaaccbddee.) Yet the odd rhyme recurrence easily becomes part of the fabric of the poem. I let this happen intentionally, for the rhymes seemed to be a part of the expression of the anger, their "mistakeness" part of the general mistakeness of repressing anger. Look at quilts or lace or medieval tapestries: for all the perfect skill are the nubs, the sew-overs, the piecings together, a revision process allowing for a conglomerate of mistakes and a final, integrated whole. To me that is what craft is.

And that is how I come by my female poetic heritage: Edna Millay smoking cigarettes in sonnets, Christina Rossetti's bald sadness, Charlotte Mew's reconsiderations on the stairs after a party, Louise Bogan's panic made palpable, all showing themselves, their humanity and the femaleness of their emotion through bending the tension of the verse strictures, either in feeling or in form, all making the decision to choose traditional verse and all to alter it to their purposes. In "How I Had To Act" I tell the story of a shopping mistake; I was so interested in getting the narrative out that I didn't set a tight frame for myself. I felt if I rhymed my two lines in a stanza I'd be doing all right, since I wasn't quite sure how it would all turn out. I needed guidance by rhyme, not entrapment; I needed to be able to play.

It is not that men cannot be playful in their formal verse enterprises (I think instantly of Robert Creeley, Philip Larkin, Auden, Richard Wilbur, Richard Howard, and James Merrill) but I often, perhaps wrongly, think of them as admiring rigor more than I do. I feel encouraged by the whimsy, the inexactitude, the changes in the type of containment women poets chose and choose and feel the female embodiment of traditional verse to be altered by a sensibility that acknowledges fluctuation and imperfection, while at the same time it values the interplay between the chaos of emotion and the order of form.

I am making two points really. One is that style is not always consonant with substance, that in fact, form can be chosen in opposition to the magnitude of feeling the poet wishes to evoke and therefore the form can embody its opposite. I do not think that it's particularly linked to one sex or the other, but that it is in the nature of the initial choice of one form over another. The other point is about the tolerance of imperfection in technique that I sense is particularly female, though heaven knows I do not prove this, and only suggest that it is there. Perhaps because it is so true of my own work, I may be generalizing too easily to others'. My aim was to inquire into the making of the beautiful blue-green feather that projects the dazzling confusion of feeling and form in the final product of a poem. This bifurcated into my two points. One was green. One was blue.

MARY JO SALTER
A Beautiful Surface

Formalism is one means of "finishing" something. The crude formalist, the versifier, may count himself finished once everything rhymes. The better poet seeks a finish that may employ, but goes beyond, the conventional tools: rhyme, meter, syllabics, stanzas. Poets who move us write not only to relieve the pressure of present feelings but to put an end to them. They write about lost lovers in order to write them off. Even the warm tribute to restless Spring freezes it. The most anguished elegy is a polished coffin to silence the poet's own heart in.

This the reader opens; for him, or her, the poet's heart beats again. With any luck, readers mistake that heart for their own. What was finished has begun somewhere else.

It's a tired misapprehension, then, that chains formalism to the dead past or to an assumed coolness of feeling. Nothing unsettles us so much — in poetry, or people — as a beautiful surface.

Robinson, Frost, and Jeffers and the New Narrative Poetry

Mark Jarman

There is a twofold difference between those Americans writing nar-
rative poetry today, especially among the younger generation who make
up what is being called increasingly the neo-narrative movement, and
their forerunners, Edwin Arlington Robinson, Robert Frost, and
Robinson Jeffers. First, whereas Robinson might have looked to George
Crabbe for his example, and Robert Frost might have looked to William
Wordsworth and over his shoulder at Robinson, and Robinson Jeffers
might well have had in mind the anonymous border ballads and the po-
ems and novels of Thomas Hardy, today's young American narrative poet
must look to Robinson, Frost, and Jeffers. If he or she looks beyond
them, to their own English masters, these modern American figures in-
tervene. The second difference is that modernism itself intervenes be-
tween Robinson, Frost, and Jeffers and the contemporary view of them.
Unlike Eliot or Pound, neither Robinson, Frost, nor Jeffers was part of
a trans-Atlantic axis or took part in describing the modernist aesthetic.
Only Frost proposed a poetics, his modest but sheerly original method of
sentence-sounds. Robinson and Jeffers worked by example and neither
would be included among what is now called the high modernists. Their
narrative approaches, like Frost's, were linear and not spatial, coherent
and not fragmented. Their intentions, too, in telling their stories might
have been recognized by Crabbe, Wordsworth, or Hardy as moral, for-
mally reflecting humanity's proper relationship to the world. It is doubt-
ful that these older English poets would have recognized much in Eliot's
and Pound's deliberately skewed and fragmented approaches to the nar-
rative mode.

Although I am convinced that Crabbe, Wordsworth, and Hardy would
have looked kindly on Robinson, Frost, and Jeffers, would Robinson, Frost,
and Jeffers approve of what is going on in the narrative movement today?
I am not sure. In fact, I have some serious doubts about whether they
would. However, despite the doubts that I can imagine they would have, I

From *The New Criterion* 1.5 (Jan. 1983): 41-46.

think their skepticism might be applied to real virtues in the neo-narrative movement and only a few shortcomings.

The successes of these three masters of American narrative poetry are notable for their difference in length. Robinson is best short, Frost at a medium stretch, and Jeffers, who reserved his narrative skill for his longer poems, is best when extending himself.

Although Robinson could and did write long narrative poems, his greatest stories are told in poems that are often shorter than "The Ballad of Sir Patrick Spens." Sometimes they are sonnets, like the one about the butcher Reuben Bright or the mysteriously happy Cliff Klingenhagen. There are the brief poems in quatrains about Richard Cory and Miniver Cheevy; there are the lyrical tetrameters about the miller and his wife who kill themselves; there is the old anthology piece, "Mr. Flood's Party," which is still a great poem, despite our familiarity and the undergraduate contempt it may have bred. Robinson's forays into the longer poem, like his Tennysonian retellings of the Camelot stories, are about as interesting, now, as Tennyson's own. An argument for the resurgence of narrative verse cannot be based on *Lancelot* as it could not be on *Idylls of the King*. There is a friendly, ambling, yet profound movement to the medium-length "Isaac and Archibald," but for narrative compression that pivots on a fully created character, sometimes complete with tragic flaw, Robinson is the master—Dickens in fourteen lines.

One looks around today for anyone who chooses to work in his mode, to set out the entire story, naming the names resonantly, in a small space. When a contemporary narrative poet works that small, and that formally, the story is usually an autobiographical portion of the life or it is a series of events involving a persona. T.R. Hummer's marvelous "Carrier," a sonnet sequence from his first book *The Angelic Orders*, is an example of the latter. Hummer displays Robinson's compassion for his characters, for their tragic as well as their comic fates. Here is "Looking in His Rearview Mirror, the Rural Carrier Thinks He Catches a Glimpse of the Angel of Death Hanging over George Gillespie's Mailbox."

> A clear day, not even a crow in the air
> Over George Gillespie's as I put the mail
> In his box. The usual stuff, except for the one bill,
> The one he's been waiting for, from the funeral parlor.
> He's asked about it twice. The first time was the day
> After his wife was buried. He came to the road

When he saw my car. Asked if I had it. Said he owed
Somebody something. Said he was ready to pay.

The second time was some days later. He just stood there,
And when I shook my head he walked off, nodding.
I haven't seen him since, though every morning
When I come by, his curtains tremble. He knows I'm here.
He knows my moves, how I hang out my window to slip
Something in his box. He knows how to add things up.

When a contemporary poet interested in telling a story invents a character
as rich as Hummer's mail carrier, he is more likely to give him an entire
series of poems than to compress everything into one sonnet. Certain char-
acters of Robinson's make more than one appearance in his poems (one
thinks of Flammonde), but he would have made the one story work—as
Hummer makes the story of George Gillespie work, albeit as an episode in
the mail carrier's life. Robinson's legacy to the neo-narrative is the episodic
power of the short form, which has now been extended to the sequence
through the contemporary interest in personae. Our current extension of
character through sequence may have been seen by Robinson as an at-
tenuation, either in search of a moral center or in flight from one. The
intervention of modernism may be seen in not wanting to round off the
life—to send Richard Cory home to the pistol or Miniver Cheevy and Eben
Flood to the bottle. The dilemma for the neo-narrative poet, then, is whether
or not to commit himself to a character's fate. Unless he does commit him-
self, he may find he has created characters more like Edgar Lee Masters'
small town stereotypes than like Robinson's sharp-edged yet three-dimen-
sional human beings.

In fact, it may be Masters who appeals to us, though I say so with great
reluctance. What intervenes between us and Robinson is modern relativism,
the reticence to judge, unless the character is part of a historical sequence
(consider the numerous historical poems of late, for example, about Nazis)
and history has already judged. Perhaps the most successful Robinsonian
character created in a narrative poem in recent years is Robert McDowell's
bootlegger in "Quiet Money," the title poem of his first book. Named "Joe,"
as in "average Joe," this character flies the Atlantic before Lindbergh; his
job is to bring liquor in from Norway. Joe is forced to endure his obscurity
while Lindbergh enjoys celebrity then suffers the tragedy of his child's kid-
nap and murder. Joe must come to terms with his own absence from history,
which he decides is preferable to Lindbergh's place in history, and thus en-

joys the rounded fate of a Robinsonian character. "Quiet Money," however, is a poem of over 200 lines and hard to imagine as a sonnet.

Robert Frost's approach to narrative, his poems of medium length in his early books, *North of Boston, Mountain Interval,* and *New Hampshire,* may be better suited to contemporary workers in the form. Many of Frost's narratives are based on the classical eclogue, a conversation between rustics, as in "Home Burial" and "Death of a Hired Man"; in others, a single voice dominates, although a narrator usually introduces the speechmaker and lets him or her go on, as in "The Black Cottage"; another example is the conversation between the mother and son in "The Witch of Coös" for the benefit of their overnight guest. The dramatic monologue takes an interesting form in Frost that can be seen in today's monologue poems. Unlike Browning's dramatic monologues, in which we can imagine the stage, the other characters, Frost's dramatic monologues tend more to be voiced ruminations about the speaker's life or inner life with no audience in mind, except the reader, as in "Wild Grapes" and "The Pauper Witch of Grafton." Only "A Servant to Servants" has Browning's sense of the full stage being acknowledged, the play being stopped for the speech, but there the poor woman uses her audience as an excuse to talk to herself. Frost does not make a point with names, either, the way Robinson does, unless the name is the point, as in the Starks who gather in "Generations of Men" and chat about the streak of madness in the family or the little girl in "Maple" who must contend with people who do not believe that "Maple" is a proper name for a child. If a name is unusual, like Toffile Lajway in "The Witch of Coös," it is only as an odd fact, to be verified on the mailbox. Frost is interested in what his people *say* and not so much in what happens to them, what their fates are or are to be. What they say and how they say it in blank verse are the pleasures of Frost's narrative poetry, more than the stories he is telling. As the critic Vereen Bell has pointed out, one does not necessarily go to Frost for his plots. This is not to say that plot does not exist in Frost's narrative poems, but it is more as a portion of a life, an episode with the rest of the life left to speculation, sometimes certain, more often not.

Frost's narrator is rarely central, but usually is along for the walk or the ride, as in "A Fountain, a Bottle, a Donkey's Ears, and Some Books," or he is the scene-setter, as in "The Witch of Coös" or, again, the person who goes along with the minister in "The Black Cottage" or who serves as an ear for the cranky mother-in-law in "The Housekeeper." This is an appealing role for the contemporary narrative poet who cannot, as Frost rarely could, completely dispense with himself or herself in a narrative poem. To serve as witness, bringing his own character or situation to bear while letting the subject shine forth, shine brighter than the poet in word or deed, was Frost's goal in his narratives, one he abandoned, as he abandoned narrative, as his fame increased and he realized that it was his pithy lyrics people wanted. Two poets who are working particularly well in the narrative tradition that Frost adapted from Wordsworth and made his own are Andrew Hudgins and Garrett Hongo.

Since Hudgins works primarily in the blank verse line, it would be good to look first at him. "Sotto Voce," from his first book *Saints and Strangers*, adapts its title from music and gives the phrase dramatic meaning. Hudgins presents himself as our narrator, but in more of a comic light than Frost ever would have presented *himself*. Like Frost, Hudgins wants to turn a phrase into a dramatic moment, to make the emotion of the poem come from the way he tells the story. Here are the poem's opening lines:

> I'm standing in the university
> library, staring at the German books
> and I don't parle eine word of Allemand.
> Actually I'm listening to a girl named Beth
> call her boyfriend in El Paso.
> He's leaving her for work in Mexico
> and other reasons. She doesn't understand,
> repeats out loud the things he says, as if
> the sound of her own voice will help make sense
> of what is happening. And even now
> her voice is airy, cool, and beautiful;
> only her humor perks into uncertainty
> as she tries to turn around his serious
> long distance voice.

Although I am not arguing that Hudgins *sounds* like Frost (there are still actual Frost imitators around), it is hard not to see the Frostian touch in how the girl repeats what her boyfriend says out loud, "as if / the sound of her own voice will help make sense / of what is happening." The simple language and the sense of that phrase fall out along the blank verse arrangement as Frost would have had it. Also, we're given a multiplicity of viewpoints: the speaker's, the girl's, the imagined party on the other end of the line, and the poet's. We're not supposed to be overhearing the girl's conversation, but how can we help it? One thinks of Frost's late and brilliant short poem, "Loud Talk," in which the speaker and his companions overhear an argument coming from a house at night as they pass by. Frost reports the substance of the fight between a married couple and some of its actual phrasing, because the phrasing contains the truth of the matter.

Hudgins watches Beth "pull pink tissues from her purse."

> With practiced hands she shreds them into strips
> then floats them to the phone booth's tiny floor,
> the phone held lovingly between her ear and shoulder.
> As if it were already painless, she's
> reminding him of the evening they made love
> (Her alto—half in music—lingers on
> the simple words) in her parents' queen-size bed.

Clearly, it is the way she is talking, the "alto" of her "sotto voce," as much as what she is talking about that moves the poet. She tells her boyfriend that she had to change the sheets and make up an excuse for her mother, saying she'd fallen asleep there herself and, for the first time since she was a child, wet the bed.

> She talks until he starts, I think, to laugh,
> and she laughs back in harmony with him,
> the laughs oddly resonant though his
> is still in Texas and I can't really hear it.

Almost everything is imagined here. One can recall Frost warning, "Let's be accurate, but not too accurate." When the girl glances up and catches the poet watching, he quickly sticks his head in a copy of *The Tin Drum*, "Which by fifty-fifty chance is right / side up." The poem ends with a parting word and a final dramatic scene.

> ...*Regret*
> is the only word that I can make out clearly,
> and even then I can't decide if it's hers
> or if she's repeating what he said.
> But with a smile she hangs the phone up and
> clicks down the hall to the elevator, leaving
> the bottom of the booth fluffed with pink tissue.
> Over the whole of German literature
> I see her smiling, framed in the closing doors;
> her afterimage holds the same sure pose,
> floating on air, in the empty shaft, and fading.

Earlier in the poem Hudgins admits, having regarded her with a stranger's intimacy, that he can understand why the boyfriend "had to run to El Paso / to leave her." The poet has fallen in love with her a little himself, as I think we do as readers, and the final depiction of her smiling and in a sure pose, floating on air, is an imagined triumph. But the poem ends, as it began, in a kind of *medias res* for the speaker; though the episode is over, the portion of the subject's life has taken shape in the speaker's own. This provisional quality, which characterizes much of Frost's narrative poetry, is attractive in a way that Robinson's fuller, tragic version may not be.

Yet Hudgins' comic self-portrait is in conflict, somewhat, with the character of the girl. It asks for our sympathy, too. Usually Frost's narrator has little or no character, and may seem much less vivid, much less alive than the character he allows us to meet. Garrett Hongo puts himself in a perfect situation to observe in this way in "Metered Onramp," from his second book, *The River of Heaven*. All that he observes in the poem, though he claims it "pursues (him) through sleep / and waking daydream," originates from his car window as he waits to get on the freeway in L.A. on the "Alondra onramp." There, he would see, in "a swale of new fieldgrass . . . / sloping under the powerlines,"

> The bums and ragpickers,
> the shopping bag people
> with their makeshift rakes
> and scavenged handtrowels,
> sifting through the loose dirt and refuse piles
> for whatever treasure they could find....

If this seems to be a typical urban desolation, consider again its roots in Frost, who could give us equally defeated places and people in New England, or Wordsworth, who could show the moors dotted with dismal little ponds where leeches bred. From such unpromising material, these poets work with a faith that meaning is inherent. Hongo discovers his leech-gatherer, his mudtime tramp.

> Her name was Sally, I think,
> and she reeked of wine and excrement
> but always had money, wadded up
> like pads of Kleenex mixed with carrot tops
> and cabbage leaves stuffed in the deep pockets
> of her long Joseph's coat.

Hongo's prosody is not the traditional one of counted feet, the one Frost would have recognized, but rather of repetition, parallelism, increment, and the laying down of interesting sentences over lines. The poem ends with a long cadenza of such free verse techniques as he remembers one day seeing Sally launch herself from the crest of the hill, as if for the delight of those waiting their turn to enter the freeway.

> She seemed to stop more than a couple of times,
> blocked by a tire or a trough in the dirt,
> splashing in the puddles,
> but kept going, shoving herself downhill
> flinging her body shoulders first
> and scuffling over the crusts of mud
> and small piles of broken fencing.
> All the while she flailed her arms,
> billowing her open coat that,
> now drenched in fresh doses of mud,
> slapped and whispered sexually
> against her spindly thighs.
> *Hallelujah*, she was saying,
> *A-le-leu*, over and over
> as we marvelled, crouching in our cars.

Certainly Frost might have cited more than one opportunity to make Hongo's poem metrical. In Hudgins, he would have taken exception to the count in some lines. But the example present in both poems is of the Frost who trusted the narrative and the mystery of the story to which he might not be able to draw a conclusion. The marvelous life that goes on as we shrink from it was a theme Frost expressed himself (think of the professor sliding down his pillow at the end of "One Hundred Collars"); it is also the life that draws us out of ourselves, out of our hiding places, like Hudgins behind his ridiculous book or Hongo in his car.

It is much more difficult to discuss Jeffers' relationship to the neo-narrative movement in American poetry because his example is at once the most daunting and least appealing. His characters act out dramas unmitigated by Robinson's compassion or Frost's moral relativism, but determined by Jeffers' merciless vision of humanity as an aberration of nature. Jeffers' determinism derives from Hardy's "Immanent Will," from his own Calvinist background (his father was an ordained Presbyterian minister), his belief in contemporary science, and his Spenglerian vision of western civilization's decline. He preferred to see man as a biological phenomenon rather than as little less than the angels. His philosophy is the moral foundation of his poetry, especially his narrative poetry. He set about in his long narratives to make humanity enact social and biological forces that he saw working to bring about the end of civilization. It is a much simpler matter to find the influence of Robinson or Frost at work today than of this austere soulmate of Thomas Hardy. Would Jeffers be more appealing if, like Hardy, he had written novels instead? For if one considers Jeffers' narrative poems beside Hardy's bleakest books, *Jude the Obscure*, *The Mayor of Casterbridge*, *Tess of the D'Urbervilles*, *The Return of the Native*, one finds the same fools damned by much the same fate. In Jeffers' case, the isolation on a coast too grand for their aspirations twists his characters to madness: man doesn't measure up to nature, to the creation. Whether we like it or not, this profound moral vision is the motivating force of Jeffers' narrative poems.

Though it is impossible to find anyone working on Jeffers' terms, some do see the long poem as a way of exploring a unified deterministic vision. Chase Twichell's "My Ruby of Lasting Sadness," from her second book *The Odds*, is held together by a scientific understanding of fate. Part narrative, part meditation, the poem relates a love affair the poet had when very young and her reunion, later in life, with the man who broke her heart. He has "laid claim / to the demimonde" and apparently is a drug dealer in Southeast Asia. She has "retired / to the regions of the north," a poet living in New England. Though the two have "divided the world" between them, a deep connection remains, one that seems to have determined who they are, and which is symbolized by a ruby in a golden lotus that he gives her as a gift. To explain their connection, Twichell appropriates one of the most speculative theories of recent physics, Bell's Theorem:

> that at a fundamental level,
> disparate parts of the universe
> may make an intimate connection,
> and furthermore
> that things once joined remain
> even over vast distances
> and through the shifts of time
> attached by an unknown force
> its speed exceeding that of light,
> a force which Bell called
> "that-which-is."

Like Jeffers, Twichell has found her own definition for God. Instead of "I am that I am," which is close to Jeffers' belief that the creation itself is God, it is "that-which-is." Thus, Twichell echoes Jeffers, but in a reductive way that resonates with a pathos I believe he would have recognized.

> The physics of connection
> is all that matters.
> The heart matters, and the mind.
> Sensation matters, as long as it lasts.
> The world does not think of us at all.
> It is animated dust, and that is all,
> a flower of atoms pulsing in space,
> a flower of ash, a flower of soot.

There are some poets working on Jeffers' scale, that of the book-length poem. Recent attempts include Frederick Turner's *The New World* and Frederick Pollack's *The Adventure*. But these poems are more properly considered epics and make use of the hero as a central figure. Both require us to imagine a science-fiction world where man is remade. Their visions are political, especially in Pollack's long poem, and veer away from Jeffers' moral absolutism for very good reasons. Jeffers' book-length and other long narrative poems hew closer to the drama and, I believe, the dramatic form of novels like Hardy's. If we think of them as naturalistic, then we can see why they must occur in their local confines; Jeffers' northern California coast is his Wessex. Thus his locality (I hesitate to say regionalism) is also essential to his vision. For Jeffers' work to be of more use to the neo-narrative movement, the terms of his great story-telling verse may have to be changed. But since those terms—the enormous beauty of creation, particularly around Carmel, California, and the insignificant ugliness of humanity—inhere in his stories, it is hard to say what a neo-narrative poem in Jeffers' style would look like without them.

My aim here has been to sketch briefly the relation of each of the American masters of narrative poetry to the current scene. It should be clear that I believe Frost is the one we find most engaging to younger poets, whether or not they recognize the influence, because of the fluidity of his medium-length narratives, especially their moral relativism when compared to Robinson's narratives or Jeffers'. Frost's own moral vision is perfectly clear in his body of work, and we might infer from it that the characters he has created express his belief in self-reliance. Still, I would argue that because of the nature of narrative as Frost uses it, there is an essential mystery of character and motivation and, in the end, meaning, that appeals to many working in the narrative verse form today. E.A. Robinson requires a fuller, more rounded story, with a manifest plot and a strong sense of closure. He feels love for his characters as human beings and pity for their fates, emotions we do not see as clearly in Frost. Finally, as I have tried to suggest, the challenge of Jeffers remains to be met. Only now that we have passed his centennial year is he being reconsidered, critically reevaluated, in a way neither Frost nor Robinson has had to be. This is all to the good. But if Jeffers is going to have the powerful effect that I, for one, believe he can have, he will have to be recognized for what he is — the most troublesome and imposing of the three figures.

The Forest for the Trees:
Preliminary Thoughts on Evaluating the Long Poem

Dick Allen

It is at once disturbing and revealing to find that contemporary attitudes toward the long poem still basically derive from Edgar Allan Poe's "The Poetic Principle," published over 150 years ago. Poe wrote, we recall, "I hold that a long poem does not exist." By maintaining poetry is only poetry when it "excites, by elevating the soul," he helped set in motion a way of composing and judging poetry which is greatly beneficial to short lyric poetry but downgrades the two other major types, the narrative and the dramatic. As a result, the short lyric has come to seem synonymous with "poetry" itself. Today's critics—whether practical or theoretical—seldom are comfortable in judging the qualities or lack of them in a poem which is "long."

Poe felt that the poem's "elevating excitement"—a quality at the heart of his aesthetic—"cannot be sustained throughout a composition of any great length. After the lapse of half an hour, at the very utmost, it flags—fails—a revulsion ensues—and then the poem is, in effect, and in fact, no longer such." A long poem such as *Paradise Lost*, he maintained, should be regarded as poetical "only when, losing sight of that vital requisite in all works of art, unity, we view it merely as a series of minor poems."

However, what Poe and the long line of critics following him (I include most of those usually discussed under the general label of "New Critics") disregarded was that, in judging the poem which extends beyond the length of the usual lyric, in judging poetry which is not written under the influence of Poe's criteria, we approach and must deal with considerations applied to judging prose fiction. The long poem is not a "pure" form, nor is it aimed to produce what Poe called "the rhythmical creation of beauty." Like the drama, the long poem is a "mixed" form and our criticism of it cannot be based solely upon its "poetical" qualities or lack of them. Most important, with the aid of critical insights and ways of evaluation taken

First published in *The Kenyon Review*—New Series, spring 1983, vol. V., no. 2. Copyright © by Kenyon College. Reprinted with permission of author and publisher.

from prose fiction, the critic can and should treat the long poem as a whole, rather than as a collection of parts.

If we grant the right of existence to the long poem, one thing becomes clear: the long poem must engage our attention and contain enough devices—usually those we associate with fiction—to hold it. The longer the poem, the more we must be interested in the story and, since involvement with character is the primary way of creating suspense and continual interest, with the characters in the poem. Unless we are to consider the long poem as a series of shorter poems, we must have some kind of plot or, as in John Ashbery's best longer poems, at the very least a sequence of actions and observations so acute that our interest is sustained, our sensibilities kept involved.

Most of the noble failures of the long poem in our century—and there have been many, Pound's *Cantos*, Williams' *Paterson*, among others—result from the poet's trying to write the long poem as if it were an extended imagistic lyric: with a minimum of explicit narrative and dramatic elements. Long poems which are pitched at high intensity, containing all the elements we have come to value in the lyric, particularly the "academic" lyric—ambiguity, layered meanings, a multitude of sophisticated rhythmic effects, concentration on the central image, primary attention to "how" a poem means —fail just as Poe said they would, and can only be treated adequately as a collection of parts. Those written more or less in "open" or "naked" form after a few pages come to seem merely rhythmical prose, interesting mainly to those interested in the poet and his or her sensibility, or as a way of shedding light on the poet's shorter works. None have achieved major importance in and of themselves.

We should, then, rightly anticipate that the longer the poem is the more we can *expect* and *welcome* sections which are not of high intensity, which exist to round out the characters, further the plot, add suspense, provide an interesting setting, enhance the mood. Just as one would not wish to remove all those elements from Shakespeare's plays—the sections seldom discussed in a classroom but utterly necessary if the play is to hold the attention of an audience not composed solely of critics and scholars—neither should we ask that the long poem be lacking in them. Critics have for too long been unchallenged when they dismiss long poems by quoting from their lesser parts—offering these, unfairly, as characteristic of the poem as a whole. Indeed, sections of lesser intensity prepare us to appreciate and be moved by sections of greater intensity—as the practiced orator's jokes and asides give us an opportunity to digest his points of major concern and relax our attention so we are ready to consider deeply what major points might follow.

Conversely, we cannot give up all the gains achieved by the century's concentration on complex language. We must expect from the long poem a form—whether this be blank verse, rhyming couplets, or even fabulously "organic" structure—which is capable of intensifying the theme, of giving a major place to the role of language in the poem's overall pattern. The contemporary long poem cannot be regarded as successful if it simply tells a story in poetic form. The commercial short story and novel have justifiably replaced such works, and we would not really wish back into vogue long poems which imitate those by Browning and Tennyson. Complex use of language, and form, however, must always be viewed as secondary to the drama of the poem as a whole. If the language, the imagery, the form of the poem obviously overwhelm the poem's plot, the poem ultimately is not successful.

A short lyric poem is a concentrated work of art which can be explicated valuably by the sensitive reader and is especially valuable in the college classroom or creative writing class. The long poem cannot be handled so easily, nor can its types of ambiguity be dredged up so neatly for consideration. The longer the poem is, the more we have a right to expect that its concerns break the bonds of literary and musical considerations. It is right to ask that the long poem justify its length. The critic can be expected to ask of the long poem a purpose beyond the poet's defense of his own position to himself. Is the poem more than reporting and more than history? Does the poem present or imply a belief it seems necessary for us to understand? Does it tell a story we have not heard told this way, with this emphasis? If it does not use traditional closed form—a form particularly suited to providing unity and technical interest to the long poem's lesser parts—what is the loss or gain? We could even be forgiven for asking that the contemporary poem in some way at least acknowledge the presence of the technological-industrial society and its impact on us; in some way explicitly or implicitly illuminate and be involved with the changes of the twentieth century; contain some understanding of such matters as television, space flight, nuclear age politics, modern astronomy, and modern physics. As Lee T. Lemon reminded us in *The Partial Critics*, "form is filled only by content."

Additionally, in evaluating the long poem the critic will fail if he dismisses, out of hand, a poem's didactic elements. Here again, he must set aside criteria for judging the lyric poem, in which didactic elements are so often scorned. Obvious didactic intention should not be cause for downgrading the poem; indeed, a lack of obvious conscious intention is a main factor in making so much of twentieth-century poetry seem irrelevant to even well-educated readers. Further, slavishly applying to the long nonlyric poem the "intentional," "affective," and "biographical" fallacies so limits our criticism that we are apt to miss completely how a poem's success or failure may depend on its persuading as well as entertaining readers.

We can expect to read the long poem differently than we do the lyric poem. For a poem of three to twenty pages, our reading should be akin to the reading of a complex short story; for a longer poem, we can expect to engage in a reading experience not dissimilar to that of reading a novella or novel, an experience which we may extend for several days, treating each new section of the poem as we would another new chapter in a novel. When we finish, we can expect to be able to turn back to particularly important and rewarding sections and episodes. But the sense of the whole should overwhelm the parts, put weaker parts into proper perspective. Again, the experience of having a work grow more unified, more important to us, is seen in fiction. We may be reminded of the way Cooper's *The Prairie*, for instance, becomes stronger and more important in retrospect (despite our having to read through many of its silly and grossly written chapters). We may also remember that when we think back on our own reading experiences with such extensive poems as *The Iliad*, *The Odyssey*, *The Divine Comedy*, individual *Canterbury Tales*, *Paradise Lost*, *Don Juan*, we remember episodes, ideas, feelings, the great interwoven themes and concerns and stories of these poems more often than the exact ways in which the poems were written, the precise lines which were used, the manner in which language and imagery were handled. To a lesser degree, the same applies to "The Rime of the Ancient Mariner," "Sunday Morning," even "Directive," "Howl," Lowell's "Skunk Hour," and Dickey's "Falling."

The achievement of imagistic poetry and the new critical methods which have so long supported it do not have to be disparaged by one interested in the long poem, so long as we realize they basically concern the lyric. The twentieth century has given us an abundance of major and minor lyric masterpieces, a golden age of lyric poetry. Yet just as the century began with the critical work of Coleridge and Poe influencing French poets' views, and these in turn influencing Pound and Eliot and a host of influential poet-critics whose sensibility persists to this day—so we have entered a time in which critical structures and methods have become so codified, so turned into classroom slogans, that we would do well to remember their limitations.

All poetry is not, to cite Robert Frost's popular observation, "a momentary stay against confusion." That "a poem should not mean / but be" is simplistic. And the famous Imagist criteria for judging poetry, necessary in its own time, have become too limiting. Too much criticism of contemporary poetry still concentrates upon the more than fifty-year-old questions of proper use of imagery. What was once revolutionary has become a method which takes few risks, excludes those who have not been classroom trained in explication methodology, and contains no new insights. What it actually does is squelch any type of poetry which is not primarily image-centered. Criticism of the lyric, centered on questions of form and image, can let us know the good from the bad, sometimes even the better from the good, but it sees trees, not forest.

And "no ideas but in things"—our key phrase for understanding modern poetry—has led too many poets and critics mistakenly to think that ideas in and of themselves have no place in poetry. Until the prevailing critical attitudes change—and they are essentially the same for judging beat, academic, new surrealistic, and confessional lyric poetry—we shall continue to have more of the same and we shall continue to discourage the understanding and furtherance of poetry which does not accept the limiting and temporal thing-oriented views of reality so strongly expressed by William Carlos Williams and Wallace Stevens.

When a critical climate has become as stale as ours has, when it actively discourages the nonlyrical longer poem (and even discourages or ignores nonlyric elements in the extended lyric), it is time to move outside prevailing frames of reference and ask of poetry—as did those in much earlier centuries—that it once more obviously entertain and instruct. Sir Philip Sidney, in "The Defense of Poesy," felt the poet was defined by his "imaginative and judging power." The poet, he wrote, is "the right popular philosopher" and "of all sciences... is our poet the monarch" who "with a tale forsooth he cometh unto you: with a tale which holdeth children from play, and old men from the chimney corner." Poetry, for Sidney as for the ancients, was inventing and prophesying. It tells "not what is or is not, but what should or should not be."

If these concepts of poetry and poets sound strange and wrong to the modern ear, they indicate what minor conceptions of poetry float on our century's final decades. It is time we ask that poets rejoin literature's major rivers and that critics judge the full journey and its accomplishments rather than concentrate on minute inspection of the often imperfect large vessels built for long passages. The small and beautiful boat of the lyric was never meant to reach and chart the larger seas.

The Dilemma of the Long Poem

Dana Gioia

American poetry prides itself on its great scope and diversity, but one wonders if an outsider might not come away with a very different notion. Imagine what an intelligent eighteenth-century reader would conclude if he surveyed the several hundred books of poetry published in America this past year. (For simplicity's sake, let us keep this long-suffering gentleman's conclusions descriptive rather than evaluative. There is no way of knowing what if anything he would actually enjoy amid this poetic avalanche.) His overall reaction, I suspect, would be a deep disappointment over the predictable sameness, the conspicuous lack of diversity in what he read. Where are the narrative poems, he would ask, the verse romances, ballads, hymns, verse dramas, didactic tracts, burlesques, satires, the songs actually meant to be sung, and even the pastoral eclogues? Are stories no longer told in poetry? Important ideas no longer discussed at length? The panoply of available genres would seem reduced to a few hardy perennials which poets worked over and over again with dreary regularity—the short lyric, the ode, the familiar verse epistle, perhaps the epigram, and one new-fangled form called the "sequence" which often seemed to be either just a group of short lyrics stuck together or an ode in the process of falling apart. Amid this myriad of shorter work he would see only a few poems longer than six or seven pages—most of them massive and complex undertakings running many times the length of the average thin volume. These, he would ascertain, are the epics of this age, but he would probably not be able to classify them further since they are mostly difficult, allusive works not governed by a narrative or expository structure. They undoubtedly belong to a genre whose rules he doesn't understand.

This hypothetical gentleman would also be perplexed by the paucity of technical means he saw employed. Most of what he read would be in free verse (some of which he would recognize as such from his familiarity with Milton, Smart, and, of course, the Old Testament) balanced by a little

First published in *The Kenyon Review*—New Series, Spring 1983, vol. V., no. 2. Copyright © by Kenyon College. Reprinted with permission of author and publisher.

irregular pentameter, an occasional sestina, and virtually nothing else. What happened to rhyme, he would ask, and all the meters ancient and modern plus all the familiar stanza forms of English? These new poets, he might conclude, are a very monotonous bunch indeed who can only manage the shorter forms and even those only within the slenderest range of technical means. Poems longer than half a dozen pages seem to be beyond their powers altogether. Yes, American poetry would seem to be a very limited enterprise. It not only lacks great poets of the stature of Shakespeare, Spenser, Milton, Dryden, and Pope, it also lacks estimable lesser writers of scope and versatility, like Dyer, Thomson, Collins, Cowper, Young, Shenstone, or Gay.

Such judgments would infuriate our poets and critics alike, but are they so inaccurate? American poetry may be bold and expansive in its moods and subject matter, but it remains timorous and short-winded in its range. Despite its enormous volume, the poetry published each year tends to be conceived almost exclusively in shorter forms. It does not take a university professor to notice this bias. Any reader familiar with at least one other period of literature in English would have to ask why the tremendous talent of contemporary poets has been so narrowly focused.

The orthodox academic reply is that the intensity and concentration of modern poetry has made the long poem impossible. An extended work in verse would perforce break up into shorter fragments. This explanation sounds plausible at first, and indeed it may even have some limited applicability to certain early modern schools such as Imagism, but careful observation proves it untrue in any general sense. Contemporary poetry is not particularly intense or concentrated on either an absolute or relative basis. Certainly concentration and intensity are characteristics of good short poetry in any age, but the twentieth century has little special claim on them. Compare half a dozen widely anthologized contemporary poems with a lyric by George Herbert or a sonnet by Milton and one will usually find the modern work relaxed and casual in comparison. Why then could a poet like Milton, an unquestioned master of the short, concentrated poem, also manage brilliant longer poems whereas our contemporaries cannot? The answer is complex and encompasses several acknowledged factors, such as the increasing identification of all poetry with the lyric mode, the subsequent rejection of narrative and didacticism as available poetic forms, and the neglect of precisely those metrical resources in English which have traditionally provided long poems with an underlying structure. There is another factor, however, which I have never heard discussed but which has had a crucial impact on our literature.

The major problem facing the long poem today is that contemporary theory allows the poet almost no middle ground between the concentration of the short lyric and the vast breadth of the epic (the modern epic, that is, in its distinctive form as the historical culture poem). Of course, our theoreticians have not banned all other kinds of poetry, but the critical emphases on lyric and epic have been so strong over the past seventy years that to poets and teachers alike they have become the distinctive forms of both the modern and so-called post-modern period. The long poem has nearly died as a result. It has become an all-or-nothing proposition, an obsessive, lifelong undertaking. The poet must confront his entire culture and prepare some vast synthesis of its history and values. There may be one or two poets in any age who are capable of bringing off so ambitious an enterprise, but how many geniuses have botched their careers trying it? To take the most conspicuous example in our century, consider Ezra Pound, who stopped writing other poetry at the height of his powers to concentrate on his never completed *Cantos*. Ultimately the *Cantos* may well be the most interesting poem in American literature, but it is surely not a success (if the word *success* has any meaning left in describing a form which has relinquished the conventional standards of literary performance and intends only to recreate an author's private sensibility without any concessions to his audience). Or consider Conrad Aiken, whose entire career was spent in trying repeatedly in vain to write the definitive long poem of his age.

Indeed the long modern poem is virtually doomed to failure by its own ground rules. Any extended work needs a strong overall form to guide both the poet in creating it and the reader in understanding it. By rejecting the traditional epic structures of narrative (as in Vergil) and didactic exposition (as in Lucretius), the modern author has been thrown almost entirely on his own resources. He must not only try to synthesize the complexity of his culture into one long poem, he must also create the form of his discourse as he goes along. It is as if a physicist were asked to make a major new discovery in quantum mechanics but prevented from using any of the established methodologies in arriving at it. Even genius cannot accomplish such a task. Could Milton have succeeded so brilliantly with *Paradise Lost* without the examples of Homer, Vergil, Dante, Tasso, and Spenser behind him? Given that the structure of the modern epic has become an elaborate nonce form, it is not surprising that one finds no incontestable masterpieces among the major long poems of this century but only a group of more or less interesting failures, none widely read in its entirety by the literary public, though all jealously guarded by some particular faction (with no group quite so rabidly partisan as those professors who have staked their academic careers on researching and explicating a particular poem): Williams's *Paterson*, Jones's *The Anathemata*, Olson's *Maximus Poems*, Zukofsky's *A*, Berryman's *Dream Songs*, Dorn's *Gunslinger*, and so forth.

Given the immensity of the commitment and the high odds of failure involved in writing the modern epic, it is hardly surprising that most poets have chosen to concentrate single-mindedly on shorter forms, especially the lyric (both in its simple and conglomerate form, the sequence). Here at least the talented poet can make a lasting place for himself. It is instructive to consider how many contemporary poets have achieved important reputations almost solely on short poems: Elizabeth Bishop, Randall Jarrell, Weldon Kees, James Wright, Sylvia Plath, Robert Graves, Richard Wilbur, Howard Nemerov, Adrienne Rich, Howard Moss, Louis Simpson, J.V. Cunningham, Philip Larkin, Charles Tomlinson, W.S. Merwin, William Stafford. The list could go on and on. Most of these writers have done extended imaginative work, but significantly they avoided poetry as the medium for it. Poets like Graves or Nemerov turned to the novel while others, like Bishop or Kees, chose the short story. Some, like Wilbur and Merwin, concentrated on verse translation or, like Rich, on polemical prose. Even drama, as in Moss's case, or autobiographical prose, as in Simpson's, served as the natural conduit for their most expansive work. The diverse extended work of these poets has only one thing in common—the avoidance of verse as its medium.

American literature needs a more modest aesthetic of the long poem, a less chauvinistic theory which does not vainly seek the great at the expense of the good and genuine. It needs to free poets from the burden of writing the definitive long poem and allow them to work in more manageable albeit limited genres like satire, comedy, unheroic autobiography, discursive writing, pure narrative—wherever, in short, their imagination takes them. It also needs to foster poems of "middle length," extended pieces not long enough to fill up an entire volume. Such poems have played an important role in English from Chaucer's *Canterbury Tales* to Browning's major dramatic monologues, but today they are shunned by editors, publishers, and critics alike. (A sad situation which parallels the almost total extinction of the novella by the novel and short story in contemporary fiction.) Poems of middle length allow a writer to explore a particular theme without over-extending it, and they do not require the Herculean effort necessary to complete an epic. Some poets work best in longer forms—Byron, Crabbe, Pope, and Dryden are a few historical examples—but even such talents may not necessarily be suited for the straight epic. Poets need a broad and various array of possible forms, an array which unfortunately does not seem available at present.

The Other Long Poem

Frederick Feirstein

Over the past two decades the only kind of long poem taken seriously by poetry's readership was the sequence: a series of lyrics thematically rather than dramatically organized and depending for its impact on the intensity of the individual moment and the accumulative effect of its images. At the same time the narrative and dramatic poem, with developed plot and character, was disregarded, much in the same way that Aristotelian drama was shoved aside for Theater of the Absurd with its loosely circular structure and its concentration on atmospheric intensity. This limiting of the form of the long poem was one of the many effects of modernism hardening into dogma.

The great modernists — Yeats, Pound, Stevens, for example — understanding the advantages of using plot, achieved some dramatic movement in their sequences by alluding to plot elements in old myths or texts or to some larger political action offstage. But their most recent followers (though they looked to myth for its primitiveness and politics for its fashionableness) discarded plot — and character as well — finding them to be "irrelevant" to the times. They backed up their practice with certain critical assumptions that the educated but intimidated lay reader learned to take for gospel. For instance, the supporter of Creeley or Ashbery would tell you that the times are chaotic and human life existential; therefore, in a poem there can't be any kind of logical structure or characters with coherent histories. Consider this statement by Reg Saner in a recent issue of *The Ohio Review*:

> Still, if poetry is to reflect where we are, it isn't likely to abandon the main feature of twentieth-century art, fragmentation. We may call it discontinuity or montage. We may refer to "aleatory" sequence or to "suppression of narrative links," but we remain tied to their devices through our sense that life is awash with random events. We admit "chance" is a word describing aspects of our ignorance, but we also admit chance in our designs, knowing that any set of objects tends to become a system.

First published in *The Kenyon Review* — New Series, spring 1983, vol. V., no. 2. Copyright © by Kenyon College. Reprinted with permission of author and publisher.

And a neosurrealist such as James Tate would tell you that there are no rules for the unconscious and, since a poem comes from the unconscious, it must be randomly arranged as well. It was almost futile to challenge these assumptions, to point out to such poets and their readers that contemporary physics and molecular biology were revealing a deep and beautiful orderliness in the universe. Or to point out what every serious student of the unconscious (from Freud to Pinchas Noy to Ephron and Carrington) has discovered: that the unconscious operates by mechanisms of selectivity that are far from random and produces an order that seems illogical only when misunderstood.

Besides these attacks on structure, a contempt for meter developed which also contributed to the abandonment of "the other long poem." It's relatively easy to create dramatic moments in free verse, and a number of poets have managed to knit them together into first-rate sequences. But anyone who's tried it knows that it's virtually impossible to develop a book-length narrative without meter—and call it poetry, not prose fiction. The conflict of opposites between the metrical line and the prose rhythm of natural speech sustains and poetically mirrors the tension in the dramatic structure itself. It establishes *in sound* a series of expectations out of which suspense, surprise, reversal, and so on, can come. In effect it does poetically what the content does dramatically. On the other hand, free verse forces the poet to rely on rhetorical devices that tend to create melodrama or to focus the reader on the poet's "voice" instead of on the action—and so distances him perhaps altogether from involvement in the intended drama.

But most of the poets, particularly the younger ones, ill-educated in workshops, simply could not master meter and therefore had no hope of succeeding with narrative. Few admitted this failing unless pressed, and only the rare exception dared do so in print. The *Ohio Review*, sensing that the free verse academy was losing its grip, published an issue (the same one in which the Saner piece appeared) devoted to challenging the notion of an unnamed poet that "free verse is dead." However, one of the essayists, Bim Ramke, had the honesty to say this:

> When I hear talk of exotic, subtle, intellectual use of forms I want to be part of it, but when I try to *do* it, I fail. Of course I fear that my failure may simply result from my laziness, lack of talent, lack of a trained ear. Stephen Spender suggests that if one has not been raised

from childhood "speaking sonnet" then the sonnets one writes will have the same order of awkwardness as the foreign language one learns too late. My sonnets are awkward.

Not only my sonnets. I once wrote a two-hundred or so line poem in smooth ballad stanzas with all the proper rhymes. It sat around a while sounding silly, so I got rid of the rhymes and roughed up the meter and sold it. It paid one month's rent so I felt less guilty. If I can't write sonnets and I can't write ballads, what can I write? And can I call whatever it is "poetry"?

But unlike Ramke most workshop poets did not even try to learn meter. In part they were dissuaded by their mentors who—usually parroting William Carlos Williams—contended that poetry must be speech, American speech. This was an odd prescription for the lyric, which traditionally was sung. It was also a comically chauvinistic pronouncement by a group of poets who insisted there was a connection between free verse and political freedom. For instance, Diane Wakoski responding (in the winter 1981-82 *Missouri Review*) to Frederick Turner's essay "'Mighty Poets in Their Misery Dead': A Polemic on the Contemporary Poetic Scene," said this:

Critics (and even some poets) obscure matters by longing for a neo-British poetry, a new England literature.... But the recognition of Dickinson and Whitman depended on readers seeing and appreciating the use of an American, rather than English, language. And the genius of the writers, themselves, had to be reckoned with in American terms—the self-involvement, the unabashed lack of concern for the classics, for other literature, and for the epic. The complete acceptance of self as important seems to be an American trait, whereas the European sensibility ... requires the writer to justify his importance.... Critics have still not accepted that those savages [Dickinson and Whitman] are the Americans, that our language is a rougher, wilder, plainer, different one, and that our myths do not go back to ancient Greece and Rome, but come out of our involvement with this immense land here, across the ocean from Europe.... I feel personally in touch with that tradition of Emily and Walt. They are ancestors I cherish and love, and it is exciting for me to see the turn of a nose here, an ankle there, the way a mouth moves when certain vowels are spoken. I could list at least a hundred poets writing today who are exciting, new and old at the same time, who give me almost the same excitement that I have writing my own poems, when I read and talk about them and their new American language.

Another reason for the neglect of "the other long poem" had to do with the popularity of confessional poetry. Strong and varied characterization is a crucial element in the narrative or dramatic poem—whether it be fictional or autobiographical. But the confessional poets and their followers had no real interest in any character but the Self, a severely damaged and unappetizing one at that. Whatever little drama inhered in their poems came from their sensationalism, from the poet's making a spectacle of him- or her-Self. Spectacle is rather low on the list of Aristotle's criteria for effective drama. After a while the work of such early confessional poets as Plath or Sexton reads as a single monologue spoken by a character who never changes, who is exhibitionistic in the throes of pathology, and tragic without compensatory release. The initial attraction to their work is understandable, particularly when seen against the background of their time — when the Self (especially the dark sides of the Self) was muted by intense social conformity. What's more, the very wretchedness of their lives titillated that odd American reader whose fascination with the artist is mixed with envy and suppressed hatred. But ultimately repeated readings of their work numbed as even good horror films numb or, in the hands of their followers, bored as soap operas bore. Even their innovative suicides became a formula their followers would imitate only with gesture or in actuality without the thrill of publicity.

These reasons for the neglect of the narrative and dramatic poem came from within the poetry world. But they were supported by factors outside that world as well. The popularity of television in the past couple of decades had a strong influence on the form and content of all the arts. The TV generation was conditioned to find emotion difficult to sustain without a commercial break. Naturally, when it came to poetry, they would gravitate toward the lyric sequence because it hit peaks of emotion for short periods and toward confessional poetry because, like television, it was sensational. Also, I might add, there was a distinct parallel between the values of commercial television and the mistaking of Williams's "no ideas but in things" to mean no ideas, and Pound's "make it new" to mean make it novel.

The rhetoric of 1960s politics also undermined the legitimacy of structure. Everything was being liberated and made new. Anything structured — worse, "linear" — was "over thirty," irrelevant. The narrative, the dramatic, was variously "bourgeois," "elitist," and "nineteenth century." Even now poets such as our friend Bim Ramke sloganeer like this:

> Is it possible that the return, if there is one, to received forms is because the elite wants its badge shined? I noticed a number of comments during the inauguration of Ronald Reagan about "class being restored to the White House." "Class," of course is to be translated "money." Whatever my fellow Georgian Carter lacked which Reagan has could not reasonably be called class, unless the word is understood in an older sense, the sense of demarcations within society. And just maybe the call for sonnets, villanelles, etc. among contemporary poets is a way of setting up class lines too.

Many of the poetry editors at major publishing houses were intimidated by this kind of reasoning. They were often recent graduates of the same schools that produced the poets or weren't sophisticated enough to sort out aesthetics from politics from fashion. Besides, they had books to sell, and what they believed sold poetry was sensationalism of content and its equivalent, "experimentation" with form. They didn't notice that sensationalism was becoming a mannerism and experimentation a convention. To defend their choices they often would talk of *new* form as they would of *relevant* content. As for the small press movement, most of its editors earnestly believed the ideology of the past twenty years and wrote according to it themselves. If the large press editors were fashionably ignorant of the long poem, the small press editors were dogmatically ignorant.

And yet there was a group of poets and critics *rebelling* — to use that dangerous word — against this new *in*formal academy. Some of the most impressive: Dick Allen, Christopher Clausen, Charles Martin, Judith Moffet, Richard Moore, and Frederick Turner. Courageously, and in almost total obscurity, they persisted in writing their narratives and dramas. When they discovered each other, they would exchange their unpublished manuscripts much as the formally censored Russian writers do. Then they began to find their way to a few daring magazines and presses. Now (while continuing to write lyrics and lyric sequences as well as narrative and dramatic poems) they have begun to publish dissident essays designed to expand the capacity of poetry and poetry criticism. Eventually they will bring plot and character back to poetry and perhaps recapture some of the audience that has been lost.

Other Lives: On Shorter Narrative Poems

David Mason

Poets are drawn to dramatic monologues and narratives when they become bored with the limitations of autobiographical writing, but they end up realizing what all good fiction writers know, that other people's lives are every bit as important as their own. Empathy, the act of inhabiting a stranger's experience, is a civilizing process. It implies connection, community, releasing the poet—who otherwise seems "Encased in talent like a uniform"— from isolation. Fiction's advantage has usually been considered its interest in society as well as the lives of specific individuals, and poets envy this particularly when the lyric "I" has become repetitious, nearly automatic. Tennyson and Browning began in Romantic subjectivity, and balanced their careers on the taut line between those early impulses and an opposing impulse toward the objectivity of storytelling. In our time the line has been stretched between similar poles; one mode of expression loses power through overuse, and poets naturally turn to the opposite mode to restore vital tension. Rather than leaping to the conclusion that the subjective lyric is dead and we can only stay aloft on the shoulders of a good story, we should admit that there are advantages and disadvantages to every genre, and that poets are better off when they can write more than one kind of poem.

Anthony Hecht and Louis Simpson have written about the use of narrative to regain literary territory that in modern times has been lost to the novel. More recently, a younger generation of poets, including Robert McDowell, Mark Jarman, and Dana Gioia, has argued that narrative may be a good way to work free of the lethargy observable in many contemporary poems. Recent uses of narrative are broader than this short list suggests, yet poets and critics have, so far, neglected fundamental questions about these practices. For example, is the poetic line as viable today for characterization as it was a century (or twenty-five centuries) ago? What are the objectives and difficulties of characterization in verse? If poets and their audience can rejoin in empathy's embrace, what sort of poem will best invite and challenge them?

Verse (winter 1990): 16-21.

There are at least two good reasons why contemporary poets might use verse to create characters and tell stories. One reason is that it can rejuvenate their art by compelling them to reevaluate the subjects they write about, to look more closely at lives usually deemed insufficiently flashy or spectacular. By involving us in the nuances of social and individual problems, narrative poetry can address issues beyond the narrow confines of the poet's life, or it can focus emotions too painfully personal to be revealed directly in a lyric. It is also possible that the line has advantages lacking in prose, the chief one being that it contributes to memorability, helping to sustain a literary culture most of us would agree is in danger of extinction. The line as a unit of sound is tremendously important, but the line is also a unit of thought and feeling; it can contribute to dramatic dynamism and plot in particular ways, adding another dimension to the process of storytelling.

These advantages are found at their fullest in shorter narratives and monologues that can be read or recited in a single session. Book-length poems, even when as well-written as Vikram Seth's Byronic novel, *The Golden Gate*, and Frederick Turner's science fiction epics, *The New World* and *Genesis*, are, in our culture, too long to be experienced whole as uninterrupted aural performances, and instead we absorb them as solitary readers over a longer period of time. If the 1980s saw the publication of several book-length poems—among them James Merrill's assembly of ghosts in *The Changing Light at Sandover*, Thomas McGrath's pseudo-autobiographical *Letter to an Imaginary Friend* and Alfred Corn's *Notes from a Child of Paradise*—it was also a period that witnessed the revival of shorter narratives by poets as various as Hecht and Simpson, and younger writers like Sydney Lea, Robert McDowell, Mark Jarman, Rita Dove and Dana Gioia. Like prose short stories, these poems have to produce their impact by memorable and economical means. They can be absorbed by an audience in their entirety, rather than in fragments or highlights. Due to their relative brevity, they cannot afford a leisurely alternation of prose-like passages and lyric moments; their line must be more consistently commanding and intense. In shorter narratives the partnership of line and narrative structure is particularly important. We can hear the adjustments of dramatic voice in relation to the line, almost a musical interplay in which the entire form of a completed story becomes audible.

Where Seth's novel owes much to Byron and Pushkin, and Turner's epics to Milton, many contemporary writers of shorter narratives look back upon Robert Frost as the most significant practitioner of their art. Frost's

"Home Burial," for example, elucidates two characters and their dramatic conflict in a mere 116 lines. With economy most fiction writers would admire, Frost plunges us into the midst of marital estrangement in his first two lines:

> He saw her from the bottom of the stairs
> Before she saw him. She was starting down....

The first line is a statement of fact, but enjambment forces us into the second line; the line break itself, and the power struggle implicit in the phrase, "Before she saw him," creates suspense. He is at the bottom of the stairs, she at the top. But she is coming down, and already we know that their meeting will produce conflict. As the poem progresses, the suspense it achieves by line breaks and withholding exposition pulls us uncomfortably close to these two people. Frost's spare dialogue uses repetition to further suspense, while also capturing the man's alienation from his wife's grief:

> He spoke
> Advancing toward her: "What is it you see
> From up there always? —for I want to know."
> She turned and sank upon her skirts at that,
> And her face changed from terrified to dull.
> He said to gain time: "What is it you see?"

The repeated question indicates the husband's helpless frustration, even trepidation, but he speaks, "Advancing toward her"—his gesture is intrusive. She, who had been "Looking over her shoulder at some fear," grows impassive, as if an impenetrable wall stood between them.

Both husband and wife know this wall intimately. He knows it even as he feigns ignorance of what put it there. Her angry grief and his coldness have built it, and though he insists that he will know what troubles her, she nests in her own bitterness, confident that he cannot know her secret. In the first twenty lines of the poem, Frost maps with scary accuracy the dimensions of their estrangement: her withdrawal into certainty that her husband cannot comprehend a mother's grief, his masculine insistence that he knows what burns in her heart. Their situation is specific. Not only does their dead child's recently-filled grave, which is visible from an upstairs window, haunt her, but her pain is multiplied by the image of her husband digging—even being able to dig. His action becomes in her mind an acknowledgement and acceptance of horrifying, unacceptable truth, and all of his attempts at sympathy, at abolishing her pain, are fresh violations.

When he speaks about the graves, then about their child's grave, his sensitivity is clumsy:

> "There are three stones of slate and one of marble,
> Broad-shouldered little slabs there in the sunlight
> On the sidehill. We haven't to mind *those*.
> But I understand: it is not the stones,
> But the child's mound—"
> > "Don't, don't, don't, don't," she cried.

The verse itself, the husband's full lines wordily groping for explanation and the wife's spondaic outburst finishing a line, contributes powerfully to the scene. Details of psychological states share space in the above passage with a detail of social milieu: as in Dickens, the gravestones almost become characters, telling of the generations of broad-shouldered farmers from whom the husband is apparently descended.

This kind of specific touch is the lifeblood of any good story, but the poet balances even more precariously, dangerously, because of the added technical difficulty of versification. Mark Jarman's dramatic monologue, "The Gift," in his book *The Black Riviera* (1990), uses blank verse as strict as Frost's to limn a specific child's point of view when she is "kidnapped" for a day by her father. As her father drives them in his car, she observes:

> Outside the windshield traffic lights hung down
> From cables, and the bushy tops of palms
> Showed at intervals that I could count.
> A pink or yellow building front skimmed past.
> But mostly I could only see the sky.

By themselves these lines are unremarkable, but in their dramatic context, given the strangeness of the event, her limited point of view and touching pride in being able to count, they carry much of the poem's disjointed mood. When the father's girlfriend shows up, Jarman's careful establishment of the speaker's voice pays off nicely:

> Then, at a stop, one of those tall palm trees
> That wears a shaggy collar of dead fronds
> Leaned down and opened up the door and got in
> Beside me. Daddy called her Charlotte dear
> And told her I was Susan.

Still, the lines themselves do not quite pay the sort of dividend Frost's do. Most contemporary narrative poets are not yet adept at milking the techniques of enjambment and metrical variation for specific dramatic effects.

Despite this weakness, Jarman has made some of the most ambitious narrative forays of any poet of his generation. In "The Death of God" he experiments with the long free verse line of Robinson Jeffers, a line that enables Jarman in his next book, *Iris* (1992), the freedom and sweep of a novelist:

> The woman sat on the bus, her daughter's hand in her lap,
>   and read a paperback of poems,
> The only book from college that she'd saved, Robinson
>   Jeffers, and talked back to him,
> As always. He was her poet. The bus crossed the two
>   lakes, and the land between them,
> Like stages of warning. Glare of water, shadow of close,
>   dense trees, glare again.
> Then entry into the isolated flatland that she'd left,
>   married, pregnant, unhurt,
> Not yet in thrall to this dead stranger from California,
>   who spoke of an end to the continent
> She had to imagine, had to summon up even more
>   strenuously while coming back
> To western Kentucky, a mother, estranged, abused and
>   wounded, hiding a black-eye behind dark glasses.

Jarman's protagonist, a woman torn between the decadent reality of contemporary life and the transcendent vision of Jeffers' ghost, begins a quest that Jarman the novelist cannot quite resolve; the book's lyrical resolution synthesizes sound, meaning, and event as only a poet could do. Indeed, if much of *Iris* has the feel of a prose novel, its conclusion almost escapes plot altogether with its lyrical loft.

Like Jarman, Robert McDowell has brought a rugged idiom and subject matter to his poetry. His first book, *Quiet Money* (1987), works by a kind of narrative architecture as much as by the devices of a poet. In blank and free verse poems, one finds here a world akin to Raymond Carver's, in which failure predominates. The title poem, about a bootlegging pilot who has made secret transatlantic flights for years before Lindbergh's famous one, becomes one of several lovely meditations on the salvation of skill and craft. It also proves beyond any doubt that real stories have indelible structures. They are like seeds containing blueprints of complex entities, and keep growing in the mind long after one has read them. Since *Quiet Money*, McDowell has published, mostly in *The Hudson Review*, more narratives with a gritty urban vision one rarely finds in poetry, particularly "The Neighborhood," "My Corporate Life," and "All the Broken Boys and Girls." These are poems in which McDowell's blank verse technique seems increasingly assured. One of the strongest of his recent poems, "The Pact," proves a dark pastoral tale combining the narrative obsession of Jeffers with the verse technique of Frost. Its vivid opening reads as follows:

> Rain bulled into the valley like a giant
> Escaping from the pages of a book.
> John-Allen in his garden watched it brawling
> Over the coastal range. Its highest peaks
> Gleamed briefly in the sun that broke above
> The Cascade Mountains fifty miles to the east,
> Then disappeared in swirling thunderheads.
> Behind him his blue house reflected deeper blue
> As all the valley darkened. He leaned the rake
> Against the cockeyed table of surplus boards
> And walked back to the fence to face the wind
> Coming in warm gusts that flattened the grass,
> Advanced on the pear tree, then on himself.
> His straw hat blew off, flew crazily away,
> Splitting the wicket of two apple trees
> Before hanging up suddenly among the roses.
> John-Allen still faced west, his hair straight back,
> His eyes tearing. He knew he should go in
> But tightened his grip on the fence. The storm inside
> Would outlast this one, which was beautiful.
> A moment's silence, then thunder came calling,
> Then all the fury of the storm broke loose.

In clean, skillfully-modulated lines, McDowell establishes his setting and the ominous potential of "the storm inside." "The Pact" achieves a powerful marriage of story and line.

The saddest moment in Frost's "Home Burial" occurs when the wife, who has been almost menacingly silent, suddenly and at length describes her husband's grave-digging. Here the verse itself is compelled by the extremity of contained emotion:

> "...you don't know how to speak.
> If you had any feelings, you that dug
> With your own hand—how could you?—his little grave;
> I saw you from that very window there,
> Making the gravel leap and leap in air,
> Leap up, like that, and land so lightly
> And roll back down the mound beside the hole.

I thought, who is that man? I didn't know you.
And I crept down the stairs and up the stairs
To look again, and still your spade kept lifting."

Now, the wife's resentment given voice, it is the husband's turn to with-
draw in bitterness, his brevity proving that language cannot bridge the
gulf between them: "I shall laugh the worst laugh I ever laughed. / I'm
cursed. God, if I don't believe I'm cursed."

Though Frost's use of the line for dramatic effect is more successful
than any of his imitators', his diction is sometimes awkward, as when the
husband says, "I don't like such things 'twixt those that love." Narrative
poets are caught between the lyric possibilities of the line and the necessi-
ties of storytelling, and occasionally one or the other of these elements suf-
fers. Two of the most remarkable recent dramatic monologues, Dana Gioia's
"The Room Upstairs" (from *Daily Horoscope*, 1986) and "Counting the Chil-
dren" (*The Gods of Winter*, 1991), blend lyric and dramatic elements almost
seamlessly. Gioia's tactic is usually to be as unobtrusive as possible, and in
both of these poems he chooses speakers well suited to his clear, meticu-
lous voice and probing intelligence. This is particularly true of "Counting
the Children," in which the speaker is, like Gioia, a businessman. Beyond
that fact we know little about Mr. Choi, a Chinese-American accountant
hired to audit the estate of an eccentric old woman who has recently died.
We do not see him interacting with other characters, as we do the husband
and wife in Frost's more dramatic poem. We hear a neighbor woman speak-
ing as she shows Mr. Choi through the house, but he does not respond
vocally to anything she says. Gioia limits the poem to the confines of Choi's
mind, so it resembles a private confession to the reader. Because of this,
Gioia's lines are not used dramatically in the manner of Frost; they are
rarely broken out of narrative necessity, but instead retain a fluid, dream-
like suppleness. Gioia's poem lacks Frost's firm grounding in a specific
milieu; instead, like Poe, he emphasizes the subjective view, linking Mr.
Choi's fevered vision to lyric moments in the verse.

No great drama propels this vision. Touring the house, Mr. Choi has
been shown the dead woman's strange collection of dolls. His function
among them is purely professional and legalistic, but the roomful of dolls
on shelves startles him out of his routine:

Where were the children who promised them love?
The small, caressing hands, the lips which whispered
Secrets in the dark? Once they were woken,

Each by name. Now they have become each other—
Anonymous except for injury,
The beautiful and headless side by side.

These are well-written lines, but the image of "The beautiful and headless side by side" does more to develop a mood than to illuminate Mr. Choi's character. Still, Gioia has pulled us into a mind that is recognizably individual. In the second section of "Counting the Children" Choi has a nightmare in which he cannot balance his ledger; his world has lost its customary order, and even numbers disobey him. The madness of that doll collection, of a mind that could assemble so many dead pairs of eyes, so many frozen little corpses, suggests a whole world unhinged, and when, in the third section, Choi awakes, his first thought is for his daughter's safety. He gropes down the hallway to her room, discovering her safely asleep. Gioia may have felt that the following openly emotional lines could not be written without the protective mask of a dramatic monologue:

How delicate this vessel in our care,
This gentle soul we summoned to the world,
A life we treasured but could not protect.

This was the terror I could not confess
Not even to my wife—and it was the joy
My daughter had no words to understand.

So standing at my pointless watch each night
In the bare nursery we had improvised,
I learned the loneliness that we call love.

Too pretty, some might say, yet in a manner that is quite unlike Frost's, Gioia has risked feelings of uncommon delicacy.

If we scarcely know Mr. Choi as a social being, it is also true that Gioia uses the man's profession, a life of columned numbers, to make specific psychological observations about dream and reality, introducing us to a world and a mind seldom seen in contemporary poetry. "And though you won't believe that an accountant / Can have a vision," he says, "I will tell you mine." The man's powerful need to shift into visionary experience, dramatized in his protective feelings for his daughter, is matched by Gioia's lyrical lines:

We long for immortality, a soul
To rise up flaming from the body's dust.
I know that it exists. I felt it there,

> Perfect and eternal in the way
> That only numbers are, intangible but real,
> Infinitely divisible yet whole.

Here the visionary sense (a restrained and muted version of what we sometimes find in Jeffers) opens the cage of the narrative, allowing the secret it contained to fly. Frost's vision is darkly realistic, Gioia's at first more hopeful, but the last image in Gioia's poem is of the daughter's lifeless dolls, their eerie faces challenging Mr. Choi's assertions. Gioia pulls us into a dramatized epiphany that teaches us about human yearning the way Frost teaches us about grief, and he does this without seeming high-handed or condescending.

The best narrative poems instruct us about life, but also about poetic practice. There must be some reason why the story had to be told in lines, some advantage to the line as a unit that is actually used by the poet to achieve effects possible by no other means. Frost's use of line breaks is a good example of this. In some cases, the lyric qualities of the line lend the narrative cohesion; the climax or crux of the story is also a climax of sound, a moment in which saying finds an extraordinary rightness, an inevitability, as it does in Gioia's "Counting the Children." Prosaic and lyric moments will undoubtedly alternate in even the best dramatic poems, and the prosaic will leave them vulnerable to the charge that what is written is not poetry. That is why there must be, at some key point or points, a benefit from the use of lines. Good narratives have been written in free verse as well as meter, but in the best of these poems there is always a moment when we know we are hearing poetry, not prose, when the line transforms thought, feeling, plot and character into memorable speech. This needn't always be a moment of high seriousness. Frost recalls laughing with Ezra Pound over the following lines from a short poem by Edwin Arlington Robinson:

> Miniver scorned the gold he sought,
>   But sore annoyed was he without it;
> Miniver thought, and thought, and thought,
>   And thought about it.

As Frost points out, the final "thought," so telling of Miniver's character, achieves its charm by being placed in another line. The line break and the shift from tetrameter to dimeter verse contribute to precision of effect.

Whatever narrative voice is used—first, second or third person—the storyteller faces a dilemma of style. In dramatic poems, rhythm and diction are not wholly governed by the poet's predilections. Rather, the poet negotiates with character, and this negotiated voice must be one in which neither poet nor character is compromised. Prose stylists have the same problem, exacerbated by our modern reliance on realism. Henry James's sentences, so adept at capturing the nuances of adult minds, fail to accommodate the child's in *What Maisie Knew*. It is too easy for the stylist to condescend to his or her subject and thereby hold at a distance what ought to be intimate knowledge. The storyteller's ego must share the stage with others. Jarman and McDowell use the diction of characters from a variety of backgrounds, while Gioia chooses speakers capable of his fluid lyricism. In either approach the poet balances on a very thin line. We don't want our stories told by nonentities, but we want even less for the characters to become nonentities. We want those other lives in their particularity, otherwise we cannot believe in them as lives. At the beginning of his short story, "The Rich Boy," F. Scott Fitzgerald writes, "Begin with an individual, and before you know it you find that you have created a type; begin with a type, and you find that you have created—nothing."

Finally, dramatic poems are often at some level personal. This is the paradox of the mask, the persona: it liberates the personal by objectifying it. A male poet may write about a middle-aged woman whose father committed suicide when she was very young, and who, as a result, has never had the opportunity to feel young herself; the poet's narrative may be fueled, as it were, by his own anxieties and neuroses stemming from family problems and their effects upon children. His father has not committed suicide, but his parents were divorced and left him feeling helpless and prematurely aged. He tells her story because he can see hers clearly, his vision unclouded by self-pity. But he too is implicated; no audience would care to listen if he weren't. I have no doubt that the death of Frost's three-year-old son gave "Home Burial" some of its accuracy and power, just as the death of Gioia's infant son gave emotional truth to the meditations of "Counting the Children."

Poetic lines remain a viable medium for characterization as well as narrative, and the necessities of fiction may contribute much of value to the poet's work, making it accessible beyond a purely literary audience. At a time when so many poets work in the academy where the very architecture of campuses sets them apart from the surrounding communities, and when poets encounter an increasingly limited and specialized range of experiences, narrative poems offer the unexplored territory of other lives. Poets may write about farmers or businessmen, children or terrorists; the point is that they look into the larger community, into the hearts of strangers, helping to restore the relation between poetry and the increasingly complicated world.

Exploration of America

Christopher Clausen

I

With a few important exceptions, nationalism as a strongly held attitude is conspicuously absent from modern poetry in English. An overtly nationalistic poem like Drayton's "Ballad of Agincourt" has hardly any parallels in the twentieth century. For a variety of reasons, skepticism about the value and an awareness of the dangers of national self-assertiveness have entered the language and attitudes available to modern poets. The cosmopolitanism of the most influential modernists and the disillusionments of the first World War are two obvious sources of this skepticism, but perhaps there are older and deeper ones as well: for example, the fact that English poetry became a trans-national enterprise precisely at the time, in the nineteenth century, when modern nationalism was taking shape. An American, Australian, or Canadian who has been educated on British poetic models finds it difficult to use them in the service of national self-assertion without some obvious ironies arising in his mind.

For whatever combination of reasons, highly regarded poetry that is explicitly nationalistic (as opposed to merely patriotic in a general way) has in the twentieth century been restricted on the whole to small or embattled nations in conditions of crisis: Yeats's poems about Irish independence, for example, or Hugh MacDiarmid's about Scotland, or the more nationalistic passages of Eliot's *Four Quartets*. "Highly regarded," of course, raises the possibility that skepticism about nationalism is an attitude of critics rather than of poets, and no doubt one could find in the twentieth century a great deal of nationalistic verse that in previous centuries would have been labeled "popular" as opposed to serious or literary poetry. Nonetheless, it is a fact that the major poets of the twentieth century, even Kipling, are far less comfortable asserting nationalistic attitudes in verse than their

---

First published in *Verse*, III 1985. Copyright © by Christopher Clausen. Reprinted with permission of the author and publisher.

predecessors from the Renaissance through the eighteenth century. If James Thomson were alive today, he might very well write a series of poems thematically similar to "The Seasons"; it is much less likely that he would write a modern equivalent of "Rule, Britannia."

None of this means that nationality and the exploration of its constituents has not been a major theme in the literature of our time. It has, perhaps all the more so as the differences between one place and another seem to lessen. I am speaking here not of the regionalism that is such a common feature in modern British and American literature, but of national self-definition. Self-definition is an entirely different activity from self-assertion, and an inevitable one in nations that have been created in recent times by settlers whose descendants are often at a loss to know what makes them a nation besides their ancestors' common, willed act of immigration. It is hardly too much to say that this need to create a national identity in the act of understanding it has obsessed the literature of America and the Commonwealth countries since their beginnings. Much American writing from the seventeenth century onwards has embodied a heroic attempt at national definition, which reached its nineteenth-century peak in the poetry of Whitman. The history of this literary theme—of an Eden settled by Europeans, who overcame the original inhabitants and declared their independent identity by an act of self-creative will—has in turn been traced exhaustively by scholars and critics, and there is neither space nor need to summarize it here.

Since Whitman's time until recently, the literary definition of America has been carried on more conspicuously and effectively by novelists than by poets. The works of Mark Twain, Henry James, F. Scott Fitzgerald, Ernest Hemingway, and William Faulkner are obvious examples, and occasional attempts at this sort of thing in the poems of Robert Frost (e.g., "The Gift Outright") and others do not weigh heavily against them. Because the adequate exploration of national identity involves history, characters, and complex attitudes, novelists are at an obvious advantage in a time when the dominant poetic form is the short or "lyric" poem. In *The Place of Poetry* (University Press of Kentucky, 1981) I described the decline of the book-length narrative or meditative poem and gave some reasons for the dominance of the short poem since the middle of the nineteenth century. Since book-length poems that tell a story or expound ideas in detail are precisely the kind best suited to the task we are discussing, we should not be surprised that prose fiction largely appropriated it, along with so many other tasks and themes, once the scale of *Leaves of Grass* had come to seem ungainly or merely impracticable by Whitman's successors.

"Are stories no longer told in poetry?" Dana Gioia asked in *The Kenyon Review* for spring 1983. "Important ideas no longer discussed at length? The panoply of available genres would seem reduced to a few hardy perennials which poets worked over and over again with dreary regularity—the short lyric, the ode, the familiar verse epistle, perhaps the epigram, and one new-fangled form called the 'sequence' which often seemed to be either just a group of short lyrics stuck together or an ode in the process of falling apart." Gioia discussed some of the advantages of longer forms and then put his finger on an important reason for their decline in the wake of modernism: "The main problem facing the long poem today is that contemporary theory allows the poet almost no middle ground between the concentration of the lyric and the vast breadth of the epic (the modern epic, that is, in its distinctive form as the historical cultural poem).... American literature needs a more modest aesthetic of the long poem, a less chauvinistic theory which does not vainly seek the great at the expense of the good and genuine. It needs to free poets from the burden of writing the definitive long poem and allow them to work in more manageable albeit limited genres like satire, comedy, unheroic autobiography, discursive writing, pure narrative—be it fictional or historic...."

Drawing attention to the eclipse of a literary form is often a step towards reviving it, and as Frederick Feirstein pointed out in the same issue of *The Kenyon Review*, most of the genres that Gioia called for are again being practiced in a variety of ways. The lyric poem could accommodate some themes and ambitions supremely well and offered many poets a welcome discipline after the verbosity of the most celebrated Victorians. But the very successes of its practitioners, from Hopkins and Yeats through Frost and Eliot to the present, exhausted many of its possibilities in the act of exploiting them. Sooner or later, new poets would wish to escape from the shadow of their immediate predecessors—just as the modernists had once done with theirs—by trying themes and forms that had fewer recent associations. One result has been a widespread but mostly unheralded revival of the book-length poem in America during the last decade or so. Another, closely related, has been a return to the theme of national identity in an era which, like Whitman's, makes that identity a matter of obsessive concern. The end of the twentieth century is in most respects a more troubling time than Whitman's, and the identity to be explored is not the same as it was in the first century of the republic. Nonetheless, Whitman, Cooper, Emerson, and their contemporaries would recognize important continuities, if only because searching for the essence of America is such a characteristically American thing to do.

From many poems that might be chosen to illustrate these assertions, I have selected three: Robert Pinsky's *An Explanation of America*, Frederick Feirstein's *Manhattan Carnival*, and Robert Penn Warren's *Chief Joseph of the Nez Perce*. They are a diverse group in their forms, in their settings, in their authors' outlooks on life in general and America in particular; yet they all embody a deep desire to get to the heart of American identity, which in varying ways all three writers (like most Americans since Jamestown) feel to be unique. None of these poems is an epic; all are ambitious "public" poems. My concern in examining them is not so much to evaluate them as to see how three contemporary poets have experimented with long forms — blank-verse meditation, fictional narrative in heroic couplets, and historical narrative in free verse — while exploring a theme of overriding significance. Looked at together, they incarnate three ways of writing a book-length poem today and also three approaches to what might be called, in medieval romance fashion, the Matter of America.

II

In *The Situation of Poetry* (1976), Robert Pinsky celebrated the bicentennial of American independence by calling for a return to the "prose virtues" in poetry. Poetry, he declared, should be as well written, and sometimes as discursive, as good prose. "Colorless and reactionary as such a position may seem," he added, mindful of the recent history of American verse, "it is worth taking up." Then he went on to explain what he had in mind by "prose virtues" and to assert that late-twentieth-century poets might find them to be necessities: "If the plural is analyzed, the virtues turn out to be a drab, unglamorous group, including perhaps Clarity, Flexibility, Efficiency, Cohesiveness . . . a puritanical assortment of shrews. They do not as a rule appear in blurbs. And yet when they are courted by those who understand them — William Carlos Williams and Elizabeth Bishop would be examples — the Prose Virtues are transformed from a supporting chorus to the performers of virtuoso marvels. They can become not merely the poem's minimum requirement, but the poetic essence." Pinsky's *An Explanation of America* (1979), subtitled in Yeatsian fashion "A Poem to My Daughter," puts most of those virtues to use in an extended meditation whose discursive purpose is proclaimed by its title.

To explain America poetically, it is necessary first to delineate the person for whom the explanation is intended. The rhetoric of explanation must be *ad hominem*, in the correct sense of that commonly abused phrase. The daughter for whom the explanation is nominally devised seems hardly the sort of child thought to be typically American: she is imaginative, solitary, infantile in many ways but with the dreams of an adult—"not / A type (the solitary flights at night; / The dreams mature, the spirit infantile) / Which America has always known to prize." She is, in short, an outsider, not a joiner, not likely to be at home with American gregariousness, a potential object of persecution, a disconcertingly intelligent child whose eyes behind their owlish glasses betray "The gaze of liberty and independence / Uneasy in groups and making groups uneasy." Already a note of alienation has been struck between the person to whom the explanation is directed (the explainer himself is not yet an issue) and the thing to be explained. We are a long way from Whitman's uncontradictory sense of America as a unified mass of individualists.

The possibility that America in the fullness of its development has become a less benign creation than Whitman hoped inheres in the daughter's childish forms of alienation. Dreams and reality have parted, leaving behind the wake of ambiguities that require the poet's explanation. Thus the first question is what, after the variety and empty vastness of the American continent, to show.

> What do I want for you to see? I want—
> Beyond the states and corporations, each
> Hiding and showing after their kind the forms
> Of their atrocities, beyond their power
> For evil—the greater evil in ourselves,
> And greater images more vast than *Time*.
> I want for you to see the thing I see
> And more, Colonial Diners, Disney, films
> Of concentration camps, the napalmed child
> Trotting through famous newsfilm in her diaper
> And tattered flaps of skin, *Deep Throat*, the rest.

In its content, its emphases, its development, its juxtaposition of the horrific and the banal, this catalogue of American realities is far different from anything in "Song of Myself." Evil and banality infect not only institutions but American selves. Television and Vietnam have both happened. If the New World was ever Eden, the Fall was a long time ago. Democracy, however desirable, has solved few problems (as the daughter puts it, "Voting *is not* fair").

> I want our country like a common dream
> to be between us in what we want to see —
> Not that I want for you to have to see
> Atrocity itself, or that its image
> Is harmless. I mean the way we need to see
> With shared, imperfect memory: the quiet
> Of tourists shuffling with their different awes
> Through well-kept Rushmore, Chiswick House, or Belsen...

Not discoverers or pioneers, not Columbus or Lewis and Clark, but tourists.

What follows is predictably fragmentary, impressions of a land and history described in the last line of the poem as "So large, and strangely broken, and unforeseen." It is not on the whole an attractive portrait.

> The plural-headed Empire, manifold
> Beyond my outrage or my admiration,
> Is like a prison which I leave to you
> (And like a shelter) — where the people vote,
> And where the threats of riot and oppression
> Inspire the inmates as they whittle, scribble,
> Jockey for places in the choir, or smile
> Passing out books on weekdays.

An empire is characterized, in Pinsky's terms, by variety, mobility, and, above all, power. Americans move around so much that regional differences, indeed all sense of place, become themselves "a kind of motion." An image of unmotivated suicide in the endless prairies of the Middle West suggests the aimlessness of so much American mobility, which is perhaps little more at bottom than a love of death. In a nation whose inhabitants have to create it imaginatively out of such a vast emptiness, a lasting individual or corporate identity is hard to come by. No wonder that the official symbol of the United States, the eagle who represents flight and power, is a "wild bird with its hardware in its claws."

What Whitman would have made of America a century after his death is anybody's guess, but he would almost certainly have resisted the notion that classical European parallels could offer useful insights. For him and his followers, America was unique in the world's history, subject to few of the limitations that affected other empires. Pinsky, however, follows many twentieth-century historians and political commentators in seeing close parallels between America and Rome, frugal republics that begat decadent empires. The center of his poem is a free translation from a letter in which Horace reflected on private versus public life in an imperial society. *Public* and *private* meant different things in an empire from what they meant in a small republic, Roman or American. For Pinsky's Horace, a detached retirement is the only way to lead a life that is both free and dignified. A public life in which those virtues can be maintained has become, if not absolutely impossible, at least very difficult. What can traditional civic virtues mean in such a civilization? At bottom, the willingness to commit suicide rather than submit to tyranny is the only solid basis for liberty—a liberty which only detached individuals can possess, not one that undergirds the whole social structure. The republic is gone forever; only in the isolated, detached self of the Stoic does anything of its spirit survive.

Republics liberate, empire imprisons. Thomas Jefferson on his mountaintop at Monticello represented an altogether different classicism from Horace at his Sabine farm. A third civic possibility is Brutus. Pinsky finds it hard to decide what kind of fortune to wish for a daughter who must live in an age of Caesarism. Whatever one's talents, to be a Jefferson is now impossible.

> Since aspirations need not (some say, should not)
> Be likely, should I wish for you to be
> A hero, like Brutus—who at the finish-line
> Declared himself to be a happy man?
> Or is the right wish health, the just proportion
> Of sun, the acorns and cold pure water, a nest
> Out in the country and a place in Rome...

The question is never resolved.

Despite the optimism of its title, "Its Everlasting Possibility," the last section of the poem remains equally uncertain. With the instincts of a classicist, Pinsky sees the denial of limit as a "pride, or failing" common to all the races, classes, and regions of America. That denial may well be what transformed America from a republic to an empire. Vietnam ought finally to have taught America a lesson about limits.

> On television, I used to see, each week,
> Americans descending in machines
> With wasted bravery and blood; to spread
> Pain and vast fires amid a foreign place...
> I think it made our country older, forever.

Older, but not wiser. The lesson was not learned. A curious amalgam of "Nostalgia and Progress" continues to dominate the collective mind. No doubt every recent observer of America has been struck by the bizarre coexistence of an unlimited faith in technology with an assertion of what are imagined to be old-fashioned family and religious values. As Pinsky puts it,

> The country, boasting that it cannot see
> The past, waits dreaming ever of the past,
> Or all the plural pasts: the way a fetus
> Dreams vaguely of heaven...

Even the ageless mountains need protection, in the form of environmental laws, from the irresponsibility of technological somnambulism.

In the epilogue, the ambiguous tale of America is tacitly compared with Shakespeare's *The Winter's Tale*. Hope may be reborn, despite appearances; the size and mobility of the country once again militate against a definitive conclusion. What can a classicist make of so unclassical a spectacle?

> Where nothing will stand still
> Nothing can end—but recoils into the past,
> Or is improvised into the dream or nightmare
> Romance of new beginnings.

A skeptical half-hope for the national future, by a mind that does not even know what it would be best to hope for, is the paradoxically patriotic conclusion to this uncertain explanation.

III

If it is to be less ambiguous, the romance of new beginnings may have to be a private rather than a national renewal. The year after Pinsky's poem was published, Ronald Reagan was elected president on the slogan, "Together, a new beginning." It seems unlikely that Pinsky's hopes for this country or his daughter were advanced by such an appropriation, but there can be no doubt that the concept of new beginnings, on the level of advertising if not of poetry, had developed a mass appeal. The public consequences of that appeal are well known. For poets and thinkers, the most important effect was probably to intensify the division between public and private life that Richard Sennett described a decade ago in *The Fall of Public Man*. We shall be looking presently at one contemporary poet's jaundiced view of public life during the period when America was transforming itself into an imperial power. Before that, however, I want to examine a more private romance of new beginnings in Frederick Feirstein's *Manhattan Carnival* (1981), a poem whose exploration of American identity rarely becomes as explicit as Pinsky's and yet is perhaps, for that very reason, all the more searching and symptomatic.

If Pinsky's points of reference are on the whole classical, Feirstein's most immediately obvious ones are eighteenth-century and neoclassical. The poem is written in heroic couplets like a satire of Pope's, but its content and idiom are 1970's New York Jewish. To confuse matters further, the subtitle is "A Dramatic Monologue." The poem's antecedents, like America's, are too various to fit clearly in a single line of development. We might best think of it as a novel in verse that begins when Mark Stern, a New York playwright whose wife has left him, wakes up one morning and decides to rediscover himself.

> I shout into the mirror football cheers:
> "You've lived on this stone island thirty years
> And loved it for its faults; you are depressed.
> Get out, discover it again, get dressed...."

If the city where he finds himself (in more senses than one) is not quite Whitman's "my own Manhattan," the search itself in its enthusiasm and inclusiveness is an expedition on which Whitman would have found himself entirely at home.

My eye is like a child's; the smog is pot.
Shining cratefuls of plum, peach, apricot
Are flung out of the fruit man's tiny store.
Behind the supermarket glass next door:
Landslides of grapefruit, orange, tangerine,
Persimmon, boysenberry, nectarine.
The florist tilts his giant crayon box
Of yellow roses, daffodils, and phlox.
A Disney sun breaks through . . .

And on and on, a Whitman catalogue in which (*pace* Pinsky) Disney is as
real and acceptable as daffodils, rock-and-roll as Mozart: contemporary
America in the eye of the beholder.

There are no villains in *Manhattan Carnival*—how could such a fre-
netically inclusive work have villains?—but not all people and things
arouse Mark Stern's sympathy equally. Landlords, bankers, sexual hypo-
crites, developers who destroy the urban landscape ("Helpless I watch
as wreckers mug and rape / The Greek Revival houses . . . ") are bad, but
not inhuman. Children, and above all childlike adults, are good, but not
unflawed. Reviving the child in himself is one of Stern's goals; the child
and the city are somehow bound together, and neither can be properly
enjoyed without the other. In the simple plot of the poem, Stern's aim is
to become childlike again partly for its own sake, partly so that his es-
tranged wife Marlene will return to him. Somehow, their lives have gone
wrong; instead of being filled with wonder and enthusiasm, both of them
were merely infantile.

We lived inside a mirrored garbage can.
Each day I grew more passive, you more wild.
The child is only father of the child.

The solution, Stern feels, is to have a child of their own.

It must be obvious by now that Manhattan is more than a setting for
this domestic drama. The exploration of self is also an exploration of the
city-state; healing the self requires a new relation to the environment.
That relation is always emotional and tactile, never political as in earlier
city-states. The mirrored garbage can has to become a carnival, not a
polis. In that sense, we are still wandering in Pinsky's empire. On the
other hand, variety and mobility are less threatening here than in Pinsky's
poem. New York is filled with all kinds of people and things, many of
them transient.

A tourist wearing giveaway white gloves,
A straw hat with a pin of turtle doves,
Asks for the flavors in a Southern drawl.
The ices-man snaps, "Just one left, that's all."
"A typical New Yorker," she replies.
Stunned by those words, tears welling in his eyes,
He lifts her hand and kisses it. "For you
—For free! Dear lady, take my special brew."
She sucks a cup of all his remnants mixed.
A rainbow "Typical New York" has fixed.
She walks away perplexed: is this one mad?
He beams, "Two years an immigrant, not bad!"

Two kinds of Americans on the move encounter each other, are baffled, but make the best of it, more or less. It may not be an ideal way to create a nation, but there is no atrocity in it.

On the whole, the city is a good place, and people who reject it are rejecting themselves. To be sure, it has its frauds, financial and artistic. As in Pinsky, though to a much lesser extent, the American refusal to recognize limits leads, if not to catastrophe, at least to bad taste.

The New World's paved with dog-shit, not with gold
And tasteless in its art. These galleries
Are filled with junk the touring Japanese
Cart home with moccasins, tin Empire States,
Key chains with footballs, paper license plates.

Nonetheless, the one point at which Stern momentarily repudiates the city is a moment of self-hatred.

I hate this Spring, rebirth, no birth, this city.
I hate my monomania, self-pity.
I hate that Hasid, hate his button shop.
I hate that jeweler, hate that traffic cop.
I hate the Gotham Bookmart, Berger's Deli.

Only the most dehumanized monuments to greed, such as Sixth Avenue (officially the Avenue of the Americas) and the Hilton Hotel, deserve this reaction.

Manhattan, like life itself, is an opportunity for affirmation in this affirmative poem. Whatever our individual and collective histories may have done to us, however flawed or impaired we may be, carnival is still possible. The relatively optimistic conclusion of the poem is effective because so much stands in its way:

In other words Corinna what I'm saying:
We're crazy, wounded, but we are a-maying.

The poem ends with the Sterns apparently in the act of begetting a child to whom America may someday have to be explained anew; but one suspects that the explanation will be less skeptical and ironic than Pinsky's. *Manhattan Carnival*, unlike *An Explanation of America*, is rooted in a place whose identity is reasonably secure. Perhaps that limit to possibility allows the poet to be less threatened by the scale and transiency of life in contemporary America.

New York City, as most Americans will concede or proclaim, is not a typically American place; but then what is? The ancestors of most living Americans entered the New World through its harbor. The identity that Mark Stern discovers and the city in which it has meaning are as centrally American as any of the other selves that rot or flourish in what F. Scott Fitzgerald defined forever as the dark fields of the republic.

IV

An Explanation of America and *Manhattan Carnival* might, in different senses, be described as poems of the Age of Carter, that humane season in which American introspection seemed to revive. Publicly and politically if not poetically, it soon became evident that the reach of the new idealism exceeded its grasp. Robert Penn Warren's *Chief Joseph of the Nez Perce* (1983)[*] is a poem for the harsher Age of Reagan, by which I mean not so much a harsher poem as one whose portrayal of American expansiveness and potentiality is bitterly ironic rather than even guardedly optimistic. The "atrocities" that Pinsky mentioned abstractly come to full historical life in this meditative narration about a nation of Indians, the Nez Perce of the Pacific Northwest, obliterated by a brutal notion of progress.

Warren would undoubtedly disagree with Pinsky that ignorance of limit is common to "all this country's regions, / Races, and classes." He would except the South. Because the South lost its war of independence,

---

[*] A shorter version was published by *The Georgia Review* in 1982. I make use here of the later text.

was devastated and conquered, its inhabitants ever since have been more aware than other Americans that the strength and boldness of a people's aspirations do not guarantee their success. Warren has made a career of writing about the durable (though perhaps not unqualified) effects of defeat on the Southern mind; his most famous novel, *All the King's Men*, is a tragedy of political corruption and hubris in Louisiana. In writing about the Nez Perce, he ascribes to them a Southern sense of the limits of self-assertion, a reverence for the earth and for their ancestors, in sharp contrast to the victorious Union veterans, insatiable conquerors of land and people, who defeat them. An advantage of writing about the traditional lives of Indians or other primitive peoples is that one can project upon them almost any set of attitudes one wishes. Their literary usefulness as a reflector of contemporary needs is unrivaled because so little is known about them. Warren has clearly mastered the few records that survive about the lives of the Nez Perce before their conquest; the mind of his Chief Joseph is an imaginative construct, however, that inevitably embodies historical realities less than the needs and anxieties of the 1980's as Warren senses them.

Thus the Indians at the beginning of the poem live in an Eden of nakedness, harmony with the natural world, truthfulness, and "unbridled glory."

> It is their land, and the bones of their fathers
> Yet love them, and in that darkness, lynxlike,
> See how their sons still thrive without fear,
> Not lying, not speaking with forked tongue.
> Men know, in night-darkness, what wisdom thrives with the fathers.

In this paradise there are no serpents until the white men come, first in the form of French trappers, then Lewis and Clark, finally the United States army and "the makers of treaties." Joseph's father signs the treaty of 1855 that guarantees the homeland of his people. For a time all is well. In 1873 President Grant again guarantees the land of Joseph's band; but the promise is not kept, and a few years later all the Nez Perce are ordered to a reservation. They fail to understand the white man's concept of truth and reality as determined by marks on paper that can be changed at will by other marks. Not only their concept of truth is different; so is their idea of national identity. By this time Joseph's father has died and Joseph himself is chief, but throughout the poem he feels himself guided by his father's voice and watched by his father's eyes.

"But then, my heart, it heard
My father's voice, like a great sky-cry
From snow-peaks in sunlight, and my voice
Was saying the Truth that no
White man can know, how the Great Spirit
Had made the earth but had drawn no lines
Of separation upon it, and all
Must remain as He made, for to each man
Earth is the Mother and Nurse, and to that spot
Where he was nursed, he must,
In love cling."

The greatest failing of white men in this poem, the flaw that motivates their brutality and greed, their perfidy and the corruptness of their public life, is their failure to love the land. For them, country and national identity are matters of documents and possession, not tradition and association—a frequent complaint of Southern writers about their Northern countrymen. America as a nation began, to be sure, with documents—the Declaration of Independence and the Constitution; the spontaneity of Joseph's feelings about his land has always been impossible for most white Americans. Ultimately the Indians fight for their land, the whites for gold and empire. Warren quotes a battlefield marker with bitter irony:

Before you . . . lies the historic battle ground of the Nez
Perce Indian War in which 34 men gave their lives in
service for their country.

Whatever they gave their lives for, Warren seems to be saying, it was not "country" in any sense that the natives who were fighting for their homeland would have understood. The white men are found "clutching earth as though they had loved her" only after they have been killed.

The flaw of the white men is also their strength, and as the story unfolds in its inevitable way we experience no surprise at the tactics by which they overcome Joseph's people. When two hostile nations track their way through mountains alien to both, the one trying to reach safety in Canada, the other trying to cut off its escape, the winner is likely to be the one who understands maps and compasses. So it proves in this case, although the Indians' instinct for the land enable them to hold off white attacks more than once and almost, in the end, to make their escape. For a time the white soldiers are more brutal than effective.

"Near dawn they struck us, new horse-soldiers. Shot
Into tepees. Women, children, old died.
Some mother might stand in the river's cold coil
And hold up the infant and weep, and cry mercy.
What heart beneath blue coat has fruited in mercy?
When the slug plugged her bosom, unfooting her
To the current's swirl and last darkness, what last
Did she hear? It was laughter...."

But we know, if we know anything at all about how the West was won,
that eventually the soldiers will surround the Indians, that the Indians will
surrender after being promised to be allowed to return to their homeland,
that the promise will be broken, that many of them will die of white men's
diseases on a reservation. The "Sky-Chief" smiles on his worshipers for a
time, then betrays them in an alien landscape. It is the endlessly depressing
story of the Indians of the West.

Although the white men act in the service of impersonal forces, not all of
them are wholly depersonalized. General O.O. Howard lost an arm in the
Civil War and feels himself driven by God's will and the love of glory. Colo-
nel Miles, even more driven, flings his men across mountain ranges in the
hope of capturing Joseph's band before Howard does. Their battle for repu-
tation is with each other rather than with the Indians, who represent (to
them) little more than a reproof and an opportunity. Both men are nearly
demented with ambition. In the end, however, both draw back from their
worst excesses. Arriving before the surrender, Howard sacrifices his longing:

Stood there, commander, enduring the only
Outlet of rage and hatred Miles
Could give vent to: ironical courtesy, cold,
Gray as snot. But Howard,
Whose sweat had soaked sheets in wrestling with God,
Laid his remaining hand on the steel-stiff shoulder
That quivered beneath it. Howard, almost
As soft as a whisper, promises him the surrender.

And hearing his own words, he knew a pure
And never-before-known bliss swell his heart.

Likewise Miles, his own ambition appeased, offers mercy to the Indians,
and later even advocacy:

And was it integrity, or some
Sad division of self, torn in ambition

And ambition's price, that at last made Miles
The only staunch friend of Joseph for all
The years? In his rising success, did something make Miles
Wonder what was the price of a star?

As at Appomattox, the conquerors are capable of mercy, charity, and
ultimately some degree of self-knowledge. But the price of serving imper-
sonal forces is irrelevance once one decides to stop serving them. Joseph
wishes throughout to be a man in the eyes of his father. The eyes in whose
gaze Howard and Miles perform—public opinion as expressed by news-
papers—are not so easily placated. The Indians find that once he has be-
friended them, Miles carries no weight.

How could they know that Miles, whom they trusted,
Was only a brigadier behind whom
Moved forces, faceless, timeless, dim,
And in such dimness, merciless?

Ambition, greed, and lust for empire are forces too powerful for mere Indi-
ans to stand in their way. Nor is any personal ideal of manhood a match for
them. Heroes like Grant, Sherman, Howard, and Miles become figures of
straw in the wind when they try to mitigate the destructiveness of their
own victories. Brooding on his long-dead father and the destiny that has
overtaken his own life, Joseph has the last word about men and nations:

"But what is a man? An autumn-tossed aspen,
Pony-fart in the wind, the melting of snow-slush?
Yes, that is all. Unless—unless —
We can learn to live the Great Spirit's meaning
As the old and wise grope for it . . ."

Glib and inadequate as this prescription may sound, Warren seems to be
saying, it represents a wisdom beyond the grasp, let alone the practice, of
the driven civilization that puts an end to the Nez Perce way of life and
simultaneously to its own public virtues.

Except in those rare cases where it arises from attachment to a place,
American identity is a matter of documents and pledges and rituals. In this
conclusion Warren, Pinsky, and Feirstein would probably all agree. The
Indians might have educated us in less destructive attitudes and ways of
living, of being a people, if we had listened before we dispossessed them.
Like Southerners, Warren's Nez Perce represent the rooted victims of an
abstract, implacable American destiny. They even get beaten by the same

men. (Of course, white Southerners are less amenable to this kind of ide-alization: they helped displace the Indians, they kept slaves, and they left more records of themselves.) When it comes to the making or maintaining of a national self, W.H. Auden put it most memorably:

> History to the defeated
> May say Alas but cannot help or pardon.

Poets, likewise, can do no more than explore and try to explain.

North American Addresses: Three Verse Narratives

Thomas M. Disch

Though narrative verse has enjoyed a small renaissance in the past decade, it continues to be regarded—or rather, disregarded—as an outmoded and déclassé art form. Reviewers encountering the rare specimen tend to fall into two camps—those who seek out some high-minded connection to the great tradition of epic verse from Homer through Milton (an effort at which the poet may have assisted by strewing his path with mythopoeic tics and homages, as Derek Walcott does in *Omeros*) and those who would permit Calliope to appear in less than full armor and who demand from narrative poetry only those pleasures they are accustomed to derive from reading novels. Since only a few long poems purvey such pleasures (Vikram Seth's *The Golden Gate* of 1986 has been the most conspicuous recent example), using such a yardstick can only yield a sense that most narrative verse offers its readers short measure.

By and large, therefore, critics of poetry simply don't interest themselves in narrative verse that is not the work of an already well-established poet like Walcott or James Merrill, and this neglect sends a clear signal to poets: Don't bother. The lyric meditation, the confessional anecdote, the barbaric yawp—these are the forms proper to contemporary poetry, and if you must aspire to write longer poems, think to create sheaves and bundles of the sanctioned shorter forms, after the manner of the longer-winded modernists, Pound, Williams, Olson. To do otherwise is to court comparison with such poetic pariahs as Robinson Jeffers, or Stephen Vincent Benét, or (if you compound the felony with rhyming stanzas) Robert Service.

That narrative verse is making a comeback despite such proscriptions can be traced to the fact that poets share our common culture, a culture saturated with fiction and make-believe. A good portion of all elementary and secondary education is devoted to teaching children to be capable readers and interpreters of prose fiction. When those children would avoid the

---

This essay originally appeared in *The Hudson Review*. Remarks on Jarman's *Iris* are interpolated from "Onegin's Children," from *The Castle of Indolence: On Poetry, Poets, and Poetasters* (Picador, 1995: 80-83).

novels they've been assigned for homework, they venture out upon the vaster sea of stories available on TV. I have known one or two poets of repute to say that they don't read novels or go to movies and subsist entirely on a diet of poetry, as once some few anorexic saints were said to have had no nourishment except the Eucharist. My reaction, in both cases, is reverence mixed with skepticism.

Poets who would embark upon a narrative career have the option of writing novels, of course, and there are compelling reasons for following that route. A novel is likelier to be published, will surely receive a better advance, and stands a far better chance of being widely reviewed and read. Poets as diverse as Robert Graves, James Dickey, Sylvia Plath, Robert Penn Warren, and D.M. Thomas have written novels that *are* novels, and bestsellers at that. By contrast, narrative poems do not—or do not usually—aspire to the condition of the novel. Nor yet is it useful (for poet or reader) to consider them as lineal descendants of the epic tradition, except insofar as all fiction, by an accident of literary history, is part of that tradition. Homer and Vergil are as little useful as role models for a narrative poet today as the ruins of Mycenae to a contemporary architect.

Theory should proceed from example. Let us consider here three books that are exemplary in both senses of that word. All are published or distributed by Story Line Press, one by Mark Jarman, one by the press's editor, Robert McDowell, and one by David Mason. As its name would suggest, Story Line Press has been an active promoter of narrative verse, having published works that have been benchmarks of the new narrative poetry. Jarman's earlier *Iris* (Story Line, 1992) so closely parallels McDowell's and Mason's poems in its taxonomy as to comprise with them the basis for a kind of esthetic triangulation.

Mark Jarman's *Iris* is a labor of love in the usual (and entirely honorable) sense. It comes close to possessing the virtues one associates with a good novel. There is a continuous action, developed characters, and a narrative momentum with none of those speed bumps that poets introduce into their longer works on purpose to slow the reader down to the statelier gait of Dame Poetry. In both its plot and its prosody *Iris* is an homage to the most successful and critically neglected practitioner of narrative verse in this century, Robinson Jeffers. It uses the same long, loping lines, and agglutinative, semicolon-encrusted syntax that gives a poem like "Roan Stallion" its bookmark-defying momentum; despite its length, *Iris* is a poem you'd be likely to read at a single sitting, for the question of what will happen next has the same import it would in an ordinary novel.

What happens is this: the eponymous heroine, fleeing an abusive husband, returns with her toddler daughter, Ruth, to her home in rural Kentucky, and for a while enjoys a neo-hillbilly country 'n' western idyll with a family consisting of her boozing Mama, her brothers, Hoy and Rice, who grow marijuana because it's the most profitable cash crop for subsistence farmers, and Mama's lover and drinking companion, Charles, a crossing guard at a shopping mall, whom Mama met in this wise:

> The day Mama found him he was like that, lackadaisical
> as a nodding thistle.
> A bad bearing on her cart made one wheel spin. Mama
> had bought too much and tried to guide
> The cart with her beer belly. Charles, ignoring her,
> motioned a car through. There was a wiry, soft
> Collision. Mama's cart tipped sideways. Groceries
> sprayed across the asphalt. Charles cursed.
> Mama grabbed his forearm like a wader caught by a
> current on shifting stones.
> When somebody appeared—the manager?—he whirled
> on Charles and Mama both and shouted.
> He grabbed Charles's hat and said he would replace the
> groceries and Charles, too.
> So, Charles had needed someone, just like Mama. Truck
> loaded, the poor boy stunned, Mama drove
> To the state line and brought them both a beer or two,
> a few games of video poker.
> Charles cheered up. You couldn't tell how old he was,
> like those boys on Lawrence Welk
> Who dance at show's end with the grandmothers, smiling
> more tenderly than any son.

The idyll ends when Hoy, Rice, and Charlie are executed by other drug dealers, whereupon Iris flees to California, with her daughter and her now autistic Mama, there to marry the first man she asks directions from. She spends the second of the poem's three sections in a state of somnambulistic housewifery. Then, the moment her daughter marries, she decamps for what had been, all this while, her secret destination, the landmark-status sea cliff home of Robinson Jeffers, whose poetry, first encountered in college, has been a talisman for Iris through the years. As she explains, towards the end of the book:

You'd think with all the death in it, my life
Would be a tragedy. But I've kept my real life a
    secret—reading Jeffers
And trying to imagine him imagining someone like me.
    It's when he says
He has been saved from human illusion and foolishness
    and passion and wants to be like a rock
That I miss something. I think I have been steadfast,
    but what does rock feel? I like him in bereavement—
When saying man can't last long, then admitting, since
    his wife's death, that he is short of patience.
Wanting to die, to lay his body down where he has found
    the wounded deer have done so,
In the hidden clearing on the cliff edge, then refusing
    to. That's when I like to read him.

That passage is a good self-reflexive critique of the book in hand as well as of Jeffers, and it also serves to illustrate an essential difference between the two narrative media, prose and poetry. In narrative poetry, the characters tend, even when they speak in a plausible, demotic way, to *think* in poetry and to share, as Iris does here, the core concerns of both the writer and the (presumed) readers, to try, in her terms, "to imagine him imagining someone like me." To put this another way, the reader of a poem is always more conscious of the shaping intelligence of the poet than the reader of the novel, whose art conceals art as best it can. The poetic storyteller also relies on his readers' imaginative cooperation in filling out those blanks that novelists can spend pages in spelling out. Imagine how long Mama's first encounter with Charles might take in the hands of even so telegraphic a prose writer as Raymond Carver. In this respect, *Iris* more resembles the punchy scene setting of a screen treatment, with the poet counting on his readers to extrapolate stage business and dialogue. The object of poetic narrative is to suggest as much as possible with maximum compression, but without becoming gnarled or gnomic and losing the flow, as in, "There was a wiry, soft collision," which conveys the impact of a car on Mama and her shopping cart with an economy that can't be taken in without a mental notation of "That's neat." It is with poets as with the splashier sort of painters, Delacroix, Rembrandt, Manet, Johns—it's not enough that their pictures fascinate us, they insist on our admiring the brushwork.

Finally, one must ask of a narrative poem the same leveling questions one asks of novels: is it a good story? Does it have a satisfying resolution?

It is, and it does, though the kind of satisfaction it affords is one of Chekhovian quietness; yet not *so* quiet that one couldn't imagine the book serving as the basis for a good movie.

Robert McDowell's *The Diviners* (Peterloo, 1995) and David Mason's *The Country I Remember* (Story Line, 1996) are of roughly equal length—55 to 57 pages, not counting blank intercalary pages in the former and twelve short poems bulking out the latter volume. *The Diviners* is told in five "chapters" of fluently variegated blank verse, each chapter set in a new decade from the fifties through the nineties. Mason's poem is less regular metrically, the predominantly pentameter lines being grouped into seven-line stanzas with an occasional singleton line serving to give closure to a dramatic sequence. There are twelve titled sections featuring, in alternation, the first-person "oral" memoirs of John Mitchell, a lieutenant in the Union Army and prisoner in the Confederacy's Libby Prison, and of his daughter, Maggie Gresham, a pioneer (with her family and on her own) of the Far West.

Both narratives are notably cool in their handling of materials that would, in the hands of most novelists, be milked for a vicarious and sensational interest. The opening chapter of *The Diviners* (which appeared first in *The Hudson Review* and was reprinted in *The Best American Poetry 1989*) has a plot line that might do duty as the kickoff for a James M. Cain thriller. A wife neglected by her businessman husband has an affair with her eight-year-old son's science teacher. A female private detective hired by the husband blackmails the wife, and the teacher has his legs broken. The wife rebels, spends half a year crisscrossing "the bleak Southwest":

> One month she deals blackjack in Las Vegas;
> Or pushes drinks in Bisbee, types in Austin.
> In Santa Fe she's fired for drinking too much.
> Her money thin, her prospects all played out,
> She calls again and says she's coming home.
> Al hears the liquor in her voice and smiles,
> And tells her not so fast.
>   "I filed last month,"
> He says to no immediate reply.
> "I asked for custody, but I'll drop it all
> If you agree to fix yourself and stay."
>
> Exhausted, bitter, Eleanor agrees.

Whereupon the story turns its attention away from the prison of Al and Eleanor's marriage and concentrates on their son, Tom, and whether he will be integrated into the society that has hollowed out his parents' souls. The sixties offer this prospect:

> The decade drowns in violence and blood,
> Conspiracies and unacknowledged coups.
> The nation seems to lie down willingly
> As Tom gets older, filling up with grief.
> The faces and the land ahead look bleak,
> And he begins to hear about the war.
> Desolated, angrier each day,
> He'd like to kill. A war is one good way.

Let us leave Tom there on the brink of the seventies for a moment (where, happily, McDowell himself switches gears, narratively, from noir—"Desolated, angrier each day"—to a tone of mellow chagrin) and consider the same nation a century earlier. Fully half of *The Country I Remember* is given to the Civil War and prison memoirs of John Mitchell. If there has been any event in American history that would seem to lend itself to an epic, neo-Homeric treatment, it would be the Civil War, and from the first, American poets have accepted the invitation. Herman Melville wrote a book of bombastic verse dioramas, *Battle-Pieces and Aspects of the War*, a literary curiosity that only his biographers could love. Even grander in manner and design is Stephen Vincent Benét's *John Brown's Body* (1927), once a staple of high school classrooms, but decisively exiled from the canon now that high school reading skills and attention spans are so much diminished.[1]

The problem with the Civil War as a theme for poetry is that its battlefields and main events have become as smooth and *known* as the turf of an often-revisited golf course. Its moral dimensions seem so monolithically clear that the poet (and reader) has little to do but choose sides, then purchase the appropriate uniform (dedicated re-enactors can spend a small fortune getting kitted up), and start pretending. David Mason confronts this problem with two ploys characteristic of the new narrative poetry: (1) his poem is artfully self-referential in that it is *about* the need of ancient mariners, war veterans, and the rest of us to tell and retell the tales that have traumatized us (about, to put it another way, our *need* for poetry);[2] (2) he favors anticlimax to a big dramatic payoff. A case in point is his account of how Mitchell, in digging an escape tunnel from Libby Prison, creates an egress prematurely. Such a plot-hinge was used as a cliffhanger to bridge the two parts of John Frankenheimer's recent television mini-series, *Andersonville*. Mason uses it as a prelude to a bout of pneumonia that prevents Mitchell joining those who escape; we are privy, instead, to his fever-dreams—and even these are rendered in his usual laconic voice. To be denied even a chance to fail is surely the height of the anticlimactic.

What, one may fairly ask of any long story, whether in verse or prose, is the point? What does the author want to tell us? Both of Mason's narrators answer that question straightforwardly on his behalf. Mitchell, dictating to an amanuensis, says:

> Sometimes I think of all the blood we've spilled,
> but thinking that way only brings bad dreams.
> It's good to have the young ones coming by
> for visits, though Maggie never had her own
> and she's still living out in California.
> Mrs. Mitchell died twelve years ago.
> It came sudden. The doctor said a stroke.
>
> Forty-eight years together, she and I,
> and most of it was work. A fellow can't
> put into words the help she gave us all.
> Not only the children. There were bad days
> when glumness got the better of me, she said,
> "Mitch, you've come too far to give up now."
> I talk a lot, but some things I can't say.

Maggie's summing-up is equally terse and stoic in its reticences. Writing in 1956 she speaks of her own surviving sibling:

> Olive's living still in Pomeroy
> and likes to call me on the telephone
> to ask about the weather. She came down
> to visit not long after Howard died
> and went to see the houses of the stars.
> My nieces and nephews are all grown up
> and like to see Aunt Maggie in L.A.
>
> They say to grow old without children is
> a curse, and sometimes I believe it's true—
> to have so much to say and no one here
> to say it to....

The lives of Mason's two protagonists (and of McDowell's Tom and Jarman's Iris, as well) are not so much uneventful as antidramatic. They eschew excitement and seek the peculiar, luminous peace associated with lyric and elegiac poetry. Confrontations are put on hold, resolutions deferred. Mason's title is taken from a poem by Trumbull Stickney, "Mnemosyne," that is a touchstone for both Mitchell and Maggie, especially its last line, "It rains across the country I remember." Mason does not quote the immediately preceding lines, though they must be considered his poem's second, secret epigraph:

> But that I knew these places are my own,
> I'd ask how came such wretchedness to cumber
> The earth, and I to people it alone.

In *Iris*, *The Diviners*, and *The Country I Remember*, children become rootless wanderers in what is seen to be a nation of drifters. The North American continent once had its own built-in teleology: "Go west, young man." "Westward the course of empire takes its way." Iris flees to California and the ocean's edge at Tor House. In Maggie's life-itinerary, from her childhood rail journey from Illinois to Oregon until, after much aleatory shunting about, her widowhood in L.A., Mason maps out a new New World, where north and south, east and west, are all one, where there are no longer any destinations but just somewhere you happen to wind up. Similarly, at the end of *The Diviners*, Tom and his wife Elaine decide to chuck it all in, trash the monitor on their home work station, and return to the barren landscapes of Ireland. (They are childless, thanks to Tom's low sperm count.)

> In bed Tom lies awake to watch the moon,
> And sees the great migrations circling back,
> The children home in lands their elders fled,
> Back home among the births and burials.

Jarman, McDowell, and Mason belong to the boomer generation, the first great cohort of Americans to have experienced disillusionment as a lifelong dietary supplement, like the Vitamin D in their milk. First, there was the Vietnam War, a crisis mirrored significantly in two of these books. The father of McDowell's Tom was a WW II veteran, with the strengths and blindnesses associated with triumphant success. Tom escapes his own baptism by fire by claiming, not quite sincerely, conscientious objector status; which, ironically, he is granted—a representative fate for boomer-age intellectuals. Mason's Mitchell, who spends his war years as a POW, represents another representative fate of the Vietnam era, for the POWs and MIAs were the only Vietnam veterans to have been accorded an unequivocal postwar status as heroes and martyrs.

The attitude towards marriage and child-rearing is similarly hedged in all three books. Parents are reverenced, even bad parents, but their examples, as procreators of the race, is looked on askance. Tom and Elaine, like Maggie, would like to have children, but it's not in their cards. Jarman's Iris has a daughter, and she goes through the motions of a loveless marriage until she's seen that daughter married, whereupon, at once, she too turns in her resignation and departs for another landscape representative of poetry and a consoling absence.

Tales of resignation and self-abnegation told by those of mature years possess a force and credibility that is not to be found in the work of younger writers, in which such sentiments too often convey a flavor of boastfulness, like the sullen triumph on the faces of those who've been multiply pierced. Resignation must be paid for by the loss of hair and faith, by deposits of cellulite, and by a host of telling details that one usually omits from one's c.v. To a degree the sadness and wisdom of middle age are a human universal (though one that has rarely been recognized as such in official American culture, where even the elderly are concerned about their tennis game), but in the nineties, sadder-but-wiser may well become a defining element of the *Zeitgeist*.

The first poets of the boomer generation to be widely celebrated were those whose work most closely resembled that of established poets of an older generation. Many came across as politically correct in an oppressive way or, the inverse, as ethically spayed. The best—Albert Goldbarth, Rodney Jones, Molly Peacock—were distinguished for the qualities one expects youth to excel in: brio, energy, pizzazz. That another *kind* of good poet should begin to emerge as the boomers mature is a reasonable expectation. That expectation is confirmed in the work of Jarman, McDowell, and Mason—work that is, like the Muse invoked by Milton in "Il Penseroso," "sober, steadfast, and demure." Nothing in recent poetry would lead us to expect a revolution so quiet, so civil, so decent, and so precisely suited to our needs.

Works Cited

1. If the renaissance of narrative verse should take deep enough root, perhaps the critical establishment may reappraise *John Brown's Body*. Modernist it's not, but Benét's poetic competence can't be brushed off as easily as that. The new narrative school of poets has already mounted a strong case for the work of Robinson Jeffers, another poet who offended academia by being too widely read.

2. In this regard, Mason's essay, "The Poetry of Life and the Life of Poetry," in the winter 1996 issue (vol. XLVIII, no. 4) of *The Hudson Review*, can be read as a pendant to his poem, since it is specifically concerned with the social utility of poetry.

BIOGRAPHICAL NOTES

Dick Allen is the author of several books of poetry including *Flight and Pursuit* and *Overnight in The Guest House of the Mystic*, a National Book Critics Circle Award nominee. *Ode to the Cold War: Poems New and Selected* appeared from Sarabande Books in 1997. He has received many national awards including a National Endowment for the Arts Fellowship and an Ingram-Merrill Fellowship in poetry. His poetry appears regularly in such magazines as *The New Yorker, Poetry, The New Criterion*, and *The Hudson Review*. In 1989 he guest-edited the special issue of *Crosscurrents* in which some of these essays first appeared.

Julia Alvarez was born in the Dominican Republic and came to the United States in 1960. After graduating from Syracuse University, she published her first collection of poems, *Homecoming*, in 1984. Alvarez has received grants from the National Endowment for the Arts and the Ingram Merrill Foundation. Her fiction includes *How the Garcia Girls Lost Their Accents*, winner of the 1991 PEN Oakland/Josephine Miles book award, *Yo!*, and *In the Time of the Butterflies*. Her most recent collection of poetry is *The Other Side: el otro lado*. She teaches at Middlebury College.

Kelly Cherry has written five books of poetry, most recently *God's Loud Hand* (LSU Press, 1993) and *Death and Transfiguration* (LSU Press 1997). Her fifth novel, *My Life and Dr. Joyce Brothers*, and her first book of nonfiction, *The Exiled Heart: A Meditative Autobiography*, both appeared in 1990. *Augusta Played: A Novel (Voices of the South)* was published in 1998. She was winner of the first Fellowship of Southern Writers Poetry Award.

Christopher Clausen is professor of English at The Pennsylvania State University. He is the author of *The Place of Poetry* (University Press of Kentucky, 1981) and *The Moral Imagination* (University of Iowa, 1986), as well as many essays, poems and reviews. *My Life with President Kennedy*, a collection of personal essays, appeared in 1994.

Thomas M. Disch has published science fiction, novels, literary criticism, and poetry. Selections from several volumes of his poems are collected in *Dark Verses and Light* from Johns Hopkins University Press. *The Priest: A Gothic Romance* and *The Castle of Indolence*, a collection of criticism of "poetry, poets, and poetasters," appeared in 1995 and 1996, respectively.

Rita Dove won the Pulitzer Prize for her 1987 collection, *Thomas and Beulah.* Dove served for two years as Poet Laureate of the United States. Her collections of poetry include *The Yellow House on the Corner, Museum, Grace Notes,* and *Selected Poems.* Dove's *The Darker Face of Earth,* a verse drama based upon Sophocles's *Oedipus the King,* was published by Story Line Press and has been produced. Dove has received Fulbright and Guggenheim Fellowships, two National Endowment for the Arts grants, the Academy of American Poets' Lavan Award, and the General Electric Foundation Award. She teaches creative writing at the University of Virginia.

Suzanne J. Doyle's third book of verse, *Dangerous Beauties,* appeared in 1992 from the Marjorie Cantor Press. She lives in Palo Alto, where she is a partner in High-Low Communications, an advertising agency. She studied poetry at Stanford with Yvor Winters.

Frederick Feirstein is a psychoanalyst in New York City. The original editor of *Expansive Poetry,* he has published seven collections of poetry, including *New and Selected Poems* (1998). He has been the recipient of a Guggenheim Fellowship in poetry, a CAPS Fellowship, the John Masefield Prize from the Poetry Society of America, and a *Quarterly Review of Literature* Colladay Award.

Annie Finch was educated at Yale University, Stanford University, and the graduate creative writing program at the University of Houston. Her manuscript of poems won the Nicholas Roerich prize and was published as *Eve* in 1997. She is also the author of the book-length poem, *The Encyclopedia of Scotland* (1982), and a critical study, *The Ghost of Meter: Culture and Prosody in American Free Verse* (University of Michigan Press, 1993), and is the editor of *A Formal Feeling Comes: Poems in Form by Contemporary Women.* She teaches at Miami University in Oxford, Ohio.

Dana Gioia is the author of *Daily Horoscope* and *The Gods of Winter,* collections of poems, and *Can Poetry Matter?,* a book of criticism. His anthology, *Formal Introductions,* was one of the earliest collections of new formalist poems. He has recently edited (with William Logan) *Certain Solitudes,* a collection of critical writings on the work of Donald Justice, and is co-author (with X. J. Kennedy) of several popular textbooks of literature. He lives in Santa Rosa, California, where he is currently working on *Nosferatu,* a libretto. Gioia's poetry now appears in *The Norton Anthology of Poetry.*

Emily Grosholz is the author of three books of poetry, *Eden* (Johns Hopkins, 1992), *Shores and Headlands* (Princeton, 1988), and *The River Painter* (University of Illinois, 1984), with a fourth, *Accidents and Essence,* forthcoming. She teaches philosophy at Pennsylvania State University and is the author of a work on the Cartesian method. Recently she edited *Telling the Barn Swallow: Poets on the Poetry of Maxine Kumin.*

R. S. Gwynn is the author of five collections of poetry and has edited several books, including two volumes of the *Dictionary of Literary Biography* on contemporary American poetry, *The Advocates of Poetry: A Reader of American Poet-Critics of the Modernist Era*, and *Poetry: A Longman Pocket Anthology*.

Marilyn Hacker is one of the most-honored of contemporary American poets, winner of the National Book Award, the Lamont Award, and the Poets' Prize. Her books of poetry include *Going Back to the River* (Random House, 1990), the verse novel *Love, Death, and the Changing of the Seasons* (Arbor House/William Morrow, 1986), and *The Hang-Glider's Daughter*, published in London by Onlywomen Press in 1990. *Winter Numbers* and *Selected Poems: 1965-1990* both appeared in 1994. She is past editor of *The Kenyon Review*.

Mark Jarman's guest-edited a special issue of *The New England Review* which examined the new narrative. He has received numerous awards in poetry, including two National Endowment for the Arts fellowships, the Joseph Henry Jackson Award, a Sotheby's International Award, and a Pushcart Prize. He teaches at Vanderbilt University. His collections of poetry include *The Black Riviera*, *Iris*, and *Questions for Ecclesiastes*. He was co-editor (with Robert McDowell) of *The Reaper* and co-editor (with David Mason) of *Rebel Angels: 25 Poets of the New Formalism*.

Paul Lake's first book of poems, *Another Kind of Travel*, was published by the University of Chicago Press in 1988. He held a Mirrielees Creative Writing Fellowship in poetry at Stanford. He has had poems in *The New Republic*, *American Scholar*, *Partisan Review*, and *Yale Review* and is a frequent contributor of criticism to such publications as *AWP Chronicle*. His novel, *Among the Immortals*, appeared in 1994. He teaches at Arkansas Tech.

Brad Leithauser is a past winner of a MacArthur Foundation grant. His collections include novels; *Penchants & Places*, a collection of critical essays; and several collections of poetry, including *Hundreds of Fireflies*, *Cats of the Temple*, and *The Mail from Anywhere*. "Metrical Illiteracy," which first appeared in *The New Criterion*, is one of the first critical essays to raise many questions central to the New Formalism. *The Odd Last Thing She Did*, a new collection of poems, appeared in 1998.

Phillis Levin is the author of *Temples and Fields* (University of Georgia Press, 1988), winner of the Poetry Society of America's Norma Farber First Book Award, and *The Afterimage* (Copper Beech, 1995). She has been a senior editor of *Boulevard* and teaches English and creative writing at the University of Maryland at College Park.

Keith Maillard was born in West Virginia and emigrated to Canada. He is an associate professor at the University of British Columbia, where he teaches creative writing. The author of seven novels and one collection of poetry, he has received the Ethel Wilson Fiction Prize and the Gerald Lampert Award for the best first book of poetry published in Canada. An eighth novel, *Gloria*, will appear in the spring of 1999.

David Mason is the co-editor (with Mark Jarman) of *Rebel Angels: 25 Poets of the New Formalism* and has published three collections of poetry and numerous personal and critical essays in periodicals, including *The Hudson Review* and *Verse*. "The Country I Remember," the award-winning title poem of his 1996 collection, has often been cited as one of the best examples of new narrative poetry. Mason teaches at Colorado College.

Robert McPhillips has written on contemporary literature for such publications as *The Sewanee Review*, *The Nation*, *Prairie Schooner*, *Crosscurrents*, *Sparrow*, and *American Literature*. For two years he wrote "The Year in Poetry" for the *Dictionary of Literary Biography Yearbook*. He is a graduate of Colgate University where he was elected to Phi Beta Kappa and received his Ph.D. in English from the University of Minnesota. He currently teaches English at Iona College.

Marilyn Nelson graduated from the University of California, Davis, and holds postgraduate degrees from the University of Pennsylvania (M.A.) and the University of Minnesota (Ph.D.). Her books are *For the Body* (1978), *Mama's Promises* (1985), *The Homeplace* (1990), and *Magnificat* (1994), all published by LSU Press, and two collections of verse for children. *The Fields of Praise: New and Selected Poems* appeared in 1997 and was a finalist for the National Book Award and winner of the Poets' Prize. She is a professor of English at the University of Connecticut, Storrs.

Ernst Pöppel is the head of the auditory research division of the Institute for Medical Psychology at the University of Munich and an internationally distinguished psychophysicist. One of his books, *Mindworks*, has been translated into English and received enthusiastic reviews in America.

Wyatt Prunty's books of poems are *Domestics of the Outer Bank*, *The Times Between*, *What Women Know*, *What Men Believe*, *Balance As Belief*, *The Run of the House*, and *Since the Noon Mail Stopped*. Oxford University Press published his critical study of figure and form in contemporary poetry, *Fallen from the Symboled World: Precedents for the New Formalism*. He teaches at the University of the South, where he is director of the Sewanee Writers Conference.

Mary Jo Salter has published three books of poetry, *Henry Purcell in Japan*, *Unfinished Painting*, and *Sunday Skaters* (Knopf, 1994), as well as a book for children and critical articles in *The New Criterion* and other periodicals. Her awards include the Lamont Prize, the Witter Bynner Award, the Peter I. B. Lavan Award, and grants from the National Endowment for the Arts, the Ingram Merrill Foundation, and the Guggenheim Foundation. She serves as poetry editor of *The New Republic* and is co-editor of *The Norton Anthology of Poetry*.

Meg Schoerke has written criticism for *Poetry after Modernism* and a forthcoming collection of essays on the poetry of Muriel Rukeyser. She also wrote the introduction to *The Reaper Reader*. Her poems have appeared in *TriQuarterly*, *River Styx*, and *The American Scholar*. She is an assistant professor of English at San Francisco State University.

Timothy Steele has received a Guggenheim Fellowship in poetry and a Lavan Younger Poets Award from the Academy of American Poets. His first two books, *Uncertainties and Rest* and *Sapphics Against Anger and Other Poems*, have recently been re-issued by the University of Arkansas Press, which also published his widely discussed book on twentieth-century versification, *Missing Measures*. *The Color Wheel*, a collection of poems, appeared in 1994 from Johns Hopkins University Press, and his edition of *The Poems of J. V. Cunningham* appeared in 1997.

Frederick Turner is an English-born American poet and scholar. He is Founders Professor of Arts and Humanities at the University of Texas at Dallas and a former editor of *The Kenyon Review*. Turner has published two epic poems, *The New World* and *Genesis*, a collection of shorter poems, *April Wind*, and three collections of criticism. "The Neural Lyre" was awarded the prestigious Levinson Award by *Poetry*. His most recent publication is *The Ballad of the Good Cowboy*, a chivalric romance incorporating the landscape and mythology of the American West.

Other Works by R. S. Gwynn

POETRY

The Drive-In. Columbia: University of Missouri Press, 1986.

EDITED BOOKS

American Poets Since World War II, Second Series: Dictionary of Literary Biography. Vol. 105, Columbia: Broccoli Clark Layman, 1991.

American Poets Since World War II, Third Series: Dictionary of Literary Biography. Vol. 120, Columbia: Broccoli Clark Layman, 1992.

Drama: A HarperCollins Pocket Anthology. New York: HarperCollins, 1993.

Fiction: A HarperCollins Pocket Anthology. New York: HarperCollins, 1993.

Poetry: A HarperCollins Pocket Anthology. New York: HarperCollins, 1993.

The Advocates of Poetry: A Reader of American Poet-Critics of the Modern Era. Fayetteville: University of Arkansas Press, 1996.

Fiction: A Longman Pocket Anthology. New York: Longman, 1997.

Poetry: A Longman Pocket Anthology. New York: Longman, 1998.

POETRY CHAPBOOKS

Bearing & Distance. New Braunfels: Cedar Rock, 1977.

The Narcissied. New Braunfels: Cedar Rock, 1981.

Body Bags. In *Texas Poets in Concert: A Quartet.* Denton: University of North Texas Press, 1990.

The Area Code of God. West Chester: Aralia, 1994.

ETC.

Regular contributor of criticism to *The Hudson Review* and *The Sewanee Review.*